Organized Networks

Organized Networks

Media Theory,
Creative Labour,
New Institutions

Ned Rossiter

NAi Publishers
Institute of Network Cultures

Design: Studio Tint, Huug Schipper, The Hague
Cover design: Léon & Loes, Rotterdam
Type setting and printing: Die Keure, Bruges, Belgium
Binding: Catherine Binding
Paper: Munken Lynx, 100 grs.
Project coordination: Barbera van Kooij, NAi Publishers
Publisher: Eelco van Welie, NAi Publishers, Rotterdam

NAi Publishers is an internationally orientated publisher specialized in developing, producing and distributing books on architecture, visual arts and related disciplines.
www.naipublishers.nl info@naipublishers.nl

It was not possible to find all the copyright holders of the illustrations used. Interested parties are requested to contact NAi Publishers, Mauritsweg 23, 3012 JR Rotterdam, The Netherlands.

Available in North, South and Central America through D.A.P./Distributed Art Publishers Inc, 155 Sixth Avenue 2nd Floor, New York, NY 10013-1507, Tel 212 6271999, Fax 212 6279484.

Available in the United Kingdom and Ireland through Art Data, 12 Bell Industrial Estate, 50 Cunnington Street, London W4 5HB, Tel 208 7471061, Fax 208 7422319.

Printed and bound in Belgium

ISBN 90-5662-526-8/978-90-5662-526-9

Contents

Acknowledgements

This book began as a PhD thesis, and I have Brian Shoesmith to thank for his long-term support and patience. Sean Cubitt, Helen Grace and McKenzie Wark examined that thesis, and their feedback has been most helpful in revising the texts gathered here. My writing has benefited from deadlines and audiences associated with many conferences, events and seminar papers, and I thank all those who either invited me to undertake some work or accepted my proposals. Much of this book has been published in earlier versions. Thanks to the many who have done editorial work on those texts, especially Jodi Dean, Chris Healy, Christiane Paul, editors at *RealTime* broadsheet as well as various journal and conference reviewers. Two images from Michael Goldberg's installation *catchingafallingknife.com* appear in this book, and I appreciate his permission to use them here.

The University of Ulster has provided working conditions that enable writing and research to be undertaken. For their ongoing support with funding and research, I thank Professor Máire Messenger Davies, Director of the Centre for Media Research and Professor Bob Welch, Dean of the Faculty of Arts. My colleagues at the Centre for Media Research and School of Media and Performing Arts have made an important difference to my life in Northern Ireland, especially Robert Porter, Daniel Jewesbury, Paul Willemen and Valentina Vitali. Thanks also to Paul Moore, Tony Langlois, Gail Baylis, Martin McLoone, Sarah Edge, Amy Davis, Barbara Butcher and Vladan Zdravkovic. I thank Dan Fleming for getting me to Northern Ireland in the first instance, even if he did leave shortly afterwards.

This book has a long prehistory that I am certain tested the limits of my dear friends: Robyn Barnacle, Brent Allpress, Pia Ednie-Brown, Gina Moore, Gillian Warden, Daniel Palmer, Mike Hayes, Simon Cooper and David Holmes. Over a period of many years Jody Berland, Allen Chun and, more recently, Ien Ang and Sally Jane Norman have been particularly supportive.

Life in Europe and Australia has also been supported by the friendship and intellectual feedback from Julian Kücklich, Maren Hartmann, Katrien Jacobs, Dominic Pettman, Akseli Virtanen, Carlos Fernández, Linda Wallace, Mieke Gerritzen, Renata Kokanovic, Grisha Dolgopolov, Brian Holmes, Sandra Braman, Simon Busch and John Hutnyk. And life in China wouldn't be the same without the friendship of Du Ping.

These texts have benefited enormously from the critical feedback of Fibreculture and Nettime mailing lists. In so many ways this book was born on those lists, which have been a source of much inspiration and learning. Fibreculture in particular provided, for the first time in my life, a sense of material connection with broader intellectual and political currents. Esther Milne, Andrew Murphie, Anna Munster, Lisa Gye, David Teh, Chris Chesher, Gillian Fuller and Danny Butt have all taught me a lot and been wonderful friends. Feedback and critique from Esther and Andrew has been crucial in bringing this book to completion, and I thank both enormously for their help. Esther provided an especially close reading of the manuscript. Thanks also to respondents to the Fibreculture survey discussed in chapter 4.

Much of this book was finished at the Wissenschaftskolleg zu Berlin/Institute for Advanced Study in July 2006. I would like to thank Christine von Arnim for making arrangements that made that stay possible. Conversations and martinis with Catherine David and Samah Selim made all the difference.

Sabine Niederer at the Institute of Network Cultures has negotiated this book through to publication, and I thank her for all her help. Thanks to Barbera van Kooij at NAi Publishers for taking this book on, and for guiding it through to print. D'Laine Camp did a fine job with copy-editing and I thank her for the hard work and care she put into this book.

This book is in so many respects a collaborative effort. This is particularly the case with the guiding political concept and project of organized networks. Geert Lovink, Brett Neilson and Soenke Zehle have been immensely important friends and intellectual companions. I have a special thanks for Geert who has been an intellectual mentor and supporter of my work over the years. This book wouldn't have happened without him.

My father, Richard Rossiter, and mother, Miranda Hamilton, and brothers Tom and Will have given me an incredible life and their love. My dad has been particularly supportive throughout this long period of research. He has also taught me how to read, how to teach and how to keep the madness of university personas at a distance.

Ned Rossiter
October, 2006

Previous versions or parts of chapters in this book have been published in other volumes, journals or magazines. I acknowledge the editors and publishers for permission to bring these texts together in this book. All chapters have been revised and developed for this book.

Part of the introduction to this book was published as 'Organised Networks, Transdisciplinarity and New Institutional Forms', *Intelligent Agent* 6.2 (2006), http://www.intelligentagent.com/. The online news feeds and text filtering sites Interactivist Info Exchange and Transform also published parts of this introduction.

A much shorter version of chapter 1 was published as 'Organized Networks and Non-Representative Democracy', in Jodi Dean, Jon Anderson and Geert Lovink (eds.), *Reformatting Politics: Networked Communications and Global Civil Society*, London and New York: Routledge, 2006. Taylor & Francis Group, Inc. The chapter also draws on material published online for *Dark Markets: Infopolitics, Electronic Media and Democracy in Times of Crisis*, International Conference by Public Netbase/to, Muesumsplatz, Vienna, 3-4 October, 2002, http://darkmarkets.to.or.at/.

Chapter 2 was published as 'WSIS and Organised Networks as New Civil Society Movements', in Jan Servaes and Nico Carpentier (eds.), *Beyond the WSIS: Towards A Sustainable Agenda for the Future Information Society*, Bristol: Intellect Books, 2006, pp. 97-116; and 'The World Summit on the Information Society and Organised Networks as New Civil Society Movements', in Michael Fine, Nicholas Smith and Amanda Wise (eds),

Mobile Boundaries/Rigid Worlds: Proceedings of the 2nd Annual Conference of the CRSI, Centre for Research on Social Inclusion, Macquarie University, 2005, http://www.crsi.mq.edu.au/mobileboundaries.htm.

Chapter 3 was published as 'Creative Industries, Comparative Media Theory, and the Limits of Critique from Within', *Topia: A Canadian Journal of Cultural Studies* 11 (Spring, 2004): 21-48. A shorter version was published as 'Creative Industries and the Limits of Critique from Within', *M/C: A Journal of Media and Culture* 6.3 (2003), http://journal.media-culture.org.au/0306/11-creativeindustries.php.

Chapter 4 was published as 'Report: Creative Labour and the Role of Intellectual Property, *Fibreculture Journal* 1 (2003), http://journal.fibreculture.org/issue1/issue1_rossiter.html. A shorter version was published as 'Creative Labour and the Role of Intellectual Property', *Noema: Technologie e Società* 31 (2003), http://www.noemalab.com/sections/ideas/ideas_articles/rossiter_creative_labour.html.

Chapter 5 was published as 'Processual Media Theory', *symploke* 11.1/2 (2003): 104-131. University of Nebraska Press; 'Processual Media Theory', *Fine Art Forum* 17.8 (August, 2003), http://www.fineartforum.org/Backissues/Vol_17/faf_v17_no8/reviews/rossiter.html; 'Processual Media Theory', in Adrian Miles (ed.), *Streaming Worlds: 5th International Digital Arts & Culture (DAC) Conference, 19-23 May, 2003*, Melbourne: RMIT University, 2003, pp. 173-184, http://hypertext.rmit.edu.au/dac/papers/Rossiter.pdf.

The chapter also draws on material published as 'Processual Media Theory and the Art of Day Trading', *Noema: Technologie e Società* 25 (2003), http://www.noemalab.com/sections/ideas/ideas_25.html; 'Review. Day Trading Aesthetics: Playing with Murdoch', *RealTime* 53 (February-March, 2003), p. 25. Also available online: http://www.realtimearts.net/rt53/rossiter.html; and 'A Code in Search of a Process', *RealTime, OnScreen* 47 (February-March, 2002), p. 22. Also available online: http://www.realtimearts.net/rt47/rossiter.html.

Parts of chapter 5 were revised for 'Processual Media Theory and the Study of New Media: Towards a New Research Approach', (with Simon Cooper) in Kwamena Kwansah-Aidoo (ed.), *Topical Issues in Communications and Media Research*, New York: Nova Science Publishers, 2005, pp. 99-119.

Chapter 6 was published as 'Virtuosity, Processual Democracy and Organised Networks', *Cultural Studies Review* 11.2 (2005): 110-128. Melbourne University Publishing Ltd.

Introduction

There is an urgent need for new institutional forms. The uncertainties of labour and life within network societies and informational economies have all too clearly exposed the limits of prevailing institutional systems and structures. The key institutions of the modern era – union, state, firm, university – have proven inadequate to the task of organizing and managing populations in the past 15-30 years.[1] During this period, many countries have undergone dramatic social change wrought by the force and impact of reforms peculiar to neoliberal governance and economic globalization.[2] The challenges of contemporary governance can be addressed through the creation of new institutional forms that are responsive to the logic of social-technical networks and non-representational democratic processes.[3] Communication within networks is about *relational processes* not representational procedures.

There is no equivalence here with the biopolitical postulate of organization and management peculiar to informatic modes of neoliberal governance. Mine are not strategies that contribute to the control of life. Rather, this book is interested in forms and expressions of governance that take the elemental force of self-organization seriously. In a sense everything is a form of self-organization in so far as the world is composed of distinct organic and inorganic patterns, processes and systems. Institutions face a particularly difficult task when it comes to adapting to changing environments. More often than not the temporal rhythm of any particular institution accumulates an asymmetrical relation to the temporality of elements internal and external to its system. It's at this point that disequilibrium characterizes the system. Arguably, many institutions struggle against this condition today and for this reason new social-technical platforms of organization are required in order to recompose labour and life in ways that furnish a sense of security and stability within informational systems subject to the unsettling force of contingency. Such an undertaking requires a transdisciplinary, distributive and collaborative institutional form. This form is called the 'organized network'.

The network models of sociality made possible by information and communication technologies have resulted in new forms of social-technical systems, or what I am calling emergent institutional forms of organized networks. While these networks can be called institutional forms in so far as they have a capacity to organize social relations, they are radically dissimilar to the moribund technics of modern institutional forms – or 'networked organizations' – such as governments, unions and firms whose logic of organization is predicated on vertical integration and representative tenets of liberal democracy.[4] Such dynamics are profoundly unsuited to the collaborative and distributive culture of networks peculiar to digital communications media and their attendant socialities.

At times in this book I adopt the unattractive language typically associated with the rhetoric of neoliberalism. I do so in the interests of a pragmatism that is necessary if network cultures are to undergo a scalar and organizational transformation. Similarly, I speak very deliberately of hierarchical and centralizing tendencies of networks. The social-technical dynamics of organized networks constitute organization in ways substantively different from networked organizations.[5] Of course ICTS are common to both forms of organization. There are some fundamental differences, however: organized networks are *co-emergent* with digital communications media, while networked organizations typically *precede* the advent of digital ICTS.[6] Of special significance is the tendency for networked organizations to adopt intellectual property rights as the regulatory architecture for commerce and institutional partnerships whereas organized networks are often staunch advocates of open source software and culture.

These kinds of differences also produce tensions within the social-technical dynamics of networks. There is a prevailing consensus that experiences of sharing, feedback, flexibility, and friendship are primary to the culture of networks. I wouldn't dispute the importance of such social-technical dynamics. However, it is a mistake to think the horizontal, decentralizing and distributive capacities of digital networks as immune from a tendency to fall back into hierarchical and centralizing modes of organization and patterns of behaviour. Indeed, there are

times when such a move is necessary. Decisions have to be made. As
I discuss in more detail below, the so-called 'open' systems of communication are frequently not only not open, they also elide hierarchical operations that enable networks to become organized. Let us not forget
that flexibility is also the operative mode of post-Fordist labour and its
attendant double-edged sword of economic precarity and ontological
precariousness.[7]

It is essential to address these challenges in order to create structures
of communication within networks that enable the distribution of resources and the income they generate. Economic models developed
from such technics are immanent to the logic of network cultures and
specific to the situation of communication and practice. In other words,
there will be no universal model that applies to the dynamics of networks, which by definition are singular, albeit with patterns, tendencies, and resources that may overlap. Collaborative economies special to
network cultures can be distinguished from the service and delivery
economies of the networked university and its educational commodities enframed within intellectual property regimes that endow education and labour with informational-commodity properties.[8]

And it's not as though networked organizations are unaware of the
need to adjust to the informational mode of management. In his foreword to a Demos think-tank report entitled *Disorganisation: Why Future
Organisations must 'Loosen Up'*, Vice-President of Business Solutions, Or-
ange UK, Mike Newnham outlines what's at stake for managers that
don't adapt their organizations to meet the force of informational capitalism:

> You may feel uncomfortable with the idea if you actually run an or-
> ganisation, but there is a clear message evident from the results of
> this report: we have to 'let go', or 'disorganise'. Otherwise the employ-
> ees that we all need, the brightest and the best, will gravitate to more
> open, more flexible set-ups that fit their values and respond to their
> aspirations. This will present some real dilemmas.[9]

You have to wonder whether the message here is for managerial losers
and knuckleheads in government. So many networked organizations
have existed for some time now through casualization and the out-

sourcing of labour. Remember, this was the logic of multinational corporations since the 1970s, reaching an apogee of delight in the late '90s dotcom bubble, and continuing in the post-crash world of Richard Florida's 'creative class'.[10] The paradoxical injunction to disorganize also results in less transparency and accountability in organizations.[11] The mechanisms of workers' representation in the form of unions or academic councils are also subject to the post-Fordist logic of flexibilization, risk and uncertainty. Disorganization within an informational mode thus corresponds with a broader crisis in representational democracy. Organization, not disorganization, is the challenge facing network cultures. How to do this within non-representational social-technical systems of communication is one of the primary vectors of inquiry throughout this book.

For political projects that wish to go beyond the comfort zones of consensus communities (as if they exist outside of fantasy, myth and self-delusion, irrespective of whether one has anarchistic or social-democratic tendencies), I maintain it is better to engage hegemonic discourses, exploit their political legitimacy, and confront the materialities of informational communication in order to make concrete the horizons of utopian speculation.[12] It would be easy to dismiss such an idea as a variation of Third Way politics, but to do so would forget the materialities of communication and sociality of networks that function as dissonances in the system, and as registrations of 'the political'.

I should make one thing clear from the outset: this book does not discuss the numerous open source software and programming practices of and possibilities for network cultures. Nor does it discuss developments of social networks and the advent of the much hyped Web 2.0 and Internet2, situated as they are within an uneven geography of information. Such work is better done in media environments that hold a more proximate relation to the digital unfolding of social-technical developments. This book is best taken as a general intervention that encourages detailed case studies whose analytical empirics is immanent to the time and space of network collaborations. This amounts to what Mario Tronti calls 'concrete research' in order to create 'a strategy of the future'.[13] One key instantiation of concrete research I foresee for organized networks consists of transdisciplinary autonomous education, of which I say more below. Alternative models as advocated in this book can learn from the histories of experimentation in organization as it relates to institutional form. Organization and its relation to the question of institutional form, it seems to me, are all too often neglected when thinking about issues of sustainability and collaboration within network cultures and social movements.

This book is a search for new technics of organization. It is about conditions of possibility, the immanent relation between theory and practice – or what used to go by the name of praxis – and a resolute belief (call it fundamentalism, if you have to) in the concrete potential of invention, of the creation of transdisciplinary institutional forms that enlist the absolute force of labour and life. I have arranged this book in three parts, and left those parts without titles precisely because the themes of media theory, creative labour and the invention of new institutional forms slide across each essay, more or less explicitly. Each part holds its distinctive curiosities of inquiry that signal what I consider the key trajectories of political intervention for organized networks.

The political concept of organized networks seeks to overcome the inadequacy of thought about radical social-political movements and their relation to institutional forms. But it is not my intention to undertake a sociological study of what is commonly referred to as 'the movement of movements'. The emphasis instead is on transdisciplinarity as an immanent practice that brings into question the tendency for network cultures to indulge self-valorisation and horizontal collaboration rather than attend to the task of governance within stratified networks.

Transdisciplinarity and the Legacy of Form

Transdisciplinarity can be understood as an experimental research methodology and pedagogy that emerges within the logic of networks as they traverse diverse institutional forms. To this end, transdisciplinarity is a practice interested in the educational capacities of network cultures. Of course there is much to learn from how other networks are undertaking their autonomous education initiatives. The accumulation of best practices is perhaps the most important lesson of all.[14] National contingencies will undoubtedly shape the approaches adopted by different networks, since the advent of open education within an informational mode is conditioned by the crisis of the modern universities as they engage the neoliberal forces of commercialization, declining state funding and the legal architecture of intellectual property regimes – all of which are regulated by the transformed sovereign power of the nation-state.[15] But critique is misplaced if it assumes the combinatory force of national sovereignty and neoliberal ideology as uniform in its effects.

The reason why there is variation of the neoliberal-sovereignty nexus across different countries has to do with the fact there is no single hue of neoliberalism, with different factors and policy responses coming into play that arise out of circumstances peculiar to the nation-state. This alone presents perhaps the biggest challenge to networks seeking to collaborate in developing autonomous educational projects, since transnational relations between networks wishing to intervene in the composition and experience of education are, to varying degrees, bound to the logic of their neoliberal states. There are precedents for independent educational networks across Europe, ranging from the autonomist learning centres in Italy and the numerous educational workshops run by migrant networks and activists (often in tandem with cultural festivals or social forums) to the upscale summer schools featuring celebrity theorists.

Rather than provide a typology of examples such as these, I wish instead to point to what I consider two seminal moments in the prehistory of organized networks. And this brings us to the question of form. First, the work of Félix Guattari and others at La Borde, an experimental institution in anti-psychiatry founded in the 1950s.[16] Here we find the development of concepts such as transversality and the practice of transdisciplinarity, both of which are primary to a network of networks. And second, the period following World War II, when the Institute for Social Research returned to Germany. This passage in which an institute travels from New York City and Los Angeles to Frankfurt interests me for the way in which the methods adopted by the Institute are shaped by, or rather, have to reconcile with the political and historical situation in which the Institute found itself. The adaptive capacity of the Institute signals the relation between immanence and transdisciplinarity.

The practice of transdisciplinarity preconditions the invention of new institutional forms. As Gary Genosko notes of the metamethodology of Félix Guattari, transdisciplinarity is predicated on experiments in institutional formation.[17] In the case of organized networks, transdisciplinarity is constituted by 'the political', by the tensions that underpin cross-sectoral, multi-institutional engagements that make possible new modes and new forms of research. Transdisciplinarity can be distinguished from interdisciplinary or multidisciplinary research. Despite all the claims in OECD reports and government and university policy rhetoric on research, interdisciplinarity is not about networks, but rather clusters, and typically takes place in 'private and public labs and research centres'.[18] The UK creative industries model of the public 'incubator' as a paternal space of gestation that hatches juvenile innovation ready for commercial application shares more with science fiction than it does with processes of invention and trade within information economies.[19] Such settings, and the institutional and political-economic conditions which shape interdisciplinary research, also result in another key difference with transdisciplinarity. Interdisciplinarity rests within the regime of intellectual property, which operates as an architecture of control. As such, the knowledge produced is locked up and contained; it refuses the social relations that make possible the development of intellectual action, and it therefore refuses the potential for social transformation because of the way knowledge is enclosed within a property relation.

The story of the Institute for Social Research predates the advent of the informational age and the inscription of culture within intellectual property regimes. Yet this was also a period that saw the industrialization of culture as a commodity-form, which, as I note below, is the precondition for the information-form characteristic of the creative industries. More particularly, the Institute embodies the constitutive relations between organizational form, transdisciplinary methods and historical, political and economic contingencies. In this regard, the work of the Institute can assist contemporary social-technical networks in search of precedents to their own experience of inventing new institutional forms.

Existing in effect as a virtual laboratory with shifting residencies at Columbia University, the American Jewish Committee's Department of Scientific Research, and a bungalow in Los Angeles, members of the Institute for Social Research undertook a number of collaborative research projects that enlisted quantitative and qualitative methods along with philosophical critique and social theory.[20] The organizational role and diplomatic efforts of Max Horkheimer are incisive here. As someone astute to the material situation of intellectual labour, Horkheimer sacrificed much of his time to the tasks of administration. From his inaugural speech as Director of the Institute in 1931, Horkheimer set out a trajectory for transdisciplinary research that combined empirical studies of social phenomena with the 'animating impulses' of philosophical analysis.[21] His ambition was nothing less than 'permanent collaboration' between philosophers, sociologists, economists, historians and psychologists.[22] Key to such 'collective research' was a proto-network structure which saw the Institute manifest as a number of international branches at any one time, ensuring also the maximum potential for survival should any node happen to collapse. Consider this as a form of packet-switching for the pre-ARPANET age.

Horkheimer's institutional role contrasts that of Adorno who, as a devotee to critical theory, adopted with much reluctance and misgiving what he considered the reductive and internally contradictory empirical methods of 'administrative research' championed by Paul Lazarsfeld and Berkeley's Public Opinion Study Group. But even Adorno, subsumed into an institutional persona, found it necessary to change tack upon returning to the situation of post-war Germany. Even if Adorno's derision of empirical research and its mechanized techniques continued in a more muted form throughout his life, the Institute – and especially Horkheimer – exploited its association with 'advanced' American empirical research methods. Government, university, industry and US occupational forces perceived such methods as worthy of financial support for the reconstruction of cities, the reform of university disciplines, and the diagnosis of fascist, anti-democratic tendencies in an emergent consumer society.[23] Rolf Wiggershaus's comprehensive study of the Frankfurt School recounts one aspect of this engagement with authorities in the effort to secure funding for the Institute:

> In 1950 the US High Commissioner, John McCloy, put DM 200,000
> at the Institute's disposal, with a further DM 235,000 for rebuilding.
> This energetic support sprang from a belief among those responsible
> for American policy in Germany that sociology, particularly when

represented by American citizens and with its emphasis on empirical research, was a factor in promoting democracy.[24]

This strategy of advancing political and economic interests through client organizations has since become a hallmark of us foreign policy, which extends to the structural adjustment programmes of the International Monetary Fund (IMF) and World Bank and auxiliary role often played by non-governmental organizations (NGOS) as civil society actors. And it was a gamble that Horkheimer was willing to take in the mixed-up world of post-war Germany. Here was the opportunity for scalar enhancement that had been unravelling for some time in the us as the Institute's funds became increasingly scarce, coupled with fragile relations with collaborating individuals and institutions. By diversifying the sources of funding from a range of authorities, the Institute sought not only to maximize its funding potential, but also to create a structure in which a prevailing discourse of practical research distributed across institutions gave legitimacy – or at least some protection – to the more speculative philosophical interests held by Institute members, Adorno in particular.

What we find here is an instance in which the institution itself takes on the capacity of an actor engaged in 'immanent critique' – another key 'metamethod' in thinking the complex relations that comprise the transdisciplinary research of organized networks. This is an experimental methodology in which the time and space of research is inseparable from the labour and life of networks. Without the scalar purchase offered by the Institute for Social Research, its individual members could hope for little to no traction with funding authorities. The tragic conclusion of Walter Benjamin's life is not only a story of exodus from Nazi Europe. It was also a consequence of an individual whose personal resources, while a catalyst for an inventive life, were insufficiently and all too irregularly connected to the supportive framework offered by the form of the Institute. In other words, Benjamin's was a life that carried the intense burden of existence external to anything but the most minimal infrastructures. The Institute for Social Research, on the other hand, conducted immanent critique by inculcating the general intellect of members who held a more proximate relation to an institutional persona. This accumulation of knowledge and know-how enabled the Institute to readily adapt to changing geopolitical circumstances, taking its members along for the ride.

At the theoretical level, immanent critique takes its primary lessons from Deleuze, Foucault and Adorno with important input from Canadian political economist and communications scholar Harold A. Innis. Immanent critique is a method of post-negativity. It retains Adorno's insistence that contradictions and tensions operate as a constituent force within any idiom of expression; yet at the same time it recognizes that sociality within network cultures and creative economies is configured not according to dualisms, but rather to patterns of distribution, rhythms of tension, transversal social relations, modulations of affect and transdisciplinary institutional practices. In this sense, immanent critique understands the antagonism of the constituent outside as a processual force of affirmation as distinct from the 'negation of negation'. On this point, my position differs from that of Slavoj Žižek, who reads the Hegelian 'negation of negation' as 'nothing but repetition at its purest: in the first move, a certain gesture is accomplished and fails; then, in the second move, this same gesture is simply repeated'.[25] Such a manoeuvre, I would argue, does not account for the indeterminacy of difference that attends the affirmative role of a network of networks as it subsists within the constituent outside. This amounts to a form of post-negativity in which the operation of a constituent outside permeates social-technical and historical conditions of the present.

All instituted forms retain a relation with the constituent outside, no matter how much their logic of organization is predicated on the containment of expression and exclusion of 'the political'. Since organized networks consist of loose affiliations where participants have the freedom to come and go, they are particularly susceptible to the disruptive force of the constituent outside. Movement across borders always enhances the chance of alien infiltrations. This is both a strength and a weakness. On the one hand, it is a source of renewal, reinvention and mitigates tendencies to excessive bureaucratization often associated with institutionalization. And on the other hand, the constituent outside holds the potential to wreak unexpected demolition. For these reasons, the scalar transformation of organized networks as new institutional forms is always a fragile, uncertain process.

Institutions function to organize social relations. It follows, then, that the social-technical dynamics peculiar to a range of digital media technologies (mailing lists, collaborative blogs, wikis, content management systems) institute new modes of networked sociality. It is easy for both leftist activists and techno-libertarians to dismiss this process of emergent institution formation. Many would assert that it simply results in a bureaucratization and rigidity of social-technical communication systems whose default setting is one of flows, decentralization, horizontality, etcetera. I would suggest such knee-jerk, technically incorrect responses risk a disengagement from the political and thus from politics. There is a passivity that attends this kind of position. Moreover, it is a position that fails the politics of reappropriating the psychic, social and semiotic territory of institutions. The process of instituting networks, on the other hand, involves a movement toward the strategic rather than tactical dimension of Net politics. Another reason to turn towards the strategic dimension has to do with the short-termism that accompanies many tactical projects. The logic of the tactic is one of situated intervention. And then it disappears. There are of course some notable exceptions – Indymedia, Makrolab and the Yes Men come to mind as quite long-term experiments in networks and tactical media; yet these exceptions are not, I would suggest, instances of transdisciplinarity.

This is not to dispense with tactics since tactics are the source of renewal. Without the tactical, organized networks collapse into stasis. Interestingly enough, tactics parallel the logic of capital. We see this operation historically time and again. Just consider core-periphery relations and the ways in which capital has to incorporate or appropriate the margins in order to replenish and reproduce itself. Such movements are similar to what Brian Holmes identifies as the cooptation of the productive efforts of the artist, cultural critic, designer.[26] It's therefore important to remember that autonomists are not somehow located outside the state but rather operating as a disruptive potentiality whose difference is defined by relations of negation, refusal, exodus, subtraction, and so forth. Certainly there are important qualitative differences in the relation individuals and peoples have with the state. Think, for instance, of the experience of migrants, precarious workers and so-called illegal movement of peoples across territories. Precarity, let's remember, is an experience that traverses a range of class scales, and may even be considered as a post-Fordist technique of border control that distinguishes 'self-managed exploitation ... from those who must be exploited (or worse) by direct coercion'.[27] The emergence internationally of creative industries over the past eight years underscores the precarious situation of creative labour in so far as informational labour is the precondition for the exploitation of intellectual property.

Informational Labour in the Creative Industries

Cultural and media research on the creative industries has tended towards a policy orientation, and it needs to be complemented with other methodologies, practices and fields of inquiry. Some are obvious, such as political economy, critiques of intellectual property regimes, the adoption of Creative Commons and the business implications of non-proprietary licenses such as Copyleft. And some are less obvious, such as the question of network socialities, the virtuosity of the general intellect, the precarity of creative labour, and so forth. By undertaking transdisciplinary practice to investigate the material conditions of international creative industries, my own approach forges connections between these complementarities with the aim of organizing new institutional forms of agency and sustainability for creative labour and life in an informational era of network cultures. This is a collaborative project that goes beyond the accounts documented in this book.

It is perhaps necessary to make a distinction between the cultural industries and the creative industries. For the occasional observer, it seems as though the cultural industries imperceptibly morphed into the creative industries at some stage during the late 1990s. But this shift was no accident. The rise of creative industries corresponds with two key moments, one to do with a Blair government policy intervention in 1998 and the other to do with the informatization of social relations inaugurated in 1995 by the WTO's Agreement on Trade-Related Aspects of Intellectual Property Rights (TRIPS). And both need to be understood in the historical context of the dotcom era – a period in which start-ups were the unsustainable virus and boosterism infiltrated any number of discourses and institutional practices.

The shift from cultural industries to creative industries is also figured in the move from negative dialectics to network socialities. Such is the passage from state-regulated culture industries and broadcast media to creative production within informational economies and network media. In a more hesitant way, perhaps the remainder common to cultural industries and creative industries is the continuum of creativity as instrumental in the policy realm and autonomous in the realm of experience.

The policy moment of the creative industries is a case in which a structural determination takes place. The vast majority of academic research and local government initiatives associated with the creative industries was, and still is, shaped by government policy directives. Within the institution of the university, creative industries are essentially a research perspective derived from government policy interventions reflecting a regulatory commitment that in many ways exceeds that of the cultural industries. Here we find yet another contradiction internal to the ideology of the neoliberal state, which purports to deregulate institutional impediments to global capital flows. Academic perspectives have only gradually and reluctantly, if at all, articulated their own critical creative industries idiom in response.[28] This stems from the mission set out by national governments for academics to undertake rather crudely understood exercises in 'mapping' the empirical scope of creative industries.

In 1998 and then revised in 2001, the Blair government's Department of Culture, Media and Sport (DCMS) produced the Task Force Mapping Documents that sought to aggregate 13 otherwise distinct sectors such as media and advertising, architecture and design, music and entertainment, interactive video games, film and even the arts and crafts, which are part of what is also known as the heritage industries. This diverse field of practices was subsumed under the primary definition of the DCMS, which has since gone on to define how the creative industries have been adopted internationally by governments and policy researchers: the creative industries, according the DCMS, consists of 'the generation and exploitation of intellectual property'.[29] The informational dimension of creative industries, and the move away from the cultural industries, is embodied in this definition – economic value in the creative industries is derived from the potential of exchange value in the form of intellectual property. In other words, the creative industries are a brand economy. Even more so, the rise of creative industries has to be understood in conjunctural terms. Witness, for example, the rise of the information-form as the dominant commodity-form, which is also how the creative industries relate back to culture industries. The WTO's regulatory architecture for intellectual property is itself a consequence of this.

But there are some important aspects to the DCMS's definition that are too frequently and easily overlooked by most researchers: namely, the conditions and experience of creative labour as it relates to intellectual property regimes, which I go on to discuss in detail in chapters 3 and 4. This analytical omission and political abandon by academics who at earlier stages in their careers were not shy about their leftist persuasion is not to be unexpected. Many, after all, have been infected by the dot-com hype, and party like it's still 1999. The reasons for this have to do with temporal rhythms that differ across institutions, and even though government and the university are firmly enmeshed in market economies, they none the less move at a speed slower than industry. And this means the crash of the NASDAQ in April 2000 might as well not have happened.

While it's healthy for social ecologies to maintain a diversity of temporal modes, it has none the less lead to a form of obscurantism in most research on the creative industries. Here, I am speaking of the invisible remainder that operates as the 'constitutive outside' of 'the generation and exploitation of intellectual property'.[30] In assuming a link between creativity and proprietarization, the analytical and political oversight of most creative industries research is that it fails to acknowledge the fact that 'the generation and exploitation of intellectual property' is conditioned by the exploitation of labour-power. For this reason, most of the empirical research on creative industries paraded by academics and policy-makers alike is not only deeply unimaginative, it also results in research that holds little correlation with the actually existing material conditions of the creative industries. And it's at this point that my arguments on creative industries take off in chapters 3 and 4.

In studying the relations between labour-power and the creative industries my interest has been twofold: first, at a theoretical and political level, I have sought to invent concepts and methodologies that address the question of the organization of labour-power within network societies and informational economies. Here, my research relates to and has been informed by what the political philosopher Paolo Virno calls 'the thorniest of problems: how to organize a plurality of "social individuals" that, at the moment, seems fragmented, constitutionally exposed to blackmail – in short, unorganizable?'[31] Out of an interest in new forms of agency in the creative industries, this book considers how currently *disorganized labour* in the creative industries might institute a mode of organizing sociality immanent to networked forms of communications media.

Secondly, my research has investigated the double-edged sword of precarity within post-Fordist economies, to which the creative industries belong as a service economy modulated through informational relations.[32] The precarity of labour-power within the creative industries is double-edged in the sense that it enables the attractions of flexibility – the escape from the Fordist time of the factory and the firm – yet accompanying these relative freedoms and expressive potential for new forms of organization is the dark side of what researchers such as Ulrich Beck, Scott Lash, John Urry and Judith Butler have variously called risk, uncertainty, complexity and insecurity. Such fields of inquiry resonate with the concept of organized networks, neither of which are rarely addressed from within creative industries research, but hold tremendous potential for the development of the kind of critical perspectives that I think are missing.

While there is a distinctive homogeneity in the way creative industries travels internationally as a policy discourse, the material, economic and cultural diversity of neoliberal capitalism – its amenability and capacities for adaptation to national and city-state modulations – enables creative industry style developments to be translated in ways that seem improbable if analysis focuses exclusively at the level of policy reproduction. Such considerations reinforce the need to understand the variable and uneven dynamics of global capitalism, whose indices include the movement of cultural commodities, labour and ideas. The modern world-system of nation-states play a significant role here in regulating such mobility through the mechanisms of trade agreements, border controls and IPRs.

Here it is necessary to analyse the constitutive power of intra-regional, international macro-structural and trans-local micro-political forces. In other words, in order to make intelligible the patterns of global neoliberalism, one must attend critically to the peculiarities of subnational scales (the micro dimension) and weigh these against international forces (the macro dimension). Only then does it become possible to assemble the complex relations that compose the shifting cartographies and life-worlds of neoliberal capitalism. One place to start such analyses is on the institutional front, for all action is embedded in institutional settings of one kind or another. For reasons that I hope become apparent, the university is my particular choice of institution when it comes to registering the force of neoliberal capitalism and the conditions of exodus and invention.

Informational Universities and Neoliberalism as a Condition of Possibility

With its symbiotic relationship with the publishing industry and professions and exclusive accreditation by the state, the university has long held what Harold Innis calls a 'monopoly of knowledge'.[33] In ways not dissimilar from the church or the state, the institutional form of the university has endured over time and, in recent years, extended over space, modelling the multinational logic of the corporation. The university's concern to assert control over space corresponds with a shift in focus from the national cultivation of the citizen-subject to a capturing of the transnational consumer-client. Within a neoliberal climate of pseudo-deregulation and increasing privatization, the institutional borders of the university become more porous. Rather than lament this transformation of the university and its monopoly of knowledge, I instead see openings and possibilities for new institutional forms. A focus on educational resources strikes me as a matter of tactics that feed strategic interests.

Knowledge contexts that for good reasons – autonomy chief among them – have resided outside the borders of the university are now presented with a scalar challenge to organize as networks in transdisciplinary ways. Here I am thinking of migrant networks, media activists, NGOs, think-tanks, small business associations, community organizations, architecture and urban design platforms, and so forth. These can all broadly be understood as social-political networks increasingly subject to, if not always thoroughly embracing, the logic of informatization. Yet they retain their distinct features and properties that imbue the educational encounter and structure of relations with qualitative differences. Organized networks are waiting to emerge as concrete research in the form of new educational institutions.

Over the past decade it has become clear that digital technologies have opened up new possibilities in the production and distribution of content and are redefining the reception and creation of knowledge. Changes in the organizational capacities of institutions have accompanied these developments. Following Bill Readings' *The University in Ruins*, Kevin Robins and Frank Webster note how the modern liberal university was coextensive with the interests of the modern nation-state and 'the reproduction of national knowledge and national culture'.[34] In a period of transnational capitalism, the capacity of the university to remain bound to such a national agenda is greatly diminished. Nowadays, the university, like so many institutions, must accommodate the complexities concomitant with global market economies. The problem is that the organizational form of the university is ill-suited to such dynamics. Despite the reform agendas of universities in advanced economies over the past 15 to 20 years, their efforts at adapting to information economies and networked socialities have proven to be largely ineffective in dealing with the challenge of innovation and problematic of contingency due to the predominant adherence to the strictures of intellectual property regimes coupled with cumbersome bureaucratic systems. In this respect, universities remain embedded within a national system, since it is the responsibility of the member states and their legal organs to regulate intellectual property violations in accordance with the TRIPS Agreement.[35]

The past thirty or so years have seen the university advance into and simultaneously condition the information economy, as witnessed by the connection between intellectual property, publishing, the informatization of labour, and the commercially driven practices of the university.[36] This has created a tension between universities as public institutions and universities as private enterprises increasingly dependent on externally generated forms of income (consultancies, quasi-state and industry research funds, commercial applications, etcetera). Furthermore, the concept of the university as an institution with an exclusive purchase on the administration and provision of knowledge and learning is undergoing transformation as countries with advanced economies open the 'market' of education to private providers. Paradoxically, perhaps, neoliberalism – with its logic of outsourcing, privatization and dissembling institutional frameworks – conditions the possibility of organized networks. Moreover, neoliberalism has resulted in a weakening of collegial bonds and organizing capacities within the institutional form of the university. And this is where the story of organized networks as new institutional forms within the field of education begins.

From a strategic perspective, then, one obvious collaborative interest of organized networks is to consider what the scalar transformation of organized networks entails vis-à-vis the aggregation of educational resources distributed within and across networks. Networks have been fantastic at developing educational resources such as documentation of open source software, course materials, health-care information, tips on political organization, and so forth. Obviously there's a lot to learn from NGOs and the revival of union organizing as seen in the 'Justice for Janitors' movement in the USA.[37] Certainly my position is not to dismiss these institutional forms outright. Here it is necessary to recognize the situation of informational politics. Just as NGOs and civil society organizations (CSOS) have filled the void created by the neoliberal state's evacuation from the social, so too must organized networks seize upon the institutional persona of the 'external provider'.[38]

For collaborative research networks situated within the context of the European Union (EU), the project of constructing new institutional forms in the field of higher education holds a substantive relation to the Bologna Process.[39] The twin tasks of aggregating educational resources common to network cultures and developing business models that enable the mobilization of these resources is central to the ambitions of the Bologna Process.[40] Despite the fact that organized networks do not register within such policy, it is strategic to recognize that universities do not hold an exclusive purchase on higher education and research. There is provision – rhetorical as it may be – for non-university networks to enter the field of formalized education. Key to such a development is an engagement with the accreditation procedures in order for organized networks to operate as new business forms in the field of education.[41] To realize this concrete ambition requires assembling a 'network of networks' as unique platforms of delivery and dissemination of educational materials premised on open source principles.

The scale of administration associated with this task can very easily appear overwhelming, and the prospect of entering into the complex slog of legal frameworks can be an immediate stumbling block to the process of scaling up. Yet incorporation as a legal entity is a necessary step if networks are to play the game of suprastate funding in the EU.[42] Though it must be said, this is not without its own hazards and complications. In this regard there is much to learn from peer-to-peer migrant networks, media activism and border academy projects such as those coordinated by Florian Schneider and Susanne Lang.[43] In a conversation earlier this year about registering networks as corporate entities, Lang informed me that in Germany at least such a task can be performed relatively swiftly once the necessary procedures are understood and then coordinated as tasks distributed within the network. This is an instance where national and possibly subnational policies on the registration of an organization may cause tensions for networks of transnational orientation. A decision has to be made about national location. Take it is as a matter of paperwork and then move on. But that option requires a hospitable and user-friendly legal system, and people who know how to work it. In many cases, this will not be the case, and there is little choice but to negotiate the legislative institutional power that regulates participation by organizations in the market of education.

There's no question that the political stakes are high in such an undertaking, and there will be many who are quick to charge such a project as selling out. The reality is that organized networks will never be funded through state subsidies in the way that much of the cultural sector, along with NGOs for that matter, has and continues to be, in Europe at least, along with its neo-imperial offshoots. As a result, organized networks have no choice but to come up with business models. Otherwise they can only amble along in parasitic mode, taking a bit here and bit there from their unwitting hosts (frequently universities). As far as I can determine, an intervention into the education market is one of the few ways in which organized networks may obtain economic autonomy, which depends upon securing an economic base. Without this, organized networks have little chance of sustainability and little possibility of scalar transformation.

There is a capacity for networks to mobilize their resources in transversal ways in the form of master classes, summer schools, and training programmes that operate both internally to and externally from universities. Universities are undergoing a process of losing their expertise, their ability to bring in new knowledge and to transform the disciplines, which have become incredibly rigid and dull. Universities can be characterized by their deficiency of thought. They don't know how to move themselves in ways that incorporate what Gregory Bateson called '*a difference which makes a difference*'.[44] The strange thing is that neoliberalism makes possible the difference which makes a difference. This is the perversity of neoliberalism. The structural logic of neoliberalism makes possible openings, and openings invite interventions that begin to enable the financing of autonomous, precarious, experimental research and teaching that shows no sign of being catered for in current OECD, government and university policy directives.

My proposal can be easily criticized for appropriating the outside – the experimental elements that so often energize networks on the frontline of invention – and closing it down again. This is the classic critique of appropriation. We see this most obviously in the fashion industries. Remember punk? If you wanted, you could pay 200 bucks for a pair of jeans with a rip in them. Hilariously, there was no shortage of idiots who went out and purchased their damaged goods. The same can be said about knowledge. What functions against the closure of minds and resources is the fact that educational business projects undertaken by a network of networks are predicated on principles of open source software, society and culture. Obviously there will be fights over how best to redistribute funds within and across networks. But that's a matter that can be sorted out. Having said this, a problem remains. There is only so much free labour that can be done within the networks.[45] Certainly it helps networks to have a parasitical relation with networked organizations (universities, for example). But eventually free labour exhausts itself. And as I go on to discuss in chapters 3 and 4, this is something researchers and policy-makers in the creative industries are highly reluctant to address.

The university is actually a vulnerable institution. It is quite uncertain, and indeed could be characterized as a place of precarity. As many have experienced, the labour force of universities is predominantly composed of casual workers whose seasonal pattern of employment resembles that of the strawberry picker. Unions typically fail to represent the interests of casual workers, since their interest is to protect the security of those with tenured positions. The work of Marc Bousquet on the constitutive relations between informal economies and the information university is instructive here in so far as he locates the economic and managerial problematic of labour as key to understanding the coincidence between neoliberal policy-making, the commercialization of education and informatization of social relations. As Bousquet writes, 'informationalization is about delivering labor in the mode of information'.[46] Thus labour, and not the advancement of technological systems, is the primary source from which surplus value of the educational commodity form is derived. Just as cyber-libertarians maintain that 'information wants to be free', so publishers in the digital games industry (and open source software businesses, for that matter) are overjoyed with the abundance of free labour and innovation in the form of 'modding' (computer game modification) by gamers.[47] Increasingly, the ontics of labour becomes inseparable from the ontology of information.

There is nothing especially new in such an observation – how can we forget the insights of Marx? – but it is an important reminder that alternative models would do well to take on board when questioning the dominance of informatized education as a commercial undertaking that severs the sociality of production from the commodity form. The role of international institutions in the governance of populations, information and trade is important here, and the World Summit on the Information Society (WSIS) serves as an instructive case for this book.

Collaboration and Governance in New Institutional Forms

Two recent reports commissioned by international institutions highlight the central importance of new institutional forms if problems of democracy, accountability, fairness and sustainability are to be addressed in the twenty-first century. The International Labour Organization's World Commission on the Social Dimension of Globalization 'warns that we have reached a crisis stage in the legitimacy of our political institutions, whether national or international. There is an urgent need to rethink current institutions of global economic governance, whose rules and policies . . . are largely shaped by powerful countries and powerful players'.[48] Similarly, an OECD report titled *Governance in the 21st Century* highlights the challenges as follows:

> Organisational and creative liberty … has very exacting precondi-
> tions. In the future, more diffused approaches to governance in all
> parts of society will only work if there are frameworks in place that
> assure very high levels of transparency, accountability and integrity.
> At the same time, for public authorities and society more broadly,
> the ability to put new forms of governance into the service of realis-
> ing people's collective good will depend on a common commitment
> to democratic values, human rights and equality of opportunity.
> Even with these frameworks and values in place, the emergence of
> new forms of governance will still depend fundamentally on the
> capacity of individuals and groups to participate actively in making
> and implementing decisions.[49]

It is precisely the issues outlined here that organized networks, as a policy intervention and social-technical practice, seek to address. Through
the primary vectors of inquiry – protocols, self-organization, scaleabili-
ty, sustainability – the project of organized networks both assesses and
undertakes the construction of new institutional forms that engage diverse populations in creating mechanisms and resources for labour and
life in information societies, bringing new models to international challenges of cultural diversity, migration, creative innovation and open education. The problem remains, however, that organized networks do
not yet exist as recognized actors either within the stratum of policy discourse or as concrete-potentialities. What we have, none the less, is a
steady accumulation of energies, best practices, concept translators, situated projects, and so forth. Along with taking on board the lessons
from pre-digital institutions of experimental research, there is also
much to learn from international efforts and failures to coordinate
cross-institutional encounters in the information society.

The collaborative project of inventing new institutional forms holds
an affinity, remote as that may be, with the experiences, process and
political form of 'multi-stakeholderism' between government, business
and csos during the un's World Summit on the Information Society.
However, multi-stakeholderism generates tension as it often requires
csos and ngos to institutionalize themselves to gain recognition from
government and business stakeholders, often decoupling decision-making processes from the grass roots networks that are these organiza-

tions' key constituency. Such an operation typifies the vertical system of communication and governance within networked organizations (as distinct from organized networks).

Again, this is not to say that hierarchies and centralizing tendencies are absent from or not intrinsic to organized networks. Rather, it is to recognize that conflicting, non-assimilable hierarchies distinguish organized networks from networked organizations. Corporations, governments, universities and unions are among the key institutions that have been able to proliferate internationally and engage each other precisely because they hold equivalent hierarchical systems of organization. A government minister talks to a chief executive officer of a corporation who also occupies a position on an academic board. Communication flows, decisions are made, and policies are set into motion. My argument is that such organizational systems do not suit the logic of information economies and network cultures. None the less, the modern political and economic success of institutions associated with networked organizations rests in their capacity to reproduce hierarchical systems of organization. This is not the case for organized networks whose only common standard resides in the Transmission Control Protocol/Internet Protocol (TCP/IP), which needs to be understood as a technical standard shaped by economic and political interests. While the accumulation of best practices suggests that organized networks may develop common platforms of communication, the pragmatic decision is one that emerges internally from the culture of dissension characteristic of a network of networks. This relational dynamic between the act of decision and the culture of dissension may be the basis upon which the scalar transformation rests. How to manage this is an open question.

Herein lies the challenge of governance and indeed collaboration. The multi-stakeholderism model does not address these tensions, and is thus unsuccessful as a governance model for networks. The political concept of organized networks, however, understands conflict as a generative force in need of both collaborative methodologies and transdisciplinary frameworks. These are key problems of communication and governance that organized networks must address if they wish to operate successfully as new institutional forms composed of diverse and fluctuating constituencies, where people hold the freedom to come and go.[50]

While the organized network has a relative institutional autonomy, it must engage, by necessity, other institutional partners who may often be opposed to their interests. Organized networks share something with NGOS, CSOS and even think-tanks. Yet there is a radical dissimilarity and qualitative difference between organized networks and these institutional forms. Take NGOS and CSOS, for example, and the techniques of governance adopted throughout the WSIS process. Within any partnership there is of course a compromise. In order to obtain the necessary discursive legitimacy required to participate within the institutional settings of WSIS, NGOS and CSOS had to engage a model of organization that was antithetical to the self-organizing logic of networks. NGOS and CSOS were thus required to adopt the representational form known throughout WSIS as multi-stakeholderism – the primary model of governance for managing, if not realizing, relations between business, government and civil society. Multi-stakeholderism is predicated on representative models of liberal democracy, and such abstraction always refers to itself and thus frequently conflicts with the grass-roots networks that characterize the constituent dimension of NGOS and CSOS. Representation does not correspond with the logic of networks, which are better understood as non-representational forms of politics.

In saying this I do not wish to valorise the horizontality of networks. The tendency to describe networks in terms of horizontality results in an occlusion of 'the political', which consists of antagonisms that underpin sociality. It is technically and socially incorrect to assume that hierarchical and centralizing architectures and practices are absent from network cultures. At the technical level, one only has to look at the debates surrounding the information society and Internet governance: hierarchical and political-economic aspects of assigning domain names, location of root servers, politics of IPRS, uneven geography of information flows, determination of standards, and effects of trade agreements on content production and distribution. The hierarchical dimension to networked sociality is easy to account for: just consider the cohort of alpha males scheming in the back rooms of so many organizational forms. Even in the case of wikis, which on the surface appear to be exemplary non-representational forms in so far as labour on content production is anonymous, again we need only to venture through the backdoor to see the ringleaders at work.[51]

Of course the technical and social aspects of ICT networks are not mutually exclusive, but rather interpenetrate one another in a plethora of ways. A challenge for organized networks is thus to address the software problem and the social problem. This is no easy feat, and can be related back to my earlier point regarding whether or not to incorporate networks as a legally registered entity – an option I suggested was necessary if networks wished to intervene in the market of higher education. Joseph Reagle's blog entry on 'Open Communities and Closed Law' signals what might be identified as the fundamental disjuncture between horizontal and vertical organization and communication systems:

> What does the recent news of a Wikipedia CEO who is also a lawyer, an 'oversight' function that makes hidden revisions to Wikipedia, and the threat of the Debian Project severing its relationship with its legally chartered non-profit have in common? A strong indication that open communities with a formal legal standing are a conflicted beast.[52]

Reagle goes on to note that such tension is a hazard of scale: 'As Wikipedia has grown in size and repute the likelihood of the Wikipedia being subject to legal action has similarly grown'. It is pointless to think that networks might somehow exist as tension-free zones. Sure, it is a matter of degree, but I see no escape from this, and consider it a variation of 'the political' that attends scalar transformation for any network. To this end, this book engages the question of democracy as constituent process that registers the political dimension of networks.

Institutions beyond Democracy

As I finished this book my reservations about concepts of democracy ran deep. What does democracy mean and consist of, after all, in the logic of networks (another term that is open to any number of meanings)? And in another register, as Antonio Negri writes, 'the problem is that the term "democracy" has been emptied of all its meaning. Democracy is said to be identified with "the people" – but what is the people?'[53] In the first and most simple instance, my problem rests with the uneasy, and what I consider as ultimately incompatible, transposition or grafting of democracy onto networks. With stupefying frequency, advocates of 'e-democracy' and community oriented Internet users and researchers are among the chief culprits who maintain the Net is synonymous with democracy. But that critique is easy. There is also a more general view on the democratizing capacity of the Internet, manifesting in the production of countless speeches, newspaper columns, policy recommendations, and everyday conversations. Such a position assumes the core principles and practices of democracy can be shunted over to networks. But can they?

In my view, the question of form is paramount here. This is as much an issue of the technical and material dimensions of Internet based communications media as it is of the processual relations through which expression takes shape. The registration of form, in other words, only becomes apparent through the movement of expression.[54] Moreover, I wish to place the emphasis here on *institutional forms* rather than institutions *per se*.[55] Forms are open to the movement of networks and the network of movements. Both are in constant tension with institutionalization, which I understand as the reification of form. Since it is only revealed through expression, form holds no relation to formalism, which is another iteration of reification, stasis and establishment. Form thus initiates a kind of border zone, a space of 'the political', and contests all efforts at containment. This is its paradox. Form gives a semblance of order and finitude, but since the individuation of expression institutes the territory of form, an uncertainty always lingers about form. Form can never rest secure that it has captured expression. Its strategy of the future is precipitated by insecurity, uncertainty, hesitation, ambivalence. At best, expression is momentarily organized within the borders of form. It is through this dynamic that I understand Sandro Mezzadra and Étienne Balibar, who maintain the border signals 'the "non-democratic" element of democracy'.[56] This is also how and why liberal democracy is precisely not coextensive with the logic of networks, whose transversal relations institute new organizational forms that cut across the struggles of the movements and the policing of the state.

Angela Mitropoulos and Brett Neilson contest this assertion on borders and the 'non-democratic' element of democracy, noting the inclusion-exclusion function of the border makes possible not only the

regulation of the market and 'foundation of citizenship and politics', but, moreover, 'there can be no democracy without the border'.[57]
In other words, it is precisely the border that joins *demos* (people) with *kratos* (sovereign authority). Democracy, then, is a political idiom of limits and its deficiencies need to be understood in the terms and conditions by which it operates. My argument is not to suggest that networks are somehow borderless or beyond limits. That particular imaginary belongs to cyber-libertarians, free marketeers, and the like. Rather, my position is simply that while networks in many ways are regulated indirectly by the sovereign interests of the state, they are also not reducible to institutional apparatuses of the state. And this is what makes possible the creation of new institutional forms as expressions of non-representational democracy.

The potential for non-representational democracy within social-technical settings of digital communication networks is predicated on the materiality of informatization and informationality. Tiziana Terranova makes this clear in her book *Network Culture* in which she locates linguistic and political representation as the mode of expression and organization peculiar to the 'perspectival and three-dimensional space of modernity'.[58] The modern episteme thus rests on distinctions between subject and object, observer and observed in order to create its grid of intelligibility. Such a paradigm is inherently insecure and insufficient as a resource to understand and act within complex systems. As Terranova notes, information theory arose in the 1920s from the fields of mathematics, physics and telecommunications, and later biology and anthropology in the 1940s-'60s as studies in cybernetics develop in parallel with the military-industrial complex and its interest in the organization and management of populations. As I discuss in chapter 5, the problem engaging these fields was how 'noise' or feedback rendered communication as an unstable, mutable system. Noise came to be recognized as the precondition for renewal and regeneration within an open system. The limit and thus crisis of representation corresponds with its incapacity to account for complexity, entropy, indeterminacy and non-linearity that characterizes immersive informational environments organized about the logic of relations.[59] To think the possibility of democracy within informational social-technical systems calls, then, for non-representational models.

I have considered removing democracy entirely in reference to networks, replacing it instead with the seemingly less formal term 'politics'. But even politics, as an articulation of 'the political', tends to presuppose a formal arrangement within which the antagonistic field of sociality is instituted. More often than not, the process of institution formation and thus determining the legitimacy of politics is attributed to a sovereign power, be that one of secular or non-secular authority. Irrespective of the various idioms of democracy (rational consensus, deliberative, procedural, direct, radical, etcetera),[60] it is typically associated with the triumph of the secular rather than non-secular state. Of course there is an historical basis and tradition of thought behind this.

My point, however, is that democracy beyond and within the secular state is a process of translation that is predicated on a hegemonic operation that, in many instances, annuls the political. Or as Tronti puts it, 'The workers' movement was not defeated by capital. The workers' movement was defeated by democracy'.[61] For this reason new institutional spaces are needed in order to give formal expression to the political without which the descent into violence, dysfunctionality and malcontent proliferates. Or even worse, acquiescence. In his Posthegemony blog, Jon Beasley-Murray phrases the impasse of politics without democracy as follows: 'The prevailing consensus would seem to be that politics is unimaginable without democracy, that it is only democracy that opens up the possibility for politics. Without democracy, all we are left with is (variously, or perhaps in combination) power, administration, fanaticism, hatred'.[62]

Just think, for instance, of the complexities and antagonisms attending the will to transform Iraq from authoritarian rule into a liberal democratic non-secular state. Failure. This is the consensus. So where lurks democracy? Similarly, though situated of course within a dramatically different field of forces (political, economic, social, cultural, technical), the translation of democracy into the social-technical form of the Internet holds its own special problems. And these are all too frequently overlooked, as if the institutional frameworks of the nation-state contour seamlessly onto the Internet.

But there are other routes to thinking politics and institutional forms. The appeal of politics without democracy rests precisely with the potential for the political to refuse the passage of becoming instituted within the state form. Politics then resides within a non- or post-democratic politics, or politics unhinged from the theatre of democracy.[63] This does not eradicate the operation of institutions *per se*, indeed my argument takes a completely opposite position. But it does bring into sharp relief the limits of democracy as the only available grammar for thinking processes of instituting politics within the social-technical settings of network cultures.

There is a correlation here with Virno's elliptical gestures to a 'non-state public sphere', an extraparliamentary space of cooperation, sharing, common resources, knowledge, customs, experiences and habits that make possible a non-representative democracy that no longer submits to 'the myths and rituals of sovereignty'.[64] But Virno does not go so far as dispensing with democracy. Instead, he speaks of a 'non-representational democracy', one that is decoupled from sovereign power. The concept of organized networks is developed throughout this book in an attempt to give a sense of an emerging institutional form within which the organization of Net politics is partially autonomous from sovereign control.

Despite the fact that the Net is far from resembling anything democratic, and along with the ambivalence I hold with the concept of democracy, my decision to retain a meditation on the relation between democracy and network cultures is also motivated by more practical concerns. To adopt *politics* as the linguistic vessel of organization would have required a substantial revision of the central argument, and in ways that I can only foresee at this moment as uncertain. Democracy remains, then, as an index of the passage of my thought on network cultures over the past six years. There is also a question of creating openings for readers into a text. To this end, democracy serves as a mutable receptacle with which both the reader and this writer are able to enter the politics of network cultures.

Diagram of Thought

Bringing together the conceptual insights into the philosophy and history of technology and theories on the politics of social movements, this book sets out to analyse how cultural practices associated with the Internet can more properly be understood by examining specific geopolitical, social and economic conditions. The work of Dutch media theorist and activist Geert Lovink has informed much of my understanding as well as experience of Net politics and culture. Similarly, Australian-American media and cultural theorist McKenzie Wark has for many years now been a benchmark for how to think and write media philosophy. Lovink and Wark are a presence throughout this book, as is the thought of friends and collaborators Brett Neilson, Soenke Zehle and Danny Butt and the mailing lists of Fibreculture and Nettime. Michael Hardt and Antonio Negri's passionate revival of an autonomist variation of Marxian political philosophy in their book *Empire* was a great source of inspiration in the early stages of this book. In her review of *Empire*, Benita Parry gently admonishes Hardt and Negri for their 'dizzying conceptual promiscuity induced by the heady cocktail of Marxist, autonomist and postmodern paradigms. In particular because the Deleuzian notion of lines or paths of flight, of flows and borderless continuums is used as a trope of thinking processes and invoked as a template of real world conditions, these disposals converge in an insouciant disregard of the actually existing circumstances in what the authors insist is a post-imperialist era'.[65]

This book could also be accused of perhaps not a dizzying, but probably a conceptually promiscuous combination of 'Marxist, autonomist and postmodern paradigms', though I would phrase these lineages differently. It also draws heavily on Deleuze, invoking notions of 'continuums' in order to speak of 'processes', and then some more. At the level of conceptual approach, this book mines a slightly different lineage within Deleuze's work, one that I think corresponds in a much more familiar and conventional way with a Marxian approach that is concerned with issues of uneven development and the politics of labour-power. By drawing on the operation of a 'constitutive outside' in Deleuze's work, this book is able to furnish a much more identifiable bridge or connection with a Marxian tradition. The notion of a constitutive outside, for instance, enables the conceptual passage of labour and its relation to organized networks within this book. While this book often makes reference to 'a continuum of relations' between that which has emerged and the conditions of possibility – especially in its discussion of processual media theory – it also insists that limits play an operative role in the formation of relations. For example, in chapter 3 I question the notion of 'immaterial labour' and argue that *disorganized labour* more accurately describes the precarious condition of labour within informational economies and the creative industries.

There can be little question that the shift from broadcast communications media to networked, digital communications media has enabled a radical transformation in the ways in which social-technical relations and modes of communication are organized within a capitalist system. That much is obvious. The ongoing authority of the state, however, can often seem less apparent within contemporary media-informational environments. Yet unlike what Hardt and Negri have often asserted, there is a strong case for the ways in which the nation-state continues to play a substantive role in regulating the movement of people and things. This is not to ignore the considerable increase in the range of actors operating across subnational, intra-regional and global scales. Rather, it is to recognize that the transformation of the state is such that it frequently extends its authority beyond the territorial borders of the nation.[66] And it does so precisely through its appeal to the sovereignty of the nation-state. This is made most clear in the numerous conflicts surrounding issues of border control vis-à-vis trade and population flows across the world.

Gramsci and Lenin do not feature in this book and they probably should, since much of the concern here is with strategies and techniques of organization. Though perhaps their absence is not so surprising. The argument for organization in this book is not premised on the logic of the party. Indeed, this book is openly hostile to the cultural and structural features of party politics. Moreover, it does not see the party form as one that corresponds with the mode of communication peculiar to networked technologies such as the Internet. This book understands the possibility of organization as that which is immanent to the media of communication. Such a focus was not the concern of Lenin or Gramsci. And how could it have been? In their time, the party headquarters, the workers' association, the factory and the streets were the primary architectonic forms of communication. Today, that has all changed. As such, the ways in which politics becomes organized has also changed. New modes of communication necessitate new theoretical tools in order to make intelligible and actionable the ongoing force of living labour.

Citing David Harvey's call for the need for a 'socialist avant-garde' to facilitate in the creation of 'organizations, institutions, doctrines, programs, formalized structures and the like', both Parry and Harvey remain wedded to a mode of political organization that is as utopian as the charges levelled against Hardt and Negri.[67] Parry and Harvey are typical of a Marxian radical intelligentsia who, for all their attentiveness to the peculiarities of materiality, so often attribute so little significance to perhaps the most important dimension to any form of organization: communication.

Political organization can never again take the form of a revived Internationalist worker's movement. Aside from the primacy granted to class as the condition of possibility, Internationalism fails to comprehend one of the central lessons of Marxist analysis: the geography of uneven development. The principle and material condition of uneven development is nothing if it does not also take into account the situation of communication. This is perhaps more so than ever, as communications technologies become the primary means by which production, distribution and exchange are managed, to say nothing of social life. From ATMS on every downtown street corner and village square to satellite and radio navigation using Global Positioning Systems (GPS) in agriculture industries and leisure cruise boats; from computer systems used in finance modelling, online domestic banking and dating services, information technologies are common to the reproduction of capital and the exploitation of labour-power. This book stages a series of interventions into the parasitic logic of capital in the passionate belief that another world is indeed possible. And it is the world we live, now.

Part 1

1 Whose Democracy?

NGOS, Information Societies and
Non-Representative Democracy

The Network Problematic

A spectre is haunting this age of informationality – the spectre of
state sovereignty. As a modern technique of governance based on territorial control, a 'monopoly of violence' and the capacity to regulate the
flow of goods, services and people, the sovereign power of the nation-
state is not yet ready to secede from the system of internationalism. The
compact of alliances among nation-states over matters of trade, security,
foreign aid, investment, and so forth, substantiates the ongoing relevance of the state form in shaping the mobile life of people and things.
As the Internet gained purchase throughout the 1990s on the everyday
experiences of those living within advanced economies in particular,
the popular imagination became entranced by the promise of a 'borderless' world of 'frictionless capitalism'. Such a view is the doxa of many:
political philosophers, economists, international relations scholars,
politicians, CEOS, activists, cyber-libertarians, advertising agencies, political spin-doctors and ecologists all have their variation on the theme of
a postnational, global world-system inter-linked by informational
flows.

Just as the nation-state appears obsolete for many, so the term *network* has become perhaps the most pervasive metaphor to describe a
range of phenomena, desires and practices in contemporary information societies. The refrain one hears on networks in recent years goes
something like this: fluid, ephemeral, transitory, innovative, flowing,
non-linear, decentralized, value adding, creative, flexible, open, collaborative, risk-taking, reflexive, informal, individualized, intense, transformative, and so on and so forth. Many of these words are used inter-
changeably as metaphors, concepts and descriptions. Increasingly, there
is a desperation evident in research on new information and communication technologies that manifests in the form of empirical research.
Paradoxically, much of this research consists of methods and epistemo-

logical frameworks that render the mobility and abstraction of information in terms of stasis.

Governments have found that the network refrain appeals to their neoliberal sensibilities, which search for new rhetorics to substitute the elimination of state infrastructures with the logic of individualized self-formation within Third Way style networks of 'social capital'.[1] Research committees at university and national levels see networks as offering the latest promise of an economic utopia in which research practice synchronically models the dynamic movement of finance capital, yet so often the outcomes of research ventures are based upon the reproduction of pre-existing research clusters and the maintenance of their hegemony for institutions and individuals with ambitions of legitimacy within the prevailing doxas. Telcos and cable TV 'providers' revel in their capacity to flaunt a communications system that is less a network than a heterogeneous mass of audiences-consumers-users connected by the content and services of private media oligopolies. Activists pursue techniques of simultaneous disaggregation and consolidation via online organization in their efforts to mobilize opposition and actions in the form of mutable affinities against the corporatization of everyday life. The US military-entertainment complex enlists strategies of organized distribution of troops and weaponry on battlefields defined by unpredictability and chaos, while maintaining the spectacle of control across the vectors of news media. The standing reserve of human misery sweeps up the remains of daily horror.

Theorists and artists of new media are not immune to these prevailing discourses, and reproduce similar network homologies in their valorisation of open, decentralized, distributed, egalitarian and emergent social-technical forms. In so doing, the discursive and social-technical form of networks is attributed an ontological status. The so-called openness, fluidity and contingency of networks is rendered in essentialist terms that function to elide the complexities and contradictions that comprise the uneven spatio-temporal dimensions and material practices of networks. Similarly, the force of the 'constitutive outside' is frequently dismissed by media and cultural theorists in favour of delirious discourses of openness and horizontality. Just as 'immanence' has been a key metaphor to describe the logic of informationalization, so can it be used to describe networks. To put it in a nutshell, the technics of networks can be described as thus: if you can sketch a diagram of relations in which connections are 'external to their terms' (Hume-Deleuze), then you get a picture of a network model.

Whatever the peculiarities the network refrain may take, there is a predominant tendency to overlook the ways in which networks are produced by regimes of power, economies of desire and the restless rhythms of global capital. How, I wonder, might the antagonisms peculiar to these varied and more often than not incommensurate political situations of informationality be formulated in terms of a political theory of networks? From a theoretical and practical point of view, how might organized networks be defined as new institutional forms of informationalism? Given that institutions throughout history function to organize social relations, what distinguishes the organized network as an institution from its modern counterparts? Obviously there are differences along lines of horizontal versus vertical, distributed versus contained, decentralized versus centralized, bureaucratic reason versus database processing, and so on. But what else is there?

It is not sufficient to identify basic structural differences without also attending to the ways in which network dynamics are conditioned by the combinatory logic of 'the political' as it is shaped by materialities of knowledge and modalities of expression. At stake here is a question of epistemology and its conditions of possibility, of how techniques of intelligibility are ordered and acquire variable layers of status and capacities to effect change. To this end, institutional settings function as an enabling force. They provide a framework and set of resources from which emergent idioms of expression can be organized in ways that offer the possibility of sustainability and renewal – something that has not, for instance, been a feature of most tactical media interventions. And for this reason, I maintain that the primary political strategy for networks at the current conjuncture is to engage in the invention of new institutional forms. This chapter – and indeed, this book overall – asserts the need for a strategic turn if network cultures are to address the problematics of scale and sustainability: *the situation of informational politics.*

The challenge for politically active network cultures is to make strategic use of new communications media in order to create new institutions of possibility. Such social-technical formations will take on the characteristics of organized networks – distributive, non-linear, situated, project-based – in order to create self-sustaining media-ecologies that are simply not on the map of established political and cultural institutions. As Gary Genosko asserts, 'the real task is to find the institutional means to incarnate new modes of subjectification while simultaneously avoiding the slide into bureaucratic sclerosis'.[2] Such a view also augurs well for the life of networks as they subsist within the political logic of informationality constituted by the force of the outside.

Networks and the Limits of Liberal Democracy

A network doesn't come out of nowhere. One of the key challenges networks present is the possibility of new institutional formations that want to make a political, social and cultural difference within the social-technical logic of networks. It's not yet clear what shape these institutions will take. To fall back into the crumbling security of traditional, established institutions is not an option. The network logic is increasingly the normative mode of organizing social-technical relations in advanced economies, and this impacts upon both the urban and rural poor within those countries as well as those in economically developing countries. So, the traditional institution is hardly a place of escape for those wishing to hide from the logic of networks.

A degree of centralization and hierarchization seems essential for a network to be characterized as organized. Can the network thus be characterized as an 'institution', or might it need to acquire additional qualities? Is institutional status even desirable for a network that aspires to intervene in debates on critical Internet research and culture? How does an organized network help us redefine our understanding of what an institution might become? Moreover, what is the political logic peculiar to organized networks? These are the primary questions I address in this section and in order to do this I develop the concept of non-representative democracy via a critique of liberal democracy.

In her book *The Democratic Paradox*, Chantal Mouffe recapitulates the key characteristics of modern democracy. The core values and ideas of democracy consist of 'equality, identity between governing and governed and popular sovereignty'.[3] Modern democracy incorporated features of the liberal tradition, which was characterized by 'the rule of law, the defence of human rights and the respect of individual liberty'.[4]

Hence, the phrase *liberal democracy*. Representational democracy in the form of democratically elected governments is the principal mode that democracy has taken across the West. Popular sovereignty grants authority to the discursive figure of 'the people'. It is a mode of rule that assumes a relationship rather than alienation between the people and the state. Indeed, it assumes the people as citizens are at once represented by the state and at the same time protected by the functioning of the state in so far as they constitute the very possibility of the state. Such a notion has frequently been called into question, since it is predominantly a myth. Who, for example, constitutes the figure of 'the people'? Women, children, minority peoples? Historically, the figure of the people is underscored by a logic of exclusion, which in turn undermines the legitimacy of popular sovereignty.

Liberal democracy is predicated on an articulation between a constituency of citizens and elected representatives. This articulation has eroded in recent years with the advent of the neoliberal state, which inculcates not so much citizens but consumer-clients into the corporate-state nexus. The ambivalence that emerges around the composition of political constituencies or subjectivities has been the topic of recent debate associated with Italian political philosophers and activist movements. Paolo Virno distinguishes between the 'multitude' (a plurality) and the 'people' (a unity). He sees the former as the basis for a politics that does not involve the transfer or delegation of power (decision-making, for example) to the sovereign, which is the model of representative politics through the mechanism of voting at elections. To varying degrees, such a model has functioned as a technique of organizing social and economic relations within the architecture of the state. But to transpose such a model over to ICT-based networks is necessarily weak, since the architectonic arrangement is composed of very different variables, dynamics, forces, spaces, temporalities and the like.

To put it bluntly, it is not possible to speak of democracy as a representative, consensus-based politics in the environment of ICT-based networks. To take one dominant example: in both a practical and theoretical sense, advocates of 'e-democracy' are investing in a phantasm with their belief that the central principles of representative democracy (citizenship, participation, equality, transparency, etcetera) can be transposed into the realm of networks. For a start, citizenship is a concept and practice co-emergent with the state form. Networks are not states. Therefore in order to think democracy within networks, it is necessary to develop in conceptual and practical ways idioms for non- or post-representative democracy. Such a task does not abandon the concept or possibility of democracy, but rather it recognizes democracy as an ongoing project that, in a historical sense, is an idiom that has undergone numerous transformations. In order to develop a concept of non-representative democracy immanent to networks of communication, the work of Mouffe is, I think, helpful to engage, particularly in terms of her elaboration of 'the political' as a field of antagonistic struggles.

Mouffe argues that *agonistic* democracy consists of that which acknowledges the power-legitimation processes of 'politics' conditioned by the possibility of 'struggle between adversaries' as distinct from the illegitimacy within deliberative or Third Way rules of democracy that refuse the 'struggle between enemies', which is special to *antagonism* and 'the violence that is inherent in sociability'.[5] In her recent book, *On the Political*, Mouffe both summarizes and develops her thesis on agonistic democracy outlined in *The Democratic Paradox*.[6] In *The Democratic Paradox*, Mouffe presents a compelling (if somewhat repetitive) critique of Third Way politics and rational consensus models of liberal democracy (Habermas, Rawls) in terms of the fundamental contradictions with those political idioms: namely, a rhetoric of tolerance and pluralism underpinned by numerous forms and techniques of exclusion inherent within rational consensus models of democracy. Mouffe argues that rational consensus, deliberative models of democracy ultimately fail due to their disengagement with 'the political', or field of antagonisms that underpin sociality. With Ernesto Laclau, her call has been for a radical democracy – one that takes antagonism as a condition of possibility for democracy. She argues for an agonistic process whereby a plurality of interests, demands, discourses, practices and forces procure a space of legitimacy whereby antagonisms are able to be addressed – not for the purpose of transcendence or consensus, but for the purpose of acknowledging that incommensurabilities and dissent are inherent to the politics of sociality.

My critique of Mouffe is based on the limits of her argument when it comes to thinking politics in relation to networks articulated by digital communications media or ICTs. Her model of radical democracy is premised on political institutions of the state as the primary institutional framework for addressing 'the political'. How, though, might such a model transpire in relation to organized networks? While I think these networks can be called institutional forms in so far as they have a capacity to organize social relations, they are radically dissimilar to the technics of modern institutional forms such as parliament and auxiliary institutions and departments. In this regard, the formation of organized networks shares much with what Virno calls a 'non-state public sphere': 'It is typical of the post-fordist multitude to provoke the collapse of political representation; not as an anarchist gesture, but as a realistic and quiet search for political institutions that elude the myths and rituals of sovereignty'.[7]

If Mouffe's model of an agonistic democracy is to have any purchase within networked, informational societies, then it is essential to address the ways in which the organization of social-political relations within such a terrain occurs within new institutional forms immanent to the media vectors of communication, and thus sociality. Unless Mouffe's thesis is recast in ways that address the political situation of informational networks in terms of emergent institutions,[8] her advancement of an agonistic democracy whose condition of existence is premised on the persistence of political institutional forms within the space of second nature is one that will remain fixed within an image of nostalgia. In effect, then, a process of translation is required in order to resituate Mouffe's agonistic model of adversaries within the 'post-institutional' terrain of networks. Such work can benefit from considering how Mouffe's notions of 'politics' and 'the political' operate as constitutive forces within networks.

Networks are predisposed toward a grammar of uncertain potentialities. The traffic in expression across networks comprises the ontic level of communication, which Mouffe and Laclau associate with 'politics' as distinct from the ontological dimension of 'the political', which 'concerns the very way in which society is instituted'.[9] The ensemble of practices, actions and discourses – or what I am calling expression – is a field of competing interests, desires and demands that undergo processes of translation of 'the political'. Conflict and dispute are not excluded from expression, as the deliberative model would have it, so much as constitute the very possibility of expression. In a negative sense, the uncertainty of networks arises in part from an incapacity to manage such tensions. At this point the network may self-destruct.[10] Mailing lists, for example, are renowned for their inability to deal with the egoistically motivated habits of 'trolls' whose primary mission is to exploit the vulnerability of list communities that aspire to principles of openness and tolerance. These are nice virtues, but have proven time and again to be barriers to decision-making. The deliberation that typically follows interventions by trolls ends up being the focus of attention and does nothing to advance any political or cultural project of networks. Frequently list members will get bored and unsubscribe. Those lists that do undertake online elections in an effective way – and here, I'm thinking of a mailing list like the Association of Internet Researchers[11] – do not resemble what I would call networks as political technologies and are not the settings for engagements with adversaries as a process of social-political transformation. Representative democracy in online settings results in nothing more than the reproduction of a status quo.

The development of new institutional forms immanent to the media of communication would, I maintain, provide a stabilizing effect for networks in so far as a limit horizon is established that organizes the sociality of networks in ways that go beyond the automated and enculturated protocols and conventions one may associate with mailing lists, for example. A limit horizon operates as a necessary antidote to the dominant assumption (and indeed valorisation) of networks as spaces of fluid, ephemeral, fleeting association and exchange.[12] Limits, moreover, are established through the operation of the constitutive outside, which is a process of engaging 'the political' as a complex of tensions through which exteriorities (other networks, NGOS, universities, IPRS, government policies, exploitation of labour-power, geopolitics of information, gender and ethnic differences, etcetera) are present within a network of relations as an 'affirmation of a difference'.[13]

In the case of organized networks this affirmation, however, is not as Mouffe would have it 'a precondition for the existence of any identity', since organized networks are not the kind of institutional forms that correspond with 'the creation of a "we"', which is a collective identity found in institutional settings such as the political party or social forms such as 'the people'. While I acknowledge Laclau's understanding (which Mouffe would share) of collective identities such as 'the people' as 'the emergence of a unity out of heterogeneity [which] presupposes the establishment of equivalential logics and the production of empty signifiers'[14] – in other words, a complex of differential relations that coalesce as a unicity ('chain of empty signifiers') in order to stake out a distinction from that which is other – the organized network can never correspond to the logic of 'we' or 'unity' precisely because it is a social-technical form instituted through the logic of immanence and not the logic of the kind of institution embodied in the party-political form of the parliamentary system that Mouffe clings to as the form best able to realize the liberal democratic project as one of democratic pluralism. Mine is not a rejection of liberal democracy *per se*, but rather a recognition of its structural, material limits as a representational form and its incompatibility with the technics of communication and the organization of sociality as found in networks.[15] That said, my position does amount to a rejection if liberal democracy cannot undergo a transformation beyond a representational form.

In advocating an adversarial model of agonistic democracy, Mouffe insists that 'very important socio-economic and political transformations, with radical implications, are possible within the context of liberal democratic institutions'.[16] In the case of networks we have already gone beyond those settings and modes of social organization. Are we to then abandon any project that seeks to institute networks as political technologies? My argument, of course, is no. The challenge is to imagine and enact a non-representative democracy whose technics of organization are internal to the logic of networks. Such a project calls for the invention of new institutional forms external to the corporate-state apparatus. These new forms are neither purely local, nor are they exclusively global. Rather, they subsist as proliferating social-technical forms between micro and macro dimensions of politics and territorial scales, defining their limits according to the contingency of the event.

With organized networks there is no possibility of representational democracy due to the architectonic properties of immanent forms of social-political organization. Instead, we find the potential for post- or non-representational forms of democracy. And contrary to Laclau's argument against Hardt and Negri's *Empire*, the logic of immanence does not aim for a 'universal *desertion*' or 'eclipse' of politics in favour of some kind post-political liberation.[17] The logic of immanence does not negate the role of externalities or 'the exterior'. Externalities are elements that coalesce as a concrete arrangement whose relations are conditioned by the force of the constitutive outside. This is a process by which the potentiality of immanence is actualized as particular forms and practices.[18] Laclau is correct in his critique of Hardt and Negri's claim that with Empire there is 'no more outside' or external enemy and thus no space of opposition,[19] but he is mistaken, in my view, to assert that the logic of immanence is unable to account for social antagonisms.[20] Since the constitutive outside is integral to the logic of immanence, so too is the potentiality of tensions, struggles and conflicts as they emerge within the plane of organization or actualization.

Similarly, non-representative democracy does not assume to have eclipsed social antagonisms that underpin the field of 'the political'. As discussed above, the force of immanence as a population of potentialities is released through the operation of the constitutive outside. This dynamic is comprised of tensions and conflict, and as such can be understood in terms of 'the political'. Nor is non-representative democracy equivalent to the 'post-political' perspectives advocated by theorists such as Ulrich Beck, Anthony Giddens and Scott Lash.[21] Rather, non-representative systems are conditioned simultaneously by the social-technical impossibility of networks to represent and the decline of the civil society-state relation as a complex of representative institutions and procedures engaged in the management of labour-power and organization of social life. While networks may have members and participants, they do not have constituencies as such who are organized around the logic of a body politic. There is no unity or identity such as 'the people' or, as Laclau would put it, no heterogeneity articulated as a chain of equivalences that seeks to have its interests and demands represented by an individual or advocacy body. Individuals may choose to contribute to the expansion and proliferation of the network, they may subsist as potentialities waiting to become unleashed, and indeed they may decide to institute representative mechanisms of governance. But when this happens the network dissembles as a grammar of uncertainty and evacuates the space of 'the political'.

The concept of the organized network is also distinct from what Mouffe terms 'organized networks of global civil society and business' undertaking the task of realizing a cosmopolitan democracy – a position that Mouffe critiques for its oversight of 'the political'.[22] Unlike the global civil society networks described by Mouffe, organized networks are not new global institutions, but more modestly and pragmatically, new institutions whose technics are modulated by the spatio-temporal dynamics of the network. As I go on to show in the section that follows and the next chapter, the key model adopted by global civil society movements has been that of 'multi-stakeholderism'. This model, I argue, is incompatible with the logic of networks precisely because it is predicated on the logic of representation.

Multi-stakeholderism and the Architecture of Net Politics

My basic argument is that networks are at a turning point and their capacity to exist depends on developing technics of organization. And it's here that I think there may be opportunities for networks to lever the discursive legitimacy that has arisen for civil society networks at the World Summit on the Information Society (WSIS). This is where specific case studies of networks and how they are operating in a post-WSIS environment at subnational, transregional levels becomes helpful. Those directly involved in project development – frequently NGOS – have had much experience, but NGOS seem to be coming under increasing pressure as they have moved into a more substantive role as political actors within a neoliberal paradigm that grants legitimacy to those who can function as 'external providers'. The multi-stakeholder model doesn't seem to me to be one that enables networks (which I would distinguish from NGOS) to negotiate the complexities of information economies, societies, and the like.

After the closing ceremony of the WSIS, the nagging question that attends all summits remains largely unaddressed: what changes will happen at local, subnational levels? The WSIS process has resulted in two key outcomes for civil society: 1) a hitherto non-existent discursive legitimacy at the supranational level for civil society values, needs and interests as they relate to the political economy and technics of ICTS, and 2) a cache of resources for dealing with trans-institutional relations made possible by the multi-stakeholderism experience. As I discuss in greater detail in the next chapter, the primary post-WSIS challenge will be the extent to which NGOS and civil society movements are able to exploit the newfound discursive legitimacy at local, intra-regional levels.

At the scalar level, this is a process of renationalizing what at the moment remains a denationalized discourse. Such a problematic is one engaged by indigenous sovereignty movements and human rights practitioners and advocates for many years now.[23] In the case of the WSIS the difference is that the political economy of ICTS has expanded the complexity of life understood as a communicative relation articulated by media forms.

Since different institutions have different temporal rhythms, the movement of discourse across institutional scales instantiates antagonisms peculiar to 'the political'. Irrespective of whatever agreements are made in the form of final recommendations, the fact remains that governments are highly unlikely to legislate WSIS policy because their bureaucracies are unable to deal with the complexity of issues that have emerged from the WSIS debates. Perhaps there might have been more concrete outcomes if the WSIS debates had somehow restricted the discussion to technical issues alone, but that would require disassociating technical issues from political and economic issues. Furthermore, any national legislation that might eventuate from the WSIS proceedings is faced with the dilemma of policy that has already been made redundant by economies of speed that attend the interrelations between technological innovation and social transformation.

What, then, is to be salvaged from the WSIS for civil society, and what is the relation to Net politics? For the most part, multi-stakeholderism is celebrated as a form of democracy in action. Wolfgang Kleinwächter captures the spirit of multi-stakeholderism:

The principle of Multistakeholderism is a new and innovative concept for the global diplomacy of the 21st century. While the concept as such is still vague and undefined, non-governmental stakeholders from the private sector and from civil society are becoming step by step an integral part of policy making in the information age. ... The WSIS process has demonstrated that when the existing legal framework has to be filled with new subject related global policies, a new triangular relationship between governments, private sector and civil society is emerging. These relationships are not hierarchical by nature but will be organized in [the] form of networks around concrete issues. It will depend from the concrete substance of an issue, how

the triangular is designed and how relevant trilateral governance
mechanism will be organized.[24]

Absent from Kleinwächter's formalistic celebration of multi-stakeholderism is the unruliness of 'the political'. Aligned with the politics of
advocacy, Kleinwächter is not able to address the tensions internal to
the logic of multi-stakeholderism as an architecture for relations between international and local NGOs and grassroots organizations.[25]
However effective multi-stakeholderism may be in policy-making for
an information society, such policy proposals are largely ineffectual unless they can infiltrate the complexity of institutions whose capacities
are organized according to incommensurate temporal speeds. Again,
this is a problematic of scale and translation.

Yet perhaps the success of multi-stakeholderism should be measured
as an accumulation of resources for negotiating issues among a range of
institutional, political and social actors, as Kleinwächter suggests? Such
an ambition is crucially dependent on the capacity of actors to collectively retain institutional memories. Assuming individuals might transcend their institutional codes of secrecy, such a feature long vacated
the realm of modern, industrial institutional forms of the state department and corporate firm with the onset of post-Fordism and new forms
of flexible organization and mobility, to say nothing of the fragility of
networks and their general condition of disorganization.

Multi-stakeholderism is too closely aligned to the fantasies of deliberative, rational consensus forms of democracy. The emptiness of multi-
stakeholderism as an architecture of change invites new forms of managing the politics of information. As I have been arguing, an alternative
model is beginning to emerge: that of the organized network, a form
whose logic of organization is internal to the dynamics of the media of
communication. Like the NGO, the organized network is expected to answer to demands of transparency and accountability. Like the Internet,
the organized network is mistakenly assumed to adopt a decentralized,
horizontal, distributed structure of communication. The organized
network is antithetical to both of these presuppositions.

This is not to advocate some kind of return to the archaic form of
party-politics, as Žižek would have it. But it is to suggest that in order
for organized networks to undertake planning and development of proj-

ects and intervene in prevailing debates, a strategic – rather than tactical – architecture is required. This is where the issue of sustainability transfigures both the discourse of development and the discourse of networks. The politics of information is common to both these realms. Sustainability requires a business model.[26] NGOs have extensive experience at obtaining funding, much more so than networks associated with tactical media activists. The latter, on the other hand, have a high degree of media literacy vis-à-vis the political economy of information, the programming of code, and the performance of critique from within the spectacle of media systems. Collaboration between NGOs and tactical media practitioners could be one of those instances of mutual benefit and scalar enhancement.

While funding possibilities may arise from global relations in the form of donors, business activities and aid, the social and political force of networks is predominantly local or intra-regional. Herein lies a tension of translation internal to networks as they traverse scales for different purposes. And this is where the demands of transparency, accountability and representation become distinct in the form of externally imposed conditions and internally generated expectations. The management of these dual constituencies brings enormous pressure upon networks and highlights the manner in which 'democracy' has multiple meanings determined by the situation of actors. Accommodating these kinds of expectations and demands can absorb huge amounts of energy, time and structural-technical reconfiguration (online voting anyone?). Democracy, here, becomes equivalent to destruction.

Mechanisms of accountability and representation conflict with the speed of capital, the flow of information and can slow the development of projects. Yet they are also sources of trust – a key foundation of networks. Can trust, then, be constituted within non-representative social-technical systems in alternative ways? Just as 'democracy' as a universal principle is rendered dysfunctional when it meets the contingencies of the particular, the question of trust can only be answered on a case by case basis that considers the taxonomy of activities and relations peculiar to any network. But taxonomies are also not enough. Networks cannot be contained, even though they have limits. Similarly, trust cannot be measured, and instead resonates as an indeterminacy within the fluctuating rhythms of network ecologies.

Any inquiry into, and active engagement with, democratic polities as they emerge within informational network societies necessitates an engagement with new social-technical relations that condition the possibility of new institutional forms. This is a theme I develop in more detail in the next chapter. But for now, it is germane to foreground the limits of Laclau and Mouffe's project of radical democracy in terms of their foreclosure of both an institutional imagination and modes of expression. Part of the difficulty of transposing Laclau and Mouffe's project of radical democracy is one of translation. They focus almost exclusively on discursive conditions as the basis of political expression. Herein lies a substantive limit to the possibility of a radical democracy within media-information situations, where information is mobilized across a range of social-technical institutional settings and user-networks, as distinct from discourse, which is frequently embedded in traditional institutional forms. If democratic politics is contingent upon a functional state infrastructure consisting of political institutions, does that mean those countries without such infrastructures have abandoned the possibility of democracy? In other words, how else might democracy be thought in ways that do not conform to Western models of representative, liberal democracy? Moreover, what sort of purchase do new civil societies, as articulated by new social movements and NGOS, have in the formation of democratic polities? Is it even appropriate to continue speaking of political projects with reference to the role of civil society, which many commentators associate as a project peculiar to the modern era of democracy formation and the nation-state in the West? These are question I address in the remainder of this chapter.

Scalar Tensions

In taking up roles that are traditionally the reserve of the state, NGOS condition the possibility of three key features, all of which undermine the economic and political sovereignty of emerging states. Firstly, the logic of flexible production, accumulation and consumption that has corresponded with the emergence of new ICTS and the capacity to organize social relations in the form of networks has resulted in an increasing liberalization of the state and the market. And with this process liberalism is decoupled from democracy, where the latter ensured a degree of transparency and accountability from the former.

Such features well and truly vanished with the onset of the 'New Economy', as spectacularly demonstrated in the dubious accountancy methods of companies associated with the tech-wreck, Enron being the most obvious example.[27]

Inflated economic returns in the form of debt management on the balance sheet have been the basis for neoliberal states to secure their ongoing pursuit of deregulation and privatization. Furthermore, hegemonic states and the supranational organizations they are aligned with have been unrelenting in imposing this structural logic of neoliberalism upon developing states as a condition of receiving financial aid from the IMF, World Bank and private investors. In the case of developing states this has led to a range of structural conditions that emulate some of the structural arrangements peculiar to neoliberal modes of organizing social relations, state bureaucracies and corporate practices. The overwhelming consensus among critical international studies scholars and political economists is that the IMF/World Bank structural adjustment programmes introduced in Sub-Saharan African countries since the 1980s resulted in a 60 per cent decline in gross capital formation by the end of the decade.[28] The unilinear flow of wealth from the 'periphery' to the 'centre' reproduces the patterns of growth that characterized the nineteenth-century imperialist era of colonial economies. As Ankie Hoogvelt writes:

> Structural adjustment has tied the physical resources of Africa more firmly into servicing the 'old' segment of the global economy. At the same time, it has oiled the financial machinery by which wealth is being transported out of the region, thereby removing the very resources which are needed by the dynamic adjustment to the 'new' global economy.[29]

Within this sort of economic climate, developing states frequently lack the financial resources necessary for establishing the institutional infrastructures and social services that are conducive to civil society formations which, in the European experience, revolved around the formation of a domestic bourgeoisie that was coextensive with the project of nation building. When the state has a limited structural relation to civilian populations, then the constitutive dimensions of modern liberal democracy are undermined. For example, the task of the modern university corresponded with the project of nation building, of establishing what Benedict Anderson called an 'imagined community'. In modern times, the university has been a key actor in the process of democracy formation within the West. The university cultivated an informed and knowledgeable bourgeoisie and citizenry, trained with the capacity to deliberate over the political and social life of the nation. The university also played a key role in the development of civil society in so far as it occupied a critical space independent of the state. Today, of course, this role has been seriously eroded as universities and academics working within them are constituted within a neoliberal paradigm as 'pseudo-corporate' institutions and 'post-intellectuals'.[30] Without these sorts of experiences and histories, the project of democracy formation in developing states does not become irrelevant or impossible; rather, it becomes a question of how democracy might emerge with different properties and possibilities.

The sort of circumstances sketched above exacerbate the dependency relation developing states have with foreign actors, including new 'global civil society' organizations such as NGOS.[31] NGOS, for example, often find themselves involved in activities in the realm of education, providing training and literacy skills to local communities. Such activities may be secondary to the key mission of NGOS. As Rececca Knuth notes with regard to information flows in 'complex emergencies': 'There is an acute awareness among relief organizations that short-term intervention to save lives must be supplemented by long-term reconstruction initiatives that reconstitute local systems and prevent future crises'.[32] However, there is a high risk that such long-term initiatives become fragmented and reproduced, at best, as a series of short-term interventions undertaken by an assortment of relief agencies in as much as there is no guarantee that NGOS have either the financial resources or enduring personnel to commit to long-term reconstruction projects.[33] This predicament resonates for the situation of organized networks.

When NGOS become responsible for educating civilian populations an almost perverse correlation with the civilizing mission of the colonizer kicks in. Indeed, at a structural level NGOS occupy a similar territory as transnational corporations (TNCS), both of which contribute to a process of recolonization of postcolonial states. This can result in tensions between well-meaning NGOs and local populations over the kind of political, social and cultural values attached to the techniques of education. Moreover, the state foregoes the hegemonic process of negotiating social-political values with civilian populations as they are articulated through and within educational apparatuses. As such, a key dimension of democracy formation is dispensed with.

Secondly, in adopting the task of educating civilian populations a process is at work that is similar to the neoliberal technique of outsourcing. At a structural level, then, the state 'leapfrogs' straight into a neoliberal frame, bypassing the temporal and spatial experiences of the modern welfare state. In other words, developing states are structurally positioned whether they like it or not in flexible modes of delivery, hence creating a dependency relation on external providers as distinct from domestically developed systems of learning and the social formations and cultural values that attend such processes.

In this sense, NGOs, when involved in auxiliary roles such as education, undermine one of the traditional roles of the state. As such, NGOs are assisting in the formation of conditions that also benefit the interests of TNCs, which seek to obtain by any means possible conditions that enable unilinear flows of capital, unrestricted by domestically determined regulatory interventions by the state. Furthermore, the presence of NGOs, as external providers of services that are traditionally the reserve of the state, reinforces the sort of conditions associated with IMF and World Bank monetary loans and their structural adjustment programmes. This raises serious questions with regard to NGOs that claim to occupy an advocacy position on behalf of civilian interests. Indeed, I would suggest that the very notion of civil society as a partially autonomous space is brought into question as NGOs find themselves in a paradoxical field of tensions in which they are at once bound to local communities while assisting in direct and indirect ways the interests of TNCs and supranational governance.

A lively debate tracked this issue on the nettime mailing list in February 1997, with a number of postings critiquing the Soros network and the interrelationships between NGOs, corporations and civil society.[34] Some of the issues and critiques from that time were synthesized in an interview with Saskia Sassen by Geert Lovink in 1999. On the issue of accountability, Lovink noted that 'One of the problems of NGOs – especially if they are linked to large international organizations – is that for people on the ground, and even for governments, they are no longer accountable for what they do. They can move very quickly and in many ways can behave like finance capital'.[35] In this sense, NGOS again can be seen to model some of the dynamics of TNCS and reproduce techniques of organization peculiar to neoliberalism.[36] Deconstructing the question of accountability, Sassen importantly notes:

> [A]ccountable to what and for what? In some cases, the fact that some of these organizations are not accountable is actually better, because it means that a different kind of political project can be enacted – whereas if an organization is accountable, it often means being accountable to existing value systems, which in some cases are the very ones best avoided. However, many of the big NGOS are profoundly accountable – by which I mean they are accountable in the kinds of ways and to the kinds of entities one might not want to demand accountability for or to.

Then, relating the question back to her own research on the architecture of global finance and the need to 'invent new systems for accountability and accountability for different kinds of aims in some of these systems', Sassen elaborates the problematic of 'transparency':

> There is an architecture, there are certain standards the players adhere to; and there is transparency, the famous term 'transparency', which implies something that's intrinsically good. But what is it? It is accountability to shareholders and their short-term profit. But do we always want this kind of accountability? No – including from global finance – so we're presented with the challenge of discovering new types of accountability, new ways of thinking the question of accountability – accountability to a larger public good, and so on.

For the purposes of this chapter, I want to highlight that while NGOS may procure tactical benefits from an absence of accountability, this has to be weighed against the correspondence such a system of organization has with informational secrecy by corporations. The consequence of this is fundamentally antithetical to the 'transparency' assumed of conventional notions of democracy.

Thirdly, the sidelining of the state is also significant at a political level, since there is no institutional residue or collective memory of things being otherwise, at least in terms of the presence of state political institutions. And at an imaginary level, the possibility of different forms of political organization that correspond with the space of the nation is not there. While the neoliberal state has seen the erosion of traditional differences between the Left and the Right and the emergence of Third Way style politics, I think it is premature to overlook the political function of pseudo-corporate institutions such as the university and the persistence of trade unions: these are institutions that are part of a collective residual memory that contribute to what Ghassan Hage has called the possibility of spaces of hope.[37] Having said this, I wouldn't want to rule out the potential for alternative political models emerging from indigenous modes of political organization.

In short, I hope the above examples illustrate the paradoxical role of NGOS within quasi-states: probably against their best wishes, NGOS are often situated in such a way that they assist the imposition of neoliberal systems of organization upon developing states. As such, these states are occluded from the sort of modernizing experiences and processes – its times and its spaces – that have been fundamental to the constitution of liberal democracy in the West. I will return to the question of democracy in the final section of this chapter, once I establish the political role of intellectual property rights for developing states and their civilian populations.

Information Flows, Intellectual Property and Economic Development

With the advent of new ICTS, particularly the Internet, NGOS have been able to consolidate and expand themselves, creating new alliances by networking with each other through distributed information flows. As I noted earlier, the rise of NGOS has coincided with the emergence of globalized economies. Similarly, the Internet has enabled NGOS to interface with local, state, military and supranational entities. This might give the impression that distinctions in scale disappear, and that tensions between and within these sectors no longer prevail. Certainly this is not the case, since NGOS often enough contest the powers of the state in the interests of the 'the people' (a politically dubious figure at best). With their enhanced capacity to gather and disseminate information, NGOs have obtained greater legitimacy as political actors, often challenging the sovereignty of authoritarian governments.[38] The horizontal expansion of informational flows has led a number of scholars to claim that a new state form has emerged – a form which Castells has termed the 'network state', one that international relations theorist Martin Shaw calls the 'global state',[39] and a form that Hardt and Negri attribute to the 'post-political' manifestation of 'Empire'.

The extent to which such a new state form can be called democratic is highly questionable, however. Moreover, such a form has not fared well for communicative relations for those civilian populations deprived of adequate IT infrastructures; nor should an intensification in informational flows be assumed to correspond with open systems of communication. The commercialization of the Internet and its regulation via intellectual property regimes functions to close information flows. But as I argue below, depending on the extent of reform, IPRS can be used as a strategic political architecture that maintains the flow of information within informal networks, while at the same time securing a closure against external exploitation. By informal networks I wish to acknowledge the ways in which information flows are governed, for example, by customary law, which in itself is a highly formal system, but it can be considered as informal in the sense that I invoke it here: that is, at a discursive level such informal systems are constituted as illegitimate in so far as they hold little political and legal purchase within systems of international and national law. The case of Africa is again instructive in terms of illuminating some of the assumptions surrounding ICTS as the generator of economic development.

By the late 1990s, the relatively dismal Internet connection rate for African states prompted Castells to make the pretty obvious point that 'Most of Africa is being left in a technological apartheid…'.[40] Such a condition has been compounded by economic circumstances, with a steady decline in economic growth in Africa throughout the 1990s, accompanied by substantial drops in the levels of Foreign Direct Investment (FDI). As Hoogvelt notes, 'Africa's share of all FDI flows to developing countries has dropped from 13 per cent in 1980 to less that 5 per cent in the late 1990s'.[41] Encouraged by the privatization and deregulation of telecommunications industries, FDI has been on the rise in recent years. Mobile phone usage and Internet connection rates have also increased considerably. Yet the combination of foreign investment and unfettered market access and trade liberalization is not without problems for domestic economies and infrastructures. Referring to the crises in Asian 'tiger' economies in the late 1990s, a report in the *International Herald Tribune* in 2002 noted that high levels of foreign investment flows are no *a priori* guarantee to fast-tracking economic development: 'developing countries that allow an inflow of foreign money into their financial markets are vulnerable to disastrous, panicky withdrawals, especially if they have not developed sound banking systems first'.[42] Such an observation remains just as pertinent today.

As much as there might be what ICT for development discourse likes to call a 'technological leap' under way in Africa, this is no guarantee that individuals and communities possess the means to function within informational or knowledge economies in which knowledge and ideas are 'embodied in products, processes and organisations', which in turn 'fuel development'.[43] Such a move requires a vast educational infrastructure and cultural apparatuses and industries if information is to be codified in symbolic forms as knowledge. It also requires investment in 'sustaining the physical state of human capital (health expenditure)'.[44] Furthermore, such investment and infrastructural needs have implications for democracy formation, since the figure of the politically enabled citizen presupposes an educated and healthy civilian; thus information flows depend upon a civic infrastructure that includes schools, technical colleges, universities, library resources, and so forth. One important precursor if not parallel to such infrastructure consists of ensuring that indigenous cultural production and biological knowledge is not alienated from local communities and individuals.

While intellectual property regimes can be understood as a form of abstraction that alienates labour from production, this is not necessarily a contradiction in terms when IPRS are considered as a strategy to ensure a degree of economic and political self-determination by indigenous peoples and those living in developing or quasi-states. Intellectual property rights enable developing states to place an economic value and regime of scarcity on their cultural and biological resources. New ICTS are the mechanism for then distributing this property and extracting financial remuneration from its use by those participating in informational economies.

Furthermore, the codification of production as property reinforces the legal authority of the state, since property cannot exist independently of state recognition.[45] That is, IPRS can assist in the development of the state apparatuses, albeit ones that are circumscribed by economic interests, and reinstate their authority to legislate progressive policy related to the privacy rights of their constituents.[46] While intellectual property in and of itself does not alleviate poverty or misery, it does provide a crucial potential for leverage out of such conditions, certainly more so than if IP is handed over to TNCS that have a monopoly on ownership of both technology and product patents and copyright of cultural production.

Of course there are numerous issues and problems associated with intellectual property regimes as they currently figure. Intellectual property law reinforces what Castells identifies as a key characteristic of the 'information age as a result of its networking form of organization': namely, 'the growing individualization of labor',[47] and this functions to undermine collective bargaining or the regulation of labour and wages by agreements between unions and the state. As I have discussed elsewhere, intellectual property regimes still attribute proprietary rights to an individual, rather than a collective.[48] In this regard, IP does not favour the social form of production peculiar to many indigenous peoples and people in the developing world, where production occurs through the form of the collective and regulated within customary law.[49] Further reform needs to occur to current intellectual property law that legitimates ownership of knowledge that is not fixed in form, and enables indigenous intellectual property to be protected in perpetuity. Herein lies a challenge for NGOS at policy and legal levels.

Conclusion

In this chapter I have questioned the extent to which Mouffe's concept of agonistic or pluralist democracy as a politics of legitimacy that enables 'the struggle between adversaries' rather than antagonistic struggles between enemies is relevant in any pragmatic sense within an informational age of network societies. Certainly, Mouffe's identification of the antagonistic dimension of 'the political' as that which is underscored by the ineradicability of violence, following the work of Carl Schmitt and others, is insightful and timely as rational consensus models have gained even greater purchase as the only legitimate models of democracy in town. But how, I have wondered, is an agonistic politics to be conditioned within the logic of informationalism?

The 'postnational' ideological terrain of network societies has seen the apparatuses of the state undergo deregulation and privatization, or, in the case of developing states, simply bypassed altogether. Mouffe's model of agonistic democracy, which is predicated on traditional institutions of the state as the place in which a democratic polity unfolds, seems problematic and decidedly modern in light of the reconfiguration of statehood at extraterritorial and networked dimensions. However, my argument in this chapter is that it is precisely through pursuing IP rights for indigenous peoples and civilian populations in quasi-states that an agonistic politics might unfold. My reasoning behind this is that IPRS constitute a hegemonic field of articulation of 'the political' in which the identities of states, peoples, NGOS, corporations and supranational entities are contested and reconstituted in ways that challenge a neoliberal order as it currently stands (for instance the imposition of structural adjustment reforms on developing states by the IMF and World Bank as the condition for financial aid). To avoid engaging with the problematic of IPRS is not a political alternative.

The auxiliary task for NGOS is to ensure that the people they represent are able to be situated as political actors within this networked terrain. Such networks, as suggested by Florian Schneider, might be considered as 'packets in agony'.[50] Political legitimacy, I would suggest, is conditioned in the first instance by indigenous peoples obtaining economic sovereignty which in turn positions them as political actors in as much as informational flows across scalar dimensions and the expansion of capital depends upon engaging with what is otherwise a community of others excluded from informational economies and network societies. Given the high uncertainty of the state form within developing countries such as those in Africa, I have argued that democracy needs to be rethought in terms of non-representational politics as it figures within the emergent institutional form of organized networks.

2 The World Summit

on the Information Society and Organized Networks
as New Civil Society Movements

There is no question that non-governmental organizations have more
often than not played vital roles in fulfilling a range of humanitarian related tasks in numerous countries that have been subject to the ravages
of colonialism, environmental disasters, agricultural failure, civil wars
and genocide, internal political and social instability, currency crises, or
a combination of all of these. In many instances, NGOs have filled a gap
in the vacuum within developing, transitionary or 'quasi-states' who,
for various reasons, do not have the capacity to provide political infrastructures and social services for their populations. As a result, NGOs
entrench an extant condition whereby developing states may often not
be equipped with the sort of institutional infrastructures and social-political formations – namely, a domestic capitalist bourgeoisie and civil
society traditions – that have enabled the formation of democracy within the project of nation building, as witnessed in the West.[1] As such,
many developing states do not have the sort of structural conditions in
place to experience the unfolding of modernity. Or rather, in a dialectical sense, these states have indeed experienced forms of modernity that
are radically dissimilar in spatio-temporal and ontological ways from
that experienced by and within Western countries, many of which have
adopted liberal democratic political cultures along with the political
economies that attend such frameworks within a capitalist system.

In many respects, the material conditions of developing states have
enabled the possibility of a range of conditions and experiences in advanced economies that could be considered as privileges constituted by
legitimately enacted violence. Mary Kaldor notes that war and violence
are both primary conditions for sustaining a civil society: 'What Norbert Elias called the "civilizing process" – the removal of violence from
everyday life within the boundaries of the state – was based on the establishment of monopolies of violence and taxation'.[2] A monopoly of
violence concentrates 'the means of violence in the hands of the state
in order to remove violence from domestic relations'.[3] 'Modern sover-

eignty', write Michael Hardt and Antonio Negri, 'was thus meant to ban war from the internal, civil terrain'.[4]

The capture of violence by the state enables civil society to develop its key values of trust, civility, individual autonomy, and so forth, though within the framework of the rule of law as it is administered by the state. Moreover, the state's monopoly of violence minimizes, though never completely eliminates, politically subversive elements and the possibility of civil war arising from within the territory of the nation. At a global level, the perversity of hegemonic states possessing a monopoly of violence operates as the basis upon which territorial sovereignty is maintained by way of subjecting violence upon alien states and their populations. A large part of this experience can be accounted for by referring to the histories of colonialism – a project whereby imperial states are able to secure the material resources and imaginary dimensions necessary for their own consolidation and prosperity.

Combining Hegel's thesis on the passage of nature/civil society/state with Foucault's notion of governmental power (the biopolitical, interpenetrative 'conduct of conduct'), political philosopher and literary theorist Hardt defines civil society in its modern incarnation in terms of its capacity to organize abstract labour through the governmental techniques of education, training and discipline:

> Civil society … is central to a form of rule, or government, as Foucault says, that focuses, on the one hand, on the identity of the citizen and the process of civilization and, on the other hand, on the organization of abstract labor. These processes are variously conceived as education, training, or discipline, but what remains common is the active engagement with social forces (through either mediation or production) to order social identities within the context of institutions.[5]

With the governmentalization of the field of the social, a special relationship between civil society and the state is effected, one in which distinctions between institutions of the state and those of civil society are indiscernible, and where intersections and connections are diagrammatic. What, however, has happened to this constitutive relationship within our current era, one in which these sorts of relationships have undergone a crisis as a result of new socio-economic forces that go by the name of neoliberalism? What sort of new institutions are best suited to the organization of social relations and creative labour within an informational paradigm? And what bearing, if any, do they have on inter-state and supranational regimes of governance and control?

In short, how do civil society movements articulate their values and how do they procure a multi-scalar legitimacy once the constitutive relationship between civil society and the state has shifted as the nation-state transmogrifies into a corporate state (or, in the case of developing countries, a state that is subject, for instance, to the structural adjustment conditions set by entities such as the World Bank and WTO)? Clearly, civil society values have not disappeared; nonetheless, the traditional modern constitutive framework has changed. Increasingly, civil society values are immanent to the social-technical movements of networks. Issues of governance, I would suggest, are thus best addressed by paying attention to the technics of communication. In the case of the WSIS project, this means shifting the debate from the 'multi-stakeholder approach' – which takes bureaucratically organized institutions (or networked organizations) as its point of departure – to one which places greater attention to the conditions of tension and dissonance as they figure with 'the political' of informationality. In other words, a focus on the materialities of networks and the ways in which they operate as self-organizing systems would reveal quite different articulations that, in my view, more accurately reflect the composition of sociality within an information society.

Within a neoliberal paradigm we have witnessed what Hardt and Negri term 'a withering of civil society' in which the structures and institutions that played the role of mediation between capital and the state have been progressively undermined. This shift has been enabled by the logic of deregulation and privatization, which has seen, in some respects, the social-political power of both state and non-state institutions decline.[6] These include institutions such as the university, health care, unions and independent mainstream media. For Hardt and Negri, the possibility of liberal democracy is seriously challenged by the hegemony of neoliberalism – or what they prefer to call the imperial, biopolitical and supranational power of 'Empire'[7] – since it threatens if not entirely eradicates traditional institutions of representation and mediation between citizens and the state. As Hardt and Negri write in their book *Empire*:

> [T]his withering can be grasped clearly in terms of the decline of the dialectic between the capitalist state and labor, that is, in the decline of the effectiveness and role of unions, the decline of collective bargaining with labor, and the decline of the representation of labor in the constitution. The withering of civil society might also be recognized as concomitant with the passage from disciplinary society to the society of control.[8]

The society of control is accompanied by techniques of data surveillance such as cookies, authcate passwords, data mining of individuals and their informational traces, CCTVs that monitor the movement of bodies in public and private spaces, and so forth. Some of these are related to the governance of intellectual property. New information and communication technologies thus play a key role in maintaining a control society. In an age of network societies and informational economies, civil society, or rather civil *societies*, have not so much disappeared as become reconfigured within this new social-technical terrain in order to address problems immanent to the social, political and economic situation of mediatized life. Civil society, as it is resides within an informational plane of abstraction, continues to act as a key counterforce to and mediator between the state and capital. Thus, civil society does not entirely disappear or become destroyed with the onset of neoliberalism from around the 1970s-'80s. Rather, there has been a maintenance of civil society within our current network societies precisely because there has been a social desire and need to do so.

While such a claim may appear self-evident, it is instructive to recall that civil society was a European invention that emerged alongside the modern state and capital.[9] In its modern form, civil society mediated between the interests of capital and the coercive powers of the state. The modern form of democracy is predicated on the notion and existence of a civil society. The two are mutually constitutive formations. Civil society functioned as a space of voluntary association and open expression. The values of civil society – 'civility', respect for individual autonomy and privacy, trust among peoples, removal of fear and violence from everyday life, and so forth – operated as a counterpoint to the rules and purposes of the state whose centralized political authority administered the lives of people within a given territory.[10] The state played the role of ensuring that those values were maintained through structures of governance and the law. Civil society was articulated to the state by the media – primarily newspapers – and as such, was able to play a role in regulating the conduct of the state. This was a hugely significant shift, at least while the distinctions between the state and the public sphere of civil society remained intact.

My argument is that with the onset of neoliberalism and the transmogrification of the state, civil society also undergoes a change. For example, the extent to which civil society plays the traditional role of mediating between the interests of capital and state is now highly questionable. With the alliance between the state and capital – as seen in the many instances of corporate welfarism, where in order to attract foreign investment, the state effectively subsidizes corporations in the form of R&D, tax incentives, cheap land leases, bankruptcy bailouts, etcetera – civil society organizations are also repositioned. This is most clear in instances where civil society organizations fulfil the role of service providers – a task traditionally undertaken by government departments, particularly during the time of the welfare state. With the shift into a neoliberal paradigm come new expectations of civil society. New rules are inscribed upon civil society organizations. The increasing frequency of so-called liberal democratic governments engaging in the routine practice of misleading parliament and the populations whose interests they are supposedly representing is paralleled by greater demands for transparency and accountability on the part of civil society organizations. As I go on to discuss, the occasion of WSIS also creates a space for new civil society actors.

The emergent civil society movements go beyond satisfying the self-interest of individuals, as represented by consumer lobby groups, for example. Instead, they derive their affective and political power from a combination of formal and informal networks of relations. Think, for instance, of the effect the no-border refugee advocacy groups have had as observers of human rights violations administered by the state. Whether one is for or against the incorporation of 'illegal immigrants' into the nation-state is secondary to the fact that civil society coalitions of activists, religious organizations and social justice advocates have played a primary role in constituting what Raymond Williams termed an emergent 'structure of feeling',[11] or what can be thought of as the social-technical organization of affect, that counters the cynical opportunism of populist conservative governments.

In an in-depth report entitled *Appropriating the Internet for Social Change*, Mark Surman and Katherine Reilly examine the strategic ways in which civil society movements are using networked technologies.[12] They identify four major online activities: collaboration, publishing, mobilization and observation. These activities are mapped along two axes: formal versus informal and distributed versus centralized (Figure 1). Collaborative filtering and collaborative publishing, for instance, fall within the formal/distributed quadrant. Open publishing, mailing lists, research networks and collective blogs are located within the distributed/informal quadrant; personal blogs within the centralized/informal quadrant; and organizational web site development, online petitions, online fundraising, e-membership databases and e-newsletters fall within the formal/centralized quadrant. Surman and Reilly consider the 'tools that fall in the formal/centralized quadrant to be used primarily by large NGOS, unions and political parties'.[13] The logic of organization, production and distribution is, according to Surman and Reilly, 'based on a "broadcast" model' of communication. The distributed/informal quadrant, on the other hand, is more typical of activities undertaken by 'informal social movements, research networks and "virtual organizations"'.

In this chapter I will argue that it is time for 'informal social movements' and 'virtual organizations' – or what I prefer to call 'organized networks' – to make a strategic turn and begin to scale up their operations in ways that would situate them within the formal/centralized quadrant, but in such a manner that retains their informal, distributed and tactical capacities.[14] The participation of civil society actors in debates and policy development associated with WSIS provides one example of how such a scalar shift can occur. There are also problems with such shifts in scale, particularly at the level of institutional composition, as I will go on to discuss.

This chapter assesses Phase 1 of the World Summit on the Information Society (WSIS) that culminated in Geneva, 2003.[15] Phase 2 of the

Strategic uses spectrum

1. Strategic uses spectrum, Surman and Reilly, 2003

wsis process focussed less on the form of participation of civil society in the information society, and more on public policy issues associated with Internet governance. Debates often became highly technical but ultimately no less separable from matters concerning infrastructure, access and participation, regulation, etcetera. The un Working Group on Internet Governance (wgig) was one of the key bodies responsible for reporting to the wsis Phase 2 process.[16] With disputes among various representatives over issues such as domain names, root servers, ip addresses, spectrum allocation, software licensing and intellectual property rights, both phases of the Summit demonstrated that the architecture of information is a hugely contested area. As evidenced in official WSIS documents, consensus between governments, civil society groups, NGOS and corporations over these issues is impossible. Representation at the Summit itself was a problem for many civil society groups and NGOS. As a UN initiative geared toward addressing the need for access to ICTS, particularly for developing countries, the problem of basic infrastructure needs such as adequate electricity supply, education and equipment requirements were not sufficiently addressed. Funding, of course, is another key issue and topic of disagreement.

Against this background, this chapter argues that the question of scale is a central condition to the obtainment and redefinition of democracy. Moreover, what models of democracy are global entities such as the WSIS aspiring to when they formulate future directions for informational policy? Given the crisis of legitimacy of rational consensus, deliberative models of democracy, this chapter argues that democracy within information societies needs to be rethought in terms of organized networks of communication that condition the possibility of new institutions that are attentive to problems of scale. Such a view does not preclude informational networks that operate across a range of scales, from subnational to intraregional to supranational; rather, it suggests that new institutional forms that can organize social-technical relations in ways that address specific needs, desires and interests are a key to obtaining informational democracy.

As noted in the previous chapter, the 'multi-stakeholder' approach, as adopted in the WSIS process through the principle of bottom-up participation and inclusion of civil society organizations in processes of decision-making with governments and businesses, in and of itself cannot fulfil the objective of, for example, 'an inclusive Information Society', as proposed in the official Plan of Action.[17] Despite the various problems associated with the WSIS, my argument is that it presents an important strategic opportunity for civil society movements: the 'denationalized' political legitimacy obtained at WSIS can, I would suggest, be deployed to political and economic advantage in the process of re-nationalization or re-localization. The emergence of organized networks as new institutional forms are best suited to the process of advancing the ambitions of WSIS.

Global Governance and the World Summit on the Information Society

The WSIS's two-stage meetings in Geneva, 2003, and Tunisia, 2005, exemplify the ways in which the political, social, economic and cultural dimensions of information and communication technologies afford civil society movements a political legitimacy in developments associated with issues of global governance that has hitherto been exclusive to supranational actors and multilateral institutions such as the WTO, the World Bank, IMF, the G8 nations, the UN, the OECD, APEC, ASEAN, NAFTA, and so forth. As the 'information society' has extended beyond the reserve of rich nations or advanced economies, actors such as the World Intellectual Property Organization (WIPO) and the Internet Corporation for Assigned Names and Numbers (ICANN) have emerged as institutions responsible for establishing common standards or information architectures that enable information to flow in relatively smooth, ordered and stable ways. Such entities have often been charged as benign advocates of neoliberal interests, as represented by powerful nation-states and corporations. As a UN initiative organized by the International Telecommunications Union (ITU), the WSIS has also been perceived by many as a further extension of neoliberal agendas into the realm of civil society. As Sasha Costanza-Chock reported in May 2003:

> [T]he ITU has always served governments and the powerful telecom conglomerates. Originally set up in 1865 to regulate telegraph standards, later radio, and then satellite orbit allocation, the ITU took on the Summit because it has recently been losing power to the telecoms that increasingly set their own rules and to the Internet Corporation for Assigned Names and Numbers (ICANN), which was created by the US government to regulate the Internet domain name system. The ITU is now facing heavy budget cuts and is desperate to remain a player in the global regulation of Information and Communication Technologies (ICTS).[18]

The neoliberal disposition of ITU is further evidenced by the primacy given at the WSIS to issues such as cybercrime, security and electronic surveillance, taxation, IP protection, digital piracy and privacy.[19] The ITU's support of a summit concerned with bringing civil society movements into the decision-making process of global information governance is one that is preconditioned by the empty centre of neoliberalism, which has seen governments in advanced economies reincorporating civil society actors and social organizations into matters of social welfare in the form of 'service providers'. Within a neoliberal framework, the interest of government and the business sector in civil society is underpinned by the appeal of civil society as a source of unregulated labour-power. This new axis of articulating civil society organizations through the logic of service provision functions to conflate 'civil society' with the 'private sector'. Such a conflation blurs or obscures what had previously been clear demarcations at the level of subjectivities, value systems and institutional practices. The conflation of civil society and the private sector is evident in much of the government documentation from the wsis. In some ways this points to the multidimensional aspects of civil society – no longer can civil society be assumed to reside outside of market relations, for instance. In other ways, it raises the question of legitimacy: can civil society be 'trusted' when its condition of existence overlaps with market interests and needs of the private sector? Similarly, can the private sector be embraced by 'the Left' when the former displays credentials as a 'corporate-friendly citizen'? Indeed, what might 'citizenship' mean within a global framework? And then there is the mutually enhancing or legitimizing function that such a convergence of actors produces: both civil society organizations and the private sector expand the discursive platforms upon which they stake out their respective claims. Ambiguities such as these point to the increasing complexity of relations between institutions, politics, the economy and sociality.

There's an urgent need to think through these issues and enact practices that go beyond the cynicism of Third Way-style approaches to politics. The Third Way, as adopted in the mid-1990s by Blair, Clinton, Schroeder and others since, is nothing but the expansion of market forces into social and cultural domains that hitherto held a degree of autonomy in terms of their articulation of different regimes of value. Moreover, there is a need for a radical pragmatism that engages civil society movements with economic possibilities in such a way that maintains a plurality of political ideologies, from Left to Right; this is something Third Way politics has undermined, the result being extremist manifestations of populist fundamentalism on both the Left and Right, but without the political institutions or processes to articulate their interests. The proliferation of terror is, in part, a symptom of this collapse in politics, a collapse which refuses the antagonisms that underpin the field of 'the political', and thus results in a situation whereby actors that might otherwise be adversaries instead become enemies. Since the antagonisms prevailing within information societies tend to be seen as distractions or debilitating to the WSIS project, I have doubts about the extent to which the 'multi-stakeholder' approach goes beyond some of the tenets of Third Way politics. Let us remember that communication systems are conditioned by the dissonance of information, or what Bateson termed 'the difference which makes a difference'.

In an optimistic light, the 'multi-stakeholder' approach adopted at the WSIS is indicative of a period of transition within supranational institutions. Yet paradoxically, the efforts of the ITU/UN to include civil society movements in the decision-making process surrounding global governance of the information society is evidence of the increasing ineffectiveness of supranational governing and policy development bodies. The United State's cynicism and self-interest in bypassing the authority of the UN during the Iraq war and the breakdown of WTO summits in a post-Seattle climate of 'anti-globalization' protests are two extremes that point to the waning effectiveness of supranational institutions to address governance issues through international mechanisms. The expanding division and inequality in living and working conditions between the global North and the global South after successive WTO meetings and rounds of international agreements on trade liberalization is further evidence of the incapacity of supranational institutions to address the complexities of global governance.

In the case of the WSIS, Costanza-Cook maintains that the ITU's decision to organize the Summit was partly motivated by their fear of redundancy as a governing body within an information society. Such a view is reiterated by Steve Cisler in his account of the tensions between ICANN and ITU at the WSIS:

ITU members like France Telecom and Deutsche Telekom long resisted the Internet. They were pushing Minitel, ISDN. African members saw (rightfully) how disruptive the Internet could be and resisted it.

The ITU was shocked by the growth of the Internet, and they have
belatedly wanted to 'control' it. The failed WSIS proposal [to shift
Internet governance away from WIPO] is just the latest attempt. Of
course during this growing awareness of the importance of the Internet, the composition of the ITU has changed from almost exclusively
government telcos (or PTT's) to a mix of old style government monopolies, dual government-private, and straight corporate telephone
companies.[20]

ICANN is a US government authorized non-profit corporation that is responsible for managing various technical aspects associated with Internet governance. These include 'Internet Protocol (IP) address space allocation, protocol identifier assignment, generic (gTLD) and country code
(ccTLD) Top-Level Domain name system management [.com., .net, .org,
and so forth], and root server system management functions'.[21] The role
of ICANN in Internet governance was disputed at the WSIS for a range of
reasons. In his informative report commissioned by one of the more
dominant civil society lobby groups at the WSIS, the Association for
Progressive Communications (APC), Adam Peake unravels the debates
that took place throughout the WSIS process about the role of ICANN in
relation to issue of Internet governance. Peake notes that many were
concerned that of the 13 Root Servers around the world that install all
'top level' domain name system (DNS) servers, ten of these are located in
the USA.[22] It becomes clear that at the level of technical infrastructure,
the vertical stratification of the Net is shaped by geopolitical, economic
and cultural interests. This tendency towards the vertical organization
of information and its protocols rubs against the grain of efforts by civil
society and open source movements to 'democratize' information and
enhance the horizontalization of information management.[23]

Alternative systems such as Anycast, which enable root servers 'to be
"cloned" in multiple locations', were proposed and implemented
throughout the 2003 planning process of WSIS.[24] In other words, regional as distinct from US concentrated root servers are possible and came
into effect in early 2003, but these only mirror or copy the US root
servers and thus are not autonomously controlled.[25] Nevertheless, such
alternatives begin to alleviate the concern that various civil society and
government stakeholders had with respect to a perception that ICANN

operates in the interests of maintaining a US control of the Internet, or at least supports the bias toward US Internet usage as represented by the location of root servers whose close geographic proximity to US-based users supports rapid response times on the Net.[26]

More significant concerns were raised about the gatekeeping role played by ICANN and the US government over the allocation of a country's top-level domain names. This was seen as undermining national sovereign control over domain names. Moreover, there is serious concern that the US Department of Commerce can potentially 'remove a country from the root, and therefore remove it from the Internet'.[27] It doesn't take much to imagine the devastating effect of removing a CCTLD in times of military and information warfare: a country's entire digital communications system is rendered useless in such an event, and social and economic impacts would come into rapid effect. A more likely scenario would see the US government intervening in the allocation of CCTLDS in instances of political or economic dispute. In this regard, the control of top-level domain names operates as a potential form of economic sanction or a real technique of unilinear leverage in business and political negotiations.

The other significant player in relation to this discussion of the WSIS is WIPO and their role in the global governance of information flows. WIPO is a UN agency with a mandate to 'harmonize' intellectual property rights across member states. In 1995 WIPO made an agreement with the WTO to assist in facilitating the implementation of the TRIPS agreement across member states. More recently, WIPO's harmonization of patent law has been criticized for the way it restricts the degree of flexibility for and imposes substantial financial burdens on developing countries.[28] In a report written by Carlos Correa for the South Centre inter-governmental organization for developing countries, the following risks and asymmetrical aspects of WIPO's Patent Agenda for developing countries were summarized as follows:

> [H]armonized standards would leave little room for developing countries to adapt their patent laws to local conditions and needs; harmonization would take place at the highest level of protection (based on standards currently applied by developed countries, especially the United States and Western European countries) meaning that the

process will exert an upward force on national laws and policies in developing countries resulting in stronger and more expansive rights of the patent holders with the corresponding narrowing of limitations and exceptions. Such higher standards are unlikely to have a positive effect on local innovation in developing countries; and also the danger that the current draft contains standards that are primarily aimed at benefiting the 'international industries' and not individual inventors or small and medium size enterprises.[29]

Since it holds no legal authority at the national level, WIPO has frequently been cast by critics as an ineffective institution, although this is always going to be the case for a supranational institution whose legitimacy is as strong as the responsiveness to IPRS by member states. In instances where intellectual property protection is violated within national industries, as in the case of ongoing digital piracy of film and software within countries such as China, the lack of legal authority by WIPO is potentially offset by the mechanism of economic sanctions that can be imposed by adjacent supranational institutions and multilateral entities. A more substantial criticism of WIPO concerns its largely negative response to the issue of open source software and collaborative information flows which are best suited to developing countries without the financial resources to adopt proprietary informational systems. Thus the relationship WIPO holds with civil society movements and advocates of open source software and 'open development' is often underpinned by conflicts in interest. Furthermore, the relationship between WIPO and the WTO casts the UN in the questionable role of advocating corporate interests over those of civil society.

This very brief overview of WIPO and some of the key issues associated with information architectures and the complex structural and institutional relationships begins to raise the question of what the relationship between global citizenship and Internet governance might mean within information societies. With stakeholders from civil society organizations, government and the private sectors, WSIS was never going to succeed as a global forum that seeks to be inclusive of diversity and difference if it was just going to focus on technical issues associated with Internet governance. The expansion of the debate on Internet governance, ICTS and issues of access and technical infrastructure to include civil society issues such as sustainability, funding, education, health, labour conditions and human rights functioned to sideline any centrality that ICANN and WIPO may have sought to hold during the Summit. Many of the UN principles on human rights, for example, migrated into the Civil Society Declaration that came out of the Summit.[30] But like the Universal Declaration of Human Rights (1948), it is only as strong as the resolve of member states to ratify and uphold such principles within national legislative and legal frameworks.

The complexities of the WSIS process exceed the possibility of engaging their diversity. While the rhetoric has been one of inclusiveness, the experience for many working within civil society movements and the private sector has been a frustrating one. As Peake writes during one of the prepcom meetings leading up the December Summit in Geneva:

> For those who don't know how WSIS works – everything happens at very short notice, situations have to be reacted to immediately, and it is very difficult for civil society to respond with the transparency and inclusiveness that we would hope. There simply is never time.

> I have one major concern. We should be very careful about how we raise issues around Internet governance in the WSIS process. We (civil society, private sector, Internet users) have a very weak voice in the process. WSIS is run by the States. Our only opportunity to speak, with *no* guarantee of being listened to, is in 1 or at best 2 10 minute sessions each day. ITU are the secretariat of the process and so have a very direct role in drafting text and framing arguments for the States to consider.[31]

Critical Internet researchers have also had cautious words to say about the extent to which the civil society activists – or what many now refer to as the 'multitudes', or movement of movements – can expect to make a substantial impact on the WSIS process. Again, the diversity of stakeholders and their competing interests brings in to question the ambitions of the 'multi-stakeholder' approach. If dissonance is taken as the condition of informationality, as distinct from deliberation and consensus as idealistic outcomes, then we begin to orient ourselves around the possibility of 'non-representative' systems of organizing social-technical relations. Co-moderator of the nettime mailing list, Ted Byfield, gives his perspective in a posting in March, 2003 – around the time the ITU began to soften its tone of market-oriented, technical-driven solutions to Internet governance:

> my own view is that the activists who think the ITU/WSIS process is just another three- or four-letter target for generic social-justice demands should be much more sensitive to the context. . . . the logic of 'multitudes' may not be representative, but the logic of monolithic organizations (at best) *is* representative, so it would be a mistake to assume that the delirious logic of the movement of movements will somehow transform the ITU into some groovy, polyvocal provisionalism. it won't. one of the most 'progressive' things the WSIS process can accomplish is to minimize the scope of ITU activities. cookie-cutter activist demands will inevitably put pressure on the ITU to expand its purview – and provide a pseudo-legitimating cover for such expansions. this would NOT be a good thing.[32]

As it turned out, the Declaration of Principles and Plan of Action articulate exactly what Byfield fears: lip service to concerns of civil society movements, which are beyond the scope of the bureaucratically driven governance structures of nation-states, who are incapable of dealing with complex social and cultural issues.[33] This situation inevitably resulted in a Tunis 2005 Summit that skirted around the serial incapacity of participating governments to implement many, if any, of the recommendations proposed in the Plan of Action. Perhaps the best thing the WSIS could have done is stick with a relatively limited agenda. In a post-WSIS environment, this might mean keeping the debate on the information society focussed on limited technical and legal issues – policy domains that nation-states do have some capacity to at least administer. It would, however, be a disaster to see Internet governance shifted in any exclusive way into the regulatory domain of nation-states. It is unclear at a technical level how necessary it is for a supranational, global institution to be steering Internet governance issues. The question that persisted throughout WSIS was whether ICANN is the body best suited to this task.

It was inevitable that the broad, inclusive ambitions of the wsis at the end of the day turned into a rhetorical machine. While this has meant that civil society movements have obtained a degree of legitimacy at a supranational, institutional level, it is highly doubtful whether the wsis itself is able to turn the tables on the broad and complex social situations that inter-relate with icts. The legitimacy obtained by civil society movements involved in the wsis process can be transferred as political and symbolic leverage within other, more focussed platforms at national and translocal levels. This process of a re-nationalization of the discursive legitimacy of civil society concerns and values is the next challenge.

All of this background summary, necessarily brief as I have presented it, finally brings me to the crux of my argument in this chapter: democracy within an informational society is challenged, perhaps more than anything, by the problematic of scale and the ways in which cumbersome, top-heavy and bureaucratic-driven supranational institutions involved in issues of global governance are frequently going to fail. From the wsis fora emerges a pattern indicating that governing institutions have substantial limits in terms of policy development that acts as a driver of democratic change. Such a problematic is partly one of scale. It also has much to do with the correspondence between institutional temporalities and the limits of practice. The temporal rhythms of the networked organization, as distinct from organized networks, are simply not well suited to the complexities of social-technical relations as they manifest within informational societies. Despite the impact of post-Fordist techniques of reorganizing institutional relations and modes of production, the networked organization persists as the dominant environment within which sociality is arranged. Such institutional formations will only continue to struggle to keep apace with the speed of transformation and the contingencies of uncertainty peculiar to the informatization of social relations.

The regimes of value internal to the operation of organized networks, as distinct from networked organizations, are only just beginning to surface. In the case of organized networks, discourses, practices and values are coextensive with the media of communication in the first instance. Networked organizations, by contrast, are a predominantly modern, industrial institutional form. Hence, the role of communications media is secondary to the technics of organization instantiated through the architectonics of bricks and mortar.

In a most reductive sense, the vertical systems of communication within modern institutional forms are the primary reason why so many institutions have had difficulties with the transition into network societies. The TCP/IP (Transmission Control Protocol/Internet Protocol) standards for the Internet enable distributed, horizontal forms of communication. This is in contrast to the domain name system (DNS), which functions as the vertical axis of governance for digital technologies using TCP/IP standards. Thus the kind of disputes and tensions that have developed out of the WSIS process, and debates around Internet governance more broadly, are substantially different from those found among institutions that operate historically within a modern institutional system.

Put simply, the scene of 'the political' in the case of organized networks is coextensive with the media of communication, whereas the boundaries of 'the political' do not extend to those modern institutional forms that have been forced to upgrade their networking capacities. Moreover, the gap between these two institutional dynamics is an exemplary instance of what Jean-François Lyotard has called 'the différend', or 'phrases of dispute'.[34]

In other words, there's a need to think democracy beyond the idiom of representation and consensus – two of the basic principles which have been carried over to the multi-stakeholder model of managing policy debates among government, business and civil society stakeholders at the World Summit on the Information Society. NGOs are also expected to adopt such practices, along with those of accountability and transparency. Again, my view is that such primary components of representative democracy in its state form do not correspond with the dynamics of networks, hence the need for a non-representative idiom of democracy. What the particularities of such a model might consist of is going to vary according to situation, needs, forces, processes, interests, demands and so on of specific networks, but at the same time they are going to be affected by larger macro and structural forces associated with the political economy of ICTS and policies around Internet governance.

One could hypothesize that the ideology of neoliberalism is symptomatic of the problem of institutional forms within a networked, informational paradigm. Neoliberalism is responsive to the problematic of governance in an informatized society that has seen an intensification of abstraction in systems of production and social life. Organized networks emerge within a neoliberal era of governance, yet at the structural level they present the horizon of post-neoliberalism, since their technics of communication and organization are beyond the reformist agenda associated with neoliberal governance. As new institutional forms, organized networks create the possibility of new subjectivities that do not correspond with the modern politico-economic subjects of either the citizen or the consumer. Similarly, the concept and social-technical form of organized networks invites a rethinking of notions of civil society. Issues such as these will only become amplified as the logic of organized networks materializes as a new institutional form.

Institutional Scale and the Technics of Governance

At best, the 'informational citizen' is one who has recourse to representative systems of governance adopted by liberal democratic nation-states. But it's well and truly time to invent new post-political, non-representative models of democracy. The crisis of liberal democracy across the West over the last 20 to 30 years is carried over to the debates occasioned by the WSIS. The distributive, non-linear capacity of the Internet shapes social-technical relations and information and knowledge economies in ways that do not correspond with the old, hierarchical structures and governance processes peculiar to the modern era. The challenge of organization and governance is intrinsically bound to the informatization of the social. Representative models of democracy do not correspond with this situation.

While it may appear as just an institution whose exclusive responsibility concerns technical architectures of Internet governance, the case of ICANN points to more substantial matters associated with models of global governance within an age of networks. Described by some as 'an experiment in democratic governance on a global scale',[35] ICANN embodies many of the challenges facing organized networks, both in terms of how they understand themselves and how they function. The contest over ICANN's monopoly of Internet governance – as raised by civil society concerns at WSIS, the interests of the ITU as a new player in Net governance, and the ambitions of the EU as a 'second-tier' super-state

– signals not just the difficulties associated with multi-stakeholder approaches to governance; more than anything, the ICANN story points to the profound mistake in assuming the Net can reproduce the pillars of 'democracy' in its idealized 'Westphalian international order'.[36] John Palfrey charts the history of ICANN and what he sees as its imminent demise. ICANN, he writes, 'sought to empower the Internet user community, including the private sector, to manage a system necessary for the stable operation of the Internet'.[37] So far so good. Things became unstuck, however, at a structural level in terms of incorporating a range of stakeholders into the decision-making process of ICANN:

> Its novel, though ultimately flawed, structure has enabled a coalition of private-sector interest groups to manage the domain name system ('DNS') with broad input from individual users and limited but growing input from nation states. However, ICANN has failed to attract and incorporate sufficient public involvement to serve as the blueprint for building legitimacy through the Internet. Those who sought through ICANN to prove a point about democracy have misplaced their emphasis, because ICANN's narrow technical mandate has not lent itself to broad-based public involvement in the decision-making process.[38]

And:

> ICANN has sought to legitimate itself as an open and representative body, striving toward a bottom-up decision-making process grounded in consensus and inclusion.[39]

The online global election in 2000 of five 'At Large' members of the 19-member directorship is a great example of the mistaken understanding of what constitutes a representative polity within a global information society that is defined, from the outset, by an uneven geography of information. Who, for instance, are the elected five members (to say nothing of the 14 unelected members) supposed to represent? Their nation-state of origin? A particular set of issues? And, to recall Negri, who is 'the public' that participates in such events? These are all questions that lead to one conclusion: attempts at reproducing a modern socio-technics of representative democracy within an informational plane of abstraction can only result in failure. The valorisation of 'openness' is not a particularly helpful libertarian mantra to maintain when dealing with the uneven geography of information.[40]

For example, many libertarians and activists insist that intellectual property laws should be universally abolished, since IP inscribes a regime of scarcity upon that which is digitally encoded and thus remains undiminished at the level of form when it is reproduced and distributed. Certainly, there are strong reasons to support such a position. There is a great need to combat the substantial financial and legal barriers that emerge with accessing information and knowledge resources associated with patents for agricultural development and vaccinations. However, there are many factors overlooked in any blanket approach to the problem of intellectual property. While I would advocate the hacker ethic of sharing resources, too often the material preconditions necessary for participation in such open systems of distribution are left unaddressed, or simply assumed as a given.

In case we've forgotten, such speculative discourses are ones associated with the 'New Economy', and we saw what that amounted to when the dotcom bubble burst and NASDAQ high-tech stocks crashed in April 2000: a spectacular tech-wreck that resulted in pretty much instant bankruptcy and overnight unemployment for many.[41] The religious faith that IT development is synonymous with instant and sustainable growth was certainly brought into question with the massive devaluation of dotcoms and telcos. But one could be forgiven for wondering if the monumental tech-wreck ever happened. Government and education institutions have been particularly slow to awaken to the fact of the NASDAQ collapse. The rhetoric of 'e-solutions' as the answer to all problems continues to run thick in these places. Part of the reason for this has to do with the way in which the deregulation of many government and education institutions has followed on from the deregulation and privatization of telcos and the media industries, which was fuelled by the market hype of what critical Internet theorist Geert Lovink calls 'dotcom mania'. In other words, the ongoing hype generated out of the IT sector seems to be the only discursive framework available for countries enmeshed in the neoliberal paradigm, be they advanced economies in the West or countries undergoing a 'leap-frogging' of modernity.

While the wsis forums have been successful in generating a new legitimacy for civil society values, too often one is reminded of the deeply unimaginative ideas driving the ambition for an inclusive information society.

Jeanette Hofmann – one of the elected At Large members of ICANN – recounts a key problem confronting organizations as they scale up their level of operations. Speaking of the paradox that comes with obtaining legitimacy within international institutions, Hofmann observes: 'As soon as civil society organizations assume formal roles in international forums, their representativeness and legitimacy are also called into question. Ironically, NGOs are charged with the democratic deficit they once set out to elevate'.[42] This notion of a 'democratic deficit' can be extended to the Association for Progressive Communications,[43] who have been one of the peak lobby groups within the Internet governance and communication rights debates associated with wsis. The effect of an increased institutional and discursive visibility is, of course, conditioned by an increased marginalization of other civil society actors. Again, this points to the limits and problem of politics that operates within a representative framework, which the APC presupposes as its mandate of governance. The APC story is also symptomatic of the structural logic of political pragmatism within a multi-stakeholder, trans-scalar supranational policy forum such as wsis.

As I am arguing in this chapter, it is time to invent non- or post-representative modalities of organization, as distinct from representative idioms of governance. In this way, the technics of communication is granted the kind of primacy that corresponds with the informatization of sociality. Moreover, the disjuncture between, if you will, the signifier and signified (or speaking positions) is sidelined in favour of collaborative and distributive technics of composition. Don't get me wrong, in no way am I proposing some kind of naïve 'ideal speech act' here. There should be no illusion that distributive networks are somehow free from vertical systems of organization, be they symbolic or material. Rather, the technics of communication within a digital era do not correspond with the kind of institutional arrangements that persist within debates on the information society and presupposed in the multi-stakeholder approach of wsis. These kinds of institutions can be understood as networked organizations. They are clumsy when it comes to the management of information.

ICANN faced a similar difficulty to that of civil society organizations, as identified by Hofmann. But what I've been suggesting is that the problematic of 'democratic practice' goes beyond the level of discursive legitimacy. More fundamentally, there is a problem with the way in which principles of democracy peculiar to the modern state system are translated into the social-technical environment of the Internet. The result is always going to be failure. Completely new understandings of organizational structures, practices and political concepts are called for with the emergence of organized networks in order to create value systems and platforms of legitimacy that are internal to networks. As I briefly sketch in my concluding comments to this chapter and develop in more detail in this book's final chapter, the concept of a 'processual democracy' offers one possibility for exploring alternative political formations that are attentive to the ways in which practice is situated within the media of communication.

The case of ICANN serves as a parallel instantiation of the kind of governance problematics faced throughout the stages of WSIS. The WSIS process embodied a shift in relations between the UN and non-state actors, which, for the past decade or so had been characterized by a 'top-down' approach by which the UN engaged NGOS. In their report on the WSIS for the Social Science Research Council, New York, Claudia Padovani and Arjuna Tuzzi consider such a mode of governance as 'institutional'.[44] By contrast, they see the 'bottom-up' or 'globalization from below' approach at the WSIS as a challenge to earlier relations between the UN and civil society actors. Both, they argue, were operating during the WSIS and the two year lead up of preparatory committee meetings (PrepComs), regional conferences and follow-up meetings.

At a reductive level, the differences between these two approaches are apparent in the range of documentation and critical responses to come out of the Summit. The two approaches are most clearly delineated in their articulation of values and modes or processes of governance. In terms of values, the institutional approach embodied by government and business representatives was predominantly interested in market-based and technically-oriented solutions to ICTS and their relationship to issues of global governance. In effect, government and business participants reproduce the neoliberal paradigm that has dominated the past two decades of government policy-making in the West. Here, one finds the international lingua franca of policy that adopts an instrumentalist faith and technologically determinist simplicity to the uneven and situated problems of social, cultural and economic development.

For example, in the government Plan of Action there is an emphasis on technical infrastructures and informational access functioning as the primary enabling devices for 'universal education' and 'lifelong learning'. This sort of Third Way rhetoric is further compounded in the Plan of Action's discourse on 'capacity building' – a phrase shared among a range of WSIS stakeholders and common to many civil society organizations, but one that is understood in terms of 'e-learning' and 'distance education' in the Plan of Action. Such phrases are firmly entrenched within neoliberal discourses that understand education as a unilinear, hypodermic communication process driven by service providers operating under the auspices of imperialist political economies. Within a dotcom paradigm, such discourses amount to no more than boosterism for the IT sector.[45] The economic and political pressures faced by the university sector in the West contribute to a dependency relationship within indigenous education systems in developing countries. 'E-learning' and 'distance education' are heavily promoted as the financial panacea for cash-strapped universities in the West, and the 'consumer' of such projects frequently consists of countries without nationally developed educational infrastructures. The need by developing countries for external providers of education is then often used as the justification for developing IT infrastructures. Education becomes subject in the first instance to the interests of market economies, and policy developments associated with civic values are then articulated in economistic terms. Throughout the Plan of Action, policy initiatives are driven by the capacity for governments to index access against targets and performance indicators. Such a technique of governance and decision-making is symptomatic of the limits of supranational entities to deal with complexity and functions to give the false impression of 'demonstrable outcomes'.

The 'bottom-up' approach, as represented by civil society organizations, NGOs and activists, was much more concerned with ensuring that social and cultural priorities were embraced in the Declaration of

Principles and Plan of Action. Civil society movements have been effective in shifting the WSIS agenda from a neoliberal, technologically determinist set of proposals to a more broad understanding of an information society that is preconditioned by the materialities of communication. The 'multi-stakeholder' approach that emerged out of the WSIS meetings has enabled issues of concern to civil society movements to migrate into the field of supranational policy-making. The primary documents produced are clear on one thing – a technological fix to social and economic problems is not going to work.

The reason such a 'discourse war' between top-down and bottom-up approaches to information governance was so significant is that the success of the WSIS process in ensuring a 'social justice and development' agenda for civil societies and their relationship with ICTS in many ways rests with governments adopting the principles and proposals outlined in the official documentation. Many oral and written submissions to the drafting of the official Declaration of Principles and Plan of Action were left out of the final documents. The decoupling of 'macro' and 'micro' actors was further reflected in the Summit itself, with activists, grassroots organizations and NGOS running meetings and workshops in parallel to the official UN programme for the Geneva meeting. Padovani and Tuzzi suggest a much more overlapping approach characterized the Summit.[46] Certainly, the WSIS has presented its own peculiarities with regard to the problematics of process, decision-making and identification of key issues.[47] But one should not see the WSIS as exceptional or unique in terms of organizing a range of stakeholders around a particular theme or issue perceived as having international significance. The UN, after all, has a history of hosting approximately one summit per year since the 1992 Earth Summit (Conference on Environment and Development) in Rio de Janeiro.[48]

It would thus be a mistake to see the 'multi-stakeholder' approach to governance at the supranational level as exceptional. Arguably, all summits have had to address the challenge of managing a range of stakeholders and their competing interests and situations. What distinguishes the WSIS from previous summits is the ways in which the process of informatization has interpenetrated the organization of social relations, economic modes of production and systems of communication. Such a situation does indeed call for new models of governance, but whether the idea of 'multi-stakeholder governance' in and of itself is sufficient to the task of social-technical complexity is, I would suggest, doubtful. A substantial challenge to this model consists of the highly variable dimensions of power and its operation across a range of scales and a diversity of actors. As Padovani and Tuzzi maintain, 'the "multi-stakeholder approach" is not yet a model and needs to be defined, not only in theory but in practice, taking into consideration the nature and level of power the different stakeholders can exercise'.

Conclusion

It is time to abandon the illusion that the myths of representational democracy might somehow be transferred and realized within networked settings. That is not going to happen. After all, the people benefiting from such endeavours as the World Summit of the Information Society are, for the most part, those on the speaking and funding circuits, not people who are supposedly represented in such a process. Business and government representatives were quite clear that civil society was not to be taken seriously. Networks call for a new logics of politics, not just based on a handpicked collection of NGOs that have identified themselves as 'global civil society'.[49]

Networks are not institutions of representative democracy, despite the frequency with which they are expected to model themselves on such failed institutions. Instead, there is a search for 'post-democratic' models of decision-making that avoid classic models of representation and related identity policies. The emerging theme of non-representational democracies places an emphasis on process over its after-effect, consensus. Certainly, there's something attractive in process-oriented forms of governance. But ultimately the process model is about as sustainable as an earthworks sculpture burrowed into a patch of dirt called the 1970s. Process is fine as far as it integrates a plurality of forces into the network. But the primary questions remain: Where does it go? How long does it last? Why do it in the first place? But also: Who is speaking? And: Why bother? A focus on the vital forces that constitute social-technical life is thus required. Herein lie the variability and wildcards of organized networks. The persistence of dispute and disagreement can be taken as a given. Rational consensus models of democracy have proven, in their failure, that such underlying conditions of social-political life cannot be eradicated.

Organized networks are the social-technical system best suited to further develop the possibility of an inclusive information society. Since they have the capacity to operate on multiple scales of practice and communication, the challenge for organized networks consists of how they will engage their counterpart – networked organizations – which, after all, are the dominant institutions. One of the first tasks for organized networks is to address the question of sustainability, which hangs off the conditions of labour. Only then can they begin to provide an operative base for their subnational, intraregional and transnational geographies of expression.

Part II

3   Creative Industries,
Comparative Media Theory and the Limits of Critique from Within

Every space has become ad space.
Steve Hayden, *Wired Magazine*, 2003.

Obsession with economic considerations illustrates the dangers of monopolies of knowledge and suggests the necessity of appraising its limitations.
Harold A. Innis, *Empire and Communications*, 1950.

The limit is not outside language, it is the outside *of* language.
Gilles Deleuze, *Essays Critical and Clinical*, 1993.

Marshall McLuhan's dictum that media technologies constitute a sensory extension of the body holds an elective affinity with Ernst Jünger's notion of '"organic construction" [which] indicates [a] synergy between man and machine' and Walter Benjamin's exploration of the mimetic correspondence between the organic and the inorganic, between human and non-human forms.[1] Today, new information and communication technologies communicate with each other, seemingly independent of human intervention. Think of the dialogue between financial transactions and interest rates in banking systems, the registration of calls in telephone bills, the updating of information in your computer system. In the world of signs, the logo or brand is co-extensive with various media of communication – billboards, TV advertisements, fashion labels, book spines, mobile phones, and so forth. Often the logo is interchangeable with the product itself or a way or life. It appears that the social life of things is always defined by relations internal to their operation within a social-technical system. Since all social relations are mediated, whether by communications technologies or architectonic forms ranging from corporate buildings to sporting grounds to family living rooms, it follows that there can be no outside to sociality. The social is and always has been in a mutually determining relationship with mediating forms. It is in this sense that there is no outside.

Such an idea has become a refrain among various contemporary media theorists. Here's a sample from three leading media theorists, Geert Lovink, McKenzie Wark, and Scott Lash:

> There is no outside position anymore, nor is this perceived as something desirable.[2]

> Both 'us' and 'them' (whoever we are, whoever they are) are all always situated in this same virtual geography. There's no outside . . . . There is nothing outside the vector.[3]

> There is no more outside. The critique of information is in the information itself.[4]

In declaring a universality for media culture and information flows,[5] all of the above statements acknowledge the political and conceptual failure of assuming a critical position outside social-technically constituted relations. Similarly, they recognize the problems associated with the 'ideology critique' of the Frankfurt School who, in their distinction between 'true' and 'false-consciousness', claimed a sort of absolute knowledge for the critic that transcended the field of ideology as it is produced by the culture industry. Althusser's conception of ideology, material practices and subject formation, while more complex than that of the Frankfurt School's, nevertheless also fell prey to the pretence of historical materialism as an autonomous 'science' that is able to analytically determine the totality of lived social relations.

One of the key failings of ideology critique, then, is its incapacity to account for the ways in which the critic, theorist or intellectual is implicated in the operations of ideology. Such approaches displace the reflexivity and power relationships between epistemology, ontology and their constitution as material practices within institutional forms, cultural expressions and social-technical historical constellations, all of which are the primary settings for the instantiation of ideology. The notion of ideology as a lived relation between people and things can be retained, I think, when it is located within this kind of non-representational, materialist analytical framework. Lash abandons the term ideology altogether because of its conceptual legacies within German dialectics and French post-structuralist aporetics, both of which 'are based in a fundamental dualism, a fundamental binary, of the two types of reason. One speaks of grounding and reconciliation, the other of unbridgeability. . . . Both presume a sphere of transcendence'.[6]

Such assertions can be made at a general level concerning these diverse and often conflicting approaches when they are reduced to categories for the purpose of a polemic. However, as I go on to discuss in chapter 5, the work of 'post-structuralists' such as Foucault, Deleuze and Guattari and the work of German systems theorist Niklas Luhmann is clearly amenable to the task of critique of and within information societies. Indeed, Lash draws on such theorists in assembling his critical *dispositif* for the information age. More concretely, Lash advances his case for a new mode of critique by noting the social-technical and historical shift from 'constitutive dualisms of the era of the national manufacturing society' to global information cultures, whose constitutive forms are immanent to informational networks and flows.[7] Such a shift, according to Lash, needs to be met with a corresponding mode of critique:

> *Ideologycritique* [*ideologiekritik*] had to be somehow outside of ideology. With the disappearance of a constitutive outside, informationcritique must be inside of information. There is no outside any more.[8]

Lash goes on to note that 'Informationcritique itself is branded, another object of intellectual property, machinically mediated'.[9] Or, as Adorno proclaimed a few decades earlier, 'No theory today escapes the marketplace'.[10] It is the political and conceptual tensions between information critique and its regulation via intellectual property regimes that condition critique as yet another brand or logo that I wish to explore in this chapter and the next. Further, I will question the supposed erasure of a 'constitutive outside' of the field of social-technical relations within network societies and informational economies. Lash is far too totalizing in supposing a break between industrial modes of production and informational flows. Moreover, the assertion that there is no more outside to information too readily and simplistically assumes informational relations as universal and horizontally organized, and hence overlooks the significant structural, cultural and economic obstacles to participation within media vectors. The outside holds an immanent relation with information. Indeed, there are a plurality of outsides. These outsides are intertwined in singular ways with the flows of capital and the operations of biopower.[11] As difficult as it may be to ascertain boundaries, they nonetheless exist. Just ask the so-called 'illegal immigrant'!

This chapter assumes that three key forces comprise a constitutive outside of any media-information system: material (uneven geographies of labour-power, disjunctive social-technical systems, and the digital divide), symbolic (cultural capital and a-signifying semiotic systems), and strategic (figures of critique, situated interventions and permanent collaborations). In a basic sense, legal and material outsides are indeed no more than just that. One may be said to be 'outside' the rule of law when downloading pornography or music files from the Internet, for instance; another is without access to a particular database due to uneven funding across and within universities, or unable to access the Net because of their remote geographical location (to say nothing of their economic circumstances); or else, as a result of an individual's social-cultural disposition, there is just no interest in such matters. Yet legal and material outsides also amount to more than this. Irrespective of how often we have heard about issues such as the digital divide, we need to hear about these outsides again and again; even better, we need to be confronted by them, and to encounter their violence – be it symbolic or material (rather than 'Real', I think, since 'the Real' is always already present, disruptively penetrating the imaginary and the symbolic order). We need to work out ways of addressing such issues if we want to engage with some of the basic ethico-political situations of contemporary life. Material and legal outsides at once articulate with and act as a constitutive force for ontological and biopolitical dimensions of life. This takes us to the challenge of thinking difference within negativity, which I address in the second half of this chapter.

Over the next two chapters my point of reference in developing this inquiry will pivot around an analysis of the importation in Australia of the British 'creative industries project' and the problematic foundation such a project presents to the branding and commercialization of intellectual labour. The Creative Industries movement – or 'Queensland Ideology',[12] as I have discussed elsewhere with Danny Butt – holds further implications for the political and economic position of the university vis-à-vis the arts and humanities. The institutional variant of creative industries – as promulgated by the likes of Tony Blair's Creative Industries Task Force (CITF) and their academic counterparts in Australia – constructs itself as inside the culture of informationalism and its concomitant economies by the fact that it is an exercise in branding. Such branding is evidenced in the discourses, rhetoric and policies of the creative industries, as adopted by university faculties and academics, government departments and the cultural industries and service sectors seeking to reposition themselves in an institutional environment that is adjusting to ongoing structural reforms. These reforms are attributed to demands by the informational economy for increased labour flexibility and specialization, institutional and economic deregulation, product customization and capital accumulation.

The content of creative industries produced by labour-power is branded as copyrights and trademarks within the system of intellectual property regimes. However, a constitutive outside operates in material, symbolic and strategic ways that condition the possibility of creative industries. The constitutive outside of creative industries marks its limit, and thereby its extent.[13] To this end, a critique of the limits of creative industries contributes to rather than detracts from the various mapping projects undertaken in the name of creative industries. In terms of media or information critique, I am not denying that the critic or intellectual is situated within a media system – social relations are always already mediated through different communications media and architectonic forms which constitute the *dispositif* of expression. However, we don't all occupy the same situation within a media system. Much of the work in media and cultural studies has examined the delimiting role played by class, ethnicity, gender, age and so forth with regard to the production of meaning and the uses of media forms.

There are also considerable political and conceptual limits to any critique that dispenses with the constitutive force of the 'outside'. Obviously, a substantial limit to any critique consists of the different theoretical and disciplinary knowledge accumulated by any intellectual or critic. Epistemic boundaries coupled with their institutional settings define different historical epochs and operate as a horizon of intelligibility within which the present may be understood by actors with varying capacities of expression. I will argue that Deleuze's notion of a plane of immanence provides a particularly rich conceptual framework with which to theorize the role of a constitutive outside within the logic of informationalism. My critique of the creative industries project also serves as a mechanism for extracting a concept of communications media that acknowledges the constitutive role of the outside – or what Deleuze terms the 'limit' – within the plane of immanence.

Finally, my approach corresponds with the 'comparative media theory' research conducted by Ian Angus, who draws on the rich tradition of media and communications theory in Canada, as pioneered by Harold Innis, Marshall McLuhan, Walter Ong and Eric Havelock. This work is characterized by its interest in the constitutive force of communications media as a social relation, and distinguishes itself from research in the field that is concerned with analysing media content and its effects. Comparative media theory, as set out by Angus, places an emphasis on the polemical role of critique of 'the dominant culture'. At times this chapter also adopts a polemical stance against aspects of the dominant culture as it is played out in the arts and humanities. My target is the creative industries and a growing tendency within media theory to ignore the constitutive force of the outside. In undertaking such a critique, my interest is in the possibilities for new institutional forms, particularly as they emerge within a field of new ICTs underpinned by antagonistic social-political and economic relations.

Creative Industries, Intellectual Property Regimes and the 'New Economy'
The creative industries project, as envisioned by the Blair government's Department of Culture, Media and Sport (DCMS) responsible for the Creative Industry Task Force Mapping Documents of 1998 and 2001, is interested in enhancing the 'creative' potential of cultural labour in order to extract a commercial value from cultural objects and services. The DCMS cast its net wide when defining creative sectors and deploys a lexicon that is as vague and unquantifiable as the next mission statement by government and corporate bodies enmeshed within a neoliberal paradigm.[14] The list of sectors identified as holding creative capacities in the CITF Mapping Document include: film, music, television and radio, publishing, software, interactive leisure software,

design, designer fashion, architecture, performing arts, crafts, arts and antique markets, architecture and advertising. The Mapping Document seeks to demonstrate how these sectors consist of 'activities which have their origin in individual creativity, skill and talent and which have the potential for wealth and job creation through generation and exploitation of intellectual property'.[15]

The CITF's identification of intellectual property (IP) as central to the creation of jobs and wealth firmly places the creative industries within informational and knowledge economies. Unlike material property, intellectual property such as artistic creations (films, music, books) and innovative technical processes (software, biotechnologies) are forms of knowledge that do not diminish when they are distributed. This is especially the case when information has been encoded in a digital form and distributed through technologies such as the Internet. In such instances, information is often attributed an 'immaterial' and nonrivalrous quality, although this can be highly misleading for both the conceptualization of information and the politics of knowledge production. I address the problematic of 'immateriality' with reference to creative labour in the next chapter.

For all the emphasis the Mapping Document places on exploiting intellectual property, it is remarkable how absent any consideration of IP is from creative industries rhetoric. It is even more astonishing that media and cultural studies academics have until recently given passing attention to the issues of IPRS.[16] Perhaps such oversights by academics associated with the creative industries can be accounted for by the fact that their own jobs rest within the modern, industrial institution of the university, which continues to offer the security of a salary award system and continuing if not tenured employment despite the onslaught of neoliberal reforms since the 1980s. Such an industrial system of traditional and organized labour, however, does not define the labour conditions for those working in the so-called creative industries. Within those sectors engaged more intensively in commercializing culture, labour practices closely resemble work characterized by the dotcom boom, which saw young people working excessively long hours without any of the sort of employment security and protection vis-à-vis salary, health benefits and pension schemes peculiar to traditional and organized labour.[17] During the dotcom mania of the mid to late 1990s, stock options were frequently offered to people as an incentive for off-setting the often minimum or even deferred payment of wages.

The attraction of stock options and the rhetorical sheen of 'shareholder democracy' adopted by neoliberal governments became brutally unstuck in 2000 with the crash of the NASDAQ, which saw the collapse in share value of high-tech stocks and telcos. This 'tech-wreck' was followed up by the negative impact of September 11 on tourism and aviation sectors. The 'market populism' of the high-tech stock bubble, as Thomas Frank explains, was defined by a delirious faith in entrepreneurial culture and the capacity for new ICTs articulated with corporate governance and financescapes to function as a policy and electoral panacea for neoliberal states obsessed with dismantling the welfare state model and severing their responsibilities for social development.[18] The creative industries project emerged out of a similar context and adopted much of the same rhetoric, with a greater orientation towards 'creative capital'. It remains questionable as to the extent to which such rhetoric is transposable on an international scale and the extent to which it is then appropriate to be adopted by countries and regions with significantly and sometimes substantially different social-political relations, industrial structures and policies, and cultural forms and practices.

Another key precondition for the growth of the creative industries consists of a crisis within the 'art system'. As new ICTs became an increasing part of social and economic life within advanced economies throughout the 1990s, the culture industry continued on oblivious to this social-technical transformation. And why not? In Australia, like much of Europe and North America, the traditional forms of artistic expression – classical music, ballet, and opera in particular – have their well-established systems of patronage and government funding. Even though one might think that it should have been the task of the arts to deal with media and creative industries, they weren't about to let anything like new media arts disrupt the comfort of the status quo. While public sectors across the board were grappling with the impact of economic rationalist ideologies, the 'high' arts held dear to their myth of somehow being autonomous from prevailing socio-economic forces. The disjuncture between art and informationization functions as a constitutive outside of the creative industries, especially once that disjuncture is articulated with other forces (outsides). Two key forces consist of, firstly, a neoliberal, post-'New Left' in Britain in search of electoral legitimacy through a Third Way discourse that sought a more comprehensive bonding between culture and the economy. And secondly, a substantial increase in both Britain and Australia of students coming out of vocationalized humanities programmes (media and cultural studies, performance studies, art and design, journalism, multimedia, IT, etcetera) who want jobs as either creative producers, service workers, or cultural intermediaries and who therefore hold government interest as an emergent electoral constituency.

While the creative industries are emergent as an institutional formation, they have in recent years gained dominance at a discursive level on an international scale. The ensemble of articulation consists of four principle components that together hold a hegemonic force: 1) government policies on higher education that privilege industry affiliation over the pursuit of core values of scholarship and pedagogy within the arts and humanities; 2) Third Way ideology that is ready to legitimate a plurality of socio-cultural values, but only if they can translate into commercial form; 3) research by the OECD and an assortment of supranational research agencies, think-tanks, corporate R&D teams and government departments that have an interest in establishing intellectual property as the architecture for a global information and knowledge economy that can extract profit from education and culture; and 4) a populist strand within the field of media and cultural studies that considers consumer (audience-student-citizen) desire as relatively autonomous and self-forming and hence the basis upon which university curricula should be shaped. This approach within media and cultural studies gained purchase in the 1980s and '90s as an alternative to the impasse of ideology critique, advocating the sovereign power of the consumer over the structural forces of the state and affiliated organizations. In this regard, the populist approach has established the preconditions necessary for a relatively smooth transition within the arts and humanities into the current era of the university as a pseudo-corporation.

Many would argue that this is all proper and good – promoting the creative industries is a truly responsible project, since rather than imposing a set of cultural values from above, it is giving students-as-consumers what they want and need in order to realize and obtain the kind of lifestyle and professional satisfaction and challenges they desire. I wouldn't deny that these are important factors; my argument is that for all the populism – which, in any case, is and always has been a great fallacy at a structural level if not a rhetorical one – of creative industries style discourses, there is a substantial constituency which holds no interest for proponents of the creative industries. A focus on the role of intellectual property regimes reveals that the labour-power of the core constituency of the creative industries – information workers, programmers, designers, media producers, and so forth – is the primary vehicle for exploitation and exclusion. Even though it is situated within the social-technical and discursive system of the creative industries, the labour-power of creative workers functions as a constitutive outside for the creative industries. Just as there is no outside for information critique, for proponents of the creative industries there is no culture that is worth its name if it is outside a market economy.[19] That is, the commercialization of 'creativity' – or indeed commerce as a creative undertaking – acts as a legitimizing function and hence plays a delimiting role for 'culture' and, by association, sociality. The institutional life of career academics is also at stake in this legitimizing process.

The valuation of culture in terms of its potential exchange value is in direct contrast to the 'aesthetic' value of culture set out in the work of nineteenth-century social reformer and school inspector Mathew Arnold and his mid-twentieth-century extension, the literary critic F. R. Leavis. The guiding principle within their paternalistic, 'civilizing' and humanistic worldview consisted of evaluating culture as 'the best of what has been thought and said'.[20] Such an evaluative regime became the basis upon which to uphold the moral and political authority of the ruling classes whose value system was perceived to be under threat by the emergent 'mass culture' of the working classes and expanding bourgeoisie. Thus elite cultural forms such as painting, classical music and sculpture were privileged over the commercial cultural technologies of popular songs, novels, newspapers, radio and the cinema that appealed to the working and middle classes. Within the 'culture and civilization' tradition exemplified by Arnold and more particularly Leavis and others involved in the literary critical journal *Scrutiny*, the 'inherent quality' or aesthetics of elite cultural forms was assumed to transcend social and economic relations. Culture in this sense was static, unchanging and exclusive. The British cultural studies tradition inaugurated by the materialist work of Williams, Hoggart and Thompson contested this view of culture. Emerging out of the growth in adult education with the return of soldiers from the Second World War, British cultural studies was interested in the everyday aspects of culture and paid particular attention to the symbolic dimensions and social uses of cultural forms. This foundation myth of cultural studies is now well rehearsed and repeated verbatim within literature in the field.[21] My purpose in re-producing this story of origins is to set out some initial parameters in which to locate the paradox of culture within the creative industries.

Despite the efforts of the creative industries' academic proponents to argue for the merits of popular cultural forms, within a creative indus-tries discourse informed by policies and rhetoric of the information or knowledge economy, 'culture' reclaims a privileged location. And it is one that is remarkably similar in a structural sense to the discursive economy that informed the Arnoldian and Leavisite concept of culture: 'quality' culture is defined within the creative industries as that which has the capacity to generate and exploit intellectual property. Because the political and economic architecture of IPRS is premised on the ca-pacity to restrict access to the object or form enclosed within the infor-mational and legal system of IP, culture that has been incorporated as IP is available only to those with the economic and cultural capital that enables them access to the particular cultural form encoded as IP. In this sense, culture is elite; it is certainly not 'working class', and while it may be 'popular' it is only popular within a particular class setting that has the means to access and control it.[22] Since access is the means to the reproduction, expansion and thus innovation of culture, the enclosure of culture as forms of knowledge within a system of IP raises questions of elitism against the populist rhetoric found within much creative industries discourse.

Intellectual property, as distinct from material property, operates as a scaling device whereby the unit cost of labour is offset by the potential for substantial profit margins realized by distribution techniques availed by new ICTS and their capacity to infinitely reproduce the digital commodity object as a property relation. Within the logic of intellec-tual property regimes, the use of content is based on the capacity of individuals and institutions to pay. The syndication of media content ensures that market saturation is optimal and competition is kept to a minimum. However, such a legal architecture has run into conflict with other network cultures such as open source movements and peer-to-peer networks that operate by alternative intellectual property codes, as seen in the examples of the Creative Commons licence, the open content Wikipedia encyclopaedias, and Linux software.[23] Other instances of political conflict that are set to become an increasing concern for hegemonic media and international diplomacy and trade agreements consist of the digital piracy of software and digitally encoded cinematic forms, particularly within China.[24] To this end, IPRS are an unstable architecture for extracting profit.

As Scott McQuire has noted, there is a 'strategic rationale' behind the creative industries project: 'It provides a means for highlighting the significant economic contribution already made collectively by areas which individually may pass unnoticed all too easily'.[25] In this respect, the creative industries concept is a welcome and responsible intervention. But as McQuire also goes on to point out, the creative industries project 'provides a template for change in educational curricula'. This aspect warrants a more circumspect approach to the largely enthusiastic embrace of the concept of creative industries. Change of course is inevitable and is often much needed. However, there is a conformist principle underpinning the concept of creative industries as it has been adopted in Australia – namely the reduction of 'creativity' to content production and the submission of the arts and humanities to the market test,[26] which involves exploiting and generating intellectual property.[27] What happens to those academic programmes that prove unsuccessful in the largely government and market-driven push to converge various media of expression into a digital form? How are the actual producers – the 'creative' workers – to be protected from the exploitation incurred from being content producers?

It is understandable that the creative industries project holds an appeal for managerial intellectuals operating in arts and humanities disciplines in Australia. The Queensland University of Technology (QUT), which claims to have established the 'world's first' Creative Industries faculty, has been particularly active in reproducing and developing the British model of creative industries.[28] The creative industries model provides a validating discourse for those suffering anxiety disorders over what Ruth Barcan has called the 'usefulness' of 'idle' intellectual pastimes.[29] As a project that endeavours to articulate graduate skills with labour markets, the creative industries project is a natural extension of the neoliberal agenda within education as advocated by successive governments in Australia since the Dawkins reforms in the mid 1980s.[30] Certainly there's a constructive dimension to this: graduates, after all, need jobs, and universities should display an awareness of market conditions; within managerial discourses of 'quality assurance' and 'accountability', academics also have a responsibility to do so. I find it remarkable that so many university departments in my own field of communications and media studies are so bold and, let's face it, stupid, as to make unwavering assertions about market demands and student needs on the basis of doing little more than sniffing the wind! Time for a reality check. This means becoming more serious about allocating funds and resources towards market analysis based on the combination of needs among students, staff, disciplinary values, university expectations, and the political economy of markets.

The extent to which there should be a wholesale shift of the arts and humanities into a creative industries model is open to debate. The arts and humanities, after all, are a set of disciplinary practices and values that operate as a constitutive outside for creative industries. Indeed, in their Creative Industries manifesto, Stuart Cunningham and John Hartley loathe the arts and humanities in such confused and paradoxical ways in order to establish the arts and humanities as a sort of cultural and ideological outside, yet without acknowledging the constitutive power of that outside.[31] To subsume the arts and humanities into the creative industries, if not eradicate them altogether, is to spell the end of creative industry as it is currently conceived at the institutional level within academe.

Too much specialization in one post-industrial sector ensures a situation of labour reserves that exceed market needs. One only needs to consider all those now unemployed web-designers who graduated from multi-media programmes in the mid to late 1990s. Vocational specialization does not augur well for the inevitable shift from or collapse of a creative industries economy. Where is the standing reserve of labour shaped by university education and training in a post-creative industries economy? Diehard neoliberals and true believers in the capacity for perpetual institutional flexibility would say that this isn't a problem. The university will just 'organically' adapt to prevailing market conditions and shape its curriculum and staff composition accordingly. Perhaps. Arguably if the university is to maintain a modality of time that is distinct from the just-in-time mode of production characteristic of informational economies – and indeed, such a difference is a quality that defines the market value of the educational commodity – then limits have to be established between institutions of education and the corporate organization or creative industry entity.

The creative industries project is a reactionary model in so far as it reinforces the status quo of labour relations within a neoliberal paradigm in which bids for industry contracts are based on a combination of rich technological infrastructures often subsidized by the state (that is, paid for by the public), high labour skills, a low currency exchange rate and the lowest possible labour costs. It is no wonder that literature on the creative industries omits discussion of the importance of unions within informational, networked economies. What is the role of unions in a labour force constituted as individualized units?[32] I will address this question at greater length in chapter 4.

There is a great need to explore alternative economic models to the content production one if wealth is to be successfully extracted and distributed from activities in the new media sectors. The suggestion that the creative industries project initiates a strategic response to the conditions of cultural production within network societies and informational economies is highly debateable. The now well-documented history of digital piracy in the film and software industries and the difficulties associated with regulating violations to proprietors of IP in the form of copyright and trademarks is enough of a reason to look for alternative models of wealth extraction. And you can be sure this will occur irrespective of the endeavours of the creative industries.

The conditions of possibility for creative industries within Australia are at the same time its frailties. A significant portion of the creative industries sector in Australia is engaged in film production associated with Hollywood's activities 'down under'. In such instances intellectual property is not owned by Australian corporations or individuals, but is held more often by US-based multinationals. The success of the creative industries sector depends upon the ongoing combination of cheap labour enabled by a low currency exchange rate and the capacity of students to access the skills and training offered by universities. Of all these factors, much depends on the Australian currency being pegged at a substantially lower exchange rate than the US dollar. The economic effects in the USA of an expensive military intervention in Iraq and the larger costs associated with the 'war on terror', along with the ongoing economic fallout from the dotcom crash and corporate collapses, have all led to a creeping increase in the value of the Australian dollar against the greenback.

Reports in *The Australian Financial Review* support these claims, noting that foreign investment – most particularly from Hollywood film studios – in Australian feature film and television drama production 'fell for the first time in eight years'.[33] The 23 per cent drop is directly attributed to the rising Australian dollar. In the case of TV productions, the lack of refundable tax incentives has had a negative effect, unlike New Zealand which adopted incentives for foreign investment in the industry. The drop in expenditure was even greater for international joint ventures: 'Expenditure on international co-productions was down 50 per cent in 2002-03, from $102 million in 2001-02 to $51 million, reducing the size of Australian TV and film production by nearly a quarter'.[34] A fall in postproduction and foreign production in studios in Sydney, Melbourne and Queensland is also expected in the coming years. The security of creative labour will also be affected by the Free Trade Agreement (FTA) between Australia and the USA, which came into effect in January 2005. The FTA will have a substantial impact on Australia's media and cultural industries. Australian copyright laws will be extended from 50 to 70 years, bringing them into so-called 'harmonization' with the USA. While the FTA has retained local content rules that require 55 per cent of all free-to-air TV programming in Australia to consist of locally produced programmes and ads, there is uncertainty over the impact this will have on pay TV, multi-channelling and new media technologies such as the Internet, mobile telephony and interactive digital cinema. The likely result for many media industries is an increase in US content and market control. As Australian new media scholar and teacher Chris Chesher has pointed out, 'This one bilateral agreement may restrict future governments from making policy that fosters the development of a new media industry in Australia'.[35]

In a globalizing economy that is substantially shaped by the US domestic economy and its transnational corporate interests, the sum effect of these developments is a downgrading of skills and experience in the media industries and fewer jobs for Australian technicians, musicians and actors – a number of whom will be graduates from creative industries programmes. The security of labour is contingent then upon the relative stability of global financial systems which are underpinned by risk, uncertainty and a faith in the hubris peculiar to discourses on growth and expansion associated with the 'New Economy'.[36] Additional contingencies emerge with government policies that seek to intervene in the supranational, regional and national regulatory fields of trade agreements, privacy rights, and so forth.

In relation to matters such as these there may appear to be no outside for the creative industries. However, a model of communications and informationality that locates points of tension, conflict, or antagonism will often discover the constitutive force of an outside at work. As I've argued above, the operation of intellectual property regimes constitutes an outside within creative industries by alienating labour from its mode of information or form of expression. Lash is apposite on this point: 'Intellectual property carries with it the right to exclude'.[37] This principle of exclusion applies not only to those outside the informational economy and culture of networks as a result of geographic, economic, infrastructural, and cultural constraints. In instances where ownership of intellectual property belongs to the commissioning agent, practitioners within the creative industries are excluded from control over their creations.[38] It is in this sense that a legal and material outside is established *within* an informational society. At the same time, this internal outside – to put it rather clumsily – operates in a constitutive manner in as much as the creative industries, by definition, depend upon the capacity to exploit the IP produced by its primary source of labour. In order to further develop a notion of a constitutive outside, I now turn to Deleuze's logic of immanence and elaborate the elective affinities it holds with Marxian post-negativity. I will then suggest how a constitutive outside is assumed within a 'comparative media theory' of technology and culture.

Post-Negativity and the Logic of Immanence

The challenge for a politics of informational cultures and social-technical systems is to define limits at the current conjuncture. In ways similar to New Age devotees, cyber-libertarians, spokespeople for the IMF and many political activists, proponents of the creative industries so often insist on and valorise 'openness'. In case we have forgotten, openness itself is conditioned by the possibility of exclusion. What are the limits of the informational inside? In the case of creative industries, what are the implications of experiencing what Giorgio Agamben calls the event-horizon, or *qualunque* ('whatever') as 'the event of an outside .. . of being-*within* an *outside*'?[39] This sort of question underpins what it means to theorize about those working with the creative industries – a cultural sector that enlists actors with multiple capacities whose innovative labour-power is the condition for their exclusion from absolute self-governance, as bequeathed upon them by a managerial intellectual class within universities, government, R&D agencies, and policy think-tanks such as Demos (UK), the Cato Institute (USA), and the Centre for Independent Studies (Australia).

In order to build a theoretical framework for thinking the role of the constitutive outside for the creative industries, I will briefly outline the notion of post-negativity and then distinguish a Deleuzian logic of immanence from Lash's problematic deployment of a concept of immanence, which he enlists as a metaphor to describe the absolute interiority of relations within information societies. Perhaps part of the problem here is that Lash invokes the metaphor of immanence as a concept, while Deleuze and Guattari insist that the plane of immanence 'is neither a concept nor the concept of concepts'.[40] The finite movement of concepts subsists within the infinite movements of the plane of immanence.[41] Thus immanence is better understood as a process of singular events rather than a ubiquitous condition, as many critics and theorists have posited.

For Lash the notion of a constitutive outside is untenable since it is overdetermined and revealed as transcendent by the action of dialectics. The outside is always already that which is beyond, impossible, false. Lash believes the social-technical time of dialectics and the technics of industrial production have been surpassed by informationalism (real-time, interactivity, flow). Though I wonder, is there a combinatory practice for media and cultural studies that goes by the name of affirmative critique? Unlike Lash, Mouffe argues that 'the "constitutive outside" cannot be reduced to a dialectical negation. In order to be a true outside, the outside has to be incommensurable with the inside, and at the same time, the condition of emergence of the latter'.[42] For Mouffe, the constitutive outside is not so much a dialectics as a *suspension* (a state of exception), a *movement* whereby that which is excluded or outside is also the condition of possibility for, and conditioned by, the inside, which incorporates the outside as it simultaneously excludes it. I argue that the emergence of creative industries is caught up in such a process.

Deleuze understands the operation of this condition in terms of a 'fold', which I discuss below. Adorno's concept of 'immanent criticism' provides a first point of connection between thinking difference within negativity, the logic of immanence as understood by Deleuze, and the constitutive outside. By my reading of Deleuze, the constitutive outside is the difference within negativity. In her recent book *Thinking Past Terror*, Susan Buck-Morss summarizes the characteristics of negative dialectics and immanent criticism as follows:

> Relying on the Hegelian dialectics of negativity, combined with a Kantian humility as to the limits of what can be known, immanent criticism as practiced by Theodor Adorno, Max Horkheimer, and others sought to transcend the untruth of the present society in a non-dogmatic, critical, hence negative mode, showing the gap between concept and reality – how, for example, so-called democracies were undemocratic; how mass culture was un-cultured; how Western civilization was barbaric; and, in a classic study, *Dialectic of Enlightenment*, written in the catastrophic context of World War II, how reason, the highest value of European modernity, had become unreason.[43]

Thus an 'immanent critique' of the creative industries would set out to prove that the creative industries are neither 'creative', nor an 'industry'. Such an undertaking is not my interest in this chapter. Rather, I am interested in unpacking the articulation between Adorno's negative immanent critique and Deleuze's affirmative logic of immanence. Adorno's technique of immanent criticism seeks to uncover the contradictions inherent within the work of Hegel, Kant and Heidegger, among others. Orthodox Marxist thinking is also given a serve of Adorno's wrath. In his magnum opus, *Negative Dialectics*, Adorno's procedure is not to critique various trajectories within Western philosophy and political theory from a position outside their terms of reference and principles of deduction. Adorno is not interested in judgement from above or the safety net of an external anti-bourgeois position. That would be too easy to feign, and even easier to dismiss. Instead, he seeks to undertake a critique from within, an 'immanent critique', that ascertains the failure of philosophical disciplines to think through questions of metaphysics and problems of ontology. Opening his immanent critique of ontology, Adorno writes: 'We have no power over the philosophy of Being if we reject it generally, from outside, instead of taking it on in its own structure – turning its force against it ...'.[44] Adorno extended this method beyond the realm of philosophy, and into a critique of 'mass culture'. Buck-Morss explains the operation of immanent critique with reference to Adorno's essay 'On the Fetish Character of Music and the Regression of Hearing':

> Adorno made the characteristics of fetishism, reification, and exchange visible 'inside' the phenomenon of listening to music. . . . Adorno claimed that 'serious' and popular music converged not simply because of the revolutions of technological reproduction, but because of the transformations in the relationship between the audience as subject and the music as object, which determined the form of the new technologies as well as being determined by them. . . . Adorno claimed that the 'positive', that is, technological progress in the mass production of music, was in fact 'negative', the development of regression in listening: the mass audience, instead of experiencing music, consumed it as a fetishized object, the value of which was determined by exchange.[45]

Interestingly, Adorno was not *ipso facto* against taking a position of critique from outside, but only if it served the purpose of immanent critique. In his rejection of the 'identity principle' underpinning the Hegelian concept of history, which contrives a coincidence of subject and object, Adorno reserves a space for the outside: 'Pure identity is that which the subject posits and thus brings up from the outside. Therefore, paradoxically enough, to criticize it immanently means to criticize it from outside as well'.[46] Perhaps in response to the elevated status Benjamin grants to the modern experience of shock, Adorno retains the possibility of an outside, so long as it holds the potential for disruption and the attainment of truth: 'No immanent critique can serve its purpose wholly without outside knowledge, of course – without a moment of immediacy, if you will, a bonus from the subjective thought that looks beyond the dialectical structure. That moment is the moment of spontaneity ...'.[47]

It is this suggestion of an outside that functions as a constitutive force that I wish to retrieve from Adorno's method of immanent critique. Rather than a negativity comprised of contradictions or antinomies whose tensions structurally determine the discontinuity of history and disintegration in Western culture, how might negativity be thought in terms of a diagrammatics of tensions that traverse and constitute overlapping fields of networks – and clusters of creative industries – as an affirmative force? Benjamin understood this process in his diagrammatic taxonomies of modern life. Benjamin's analytical method consisted of identifying tensions located at the intersection between the 'axis of transcendence' (theology) and the 'the axis of empirical history' (Marxism).[48] Thus while he also worked with a model of negative dialectics (a theological, historical materialism of the 'dialectical image'[49]), Benjamin was more open than Adorno to the possibility of different arrangements of collision, of splintering, of resonance. His technics of 'profane illumination' carried the possibility of mobile, though not arbitrary, combinations and ethico-aesthetic renewal or redemption.[50] In this respect, one can detect an affirmative, as distinct from wholly negative, reworking of historical materialism.

Post-negativity is a mode of critique that thinks beyond the dualisms of subject/object, culture/nature, friend/enemy, us/them, life/death and so forth. Post-negativity defines not just a mode of thought, but thought that emerges from and permeates social-technical and historical conditions of the present. Post-negativity retains the concept of a constitutive outside. This is an outside that is configured not according to dualisms, but rather to patterns of distribution, series of encounters, rhythms of tension, spaces of dispute. Negativity persists within informational societies since the informational society is a continuum of the capitalist trajectory in which Negativity, in its modern incarnation, emerged as a concept to address problems as they were perceived.[51] The correspondence between negativity and emergent problems figures as an elective affinity within the work of Marx and Deleuze and Guattari. As Deleuze and Guattari write, 'All concepts are connected to problems without which they would have no meaning and which can themselves only be isolated or understood as their solution emerges'.[52] In a similar vein, Marx writes: 'Mankind always takes up only such problems as it can solve, since, looking at the matter more closely, we will always find that the problem itself arises only when the material conditions necessary for its solution already exist or are at least in the process of formation'.[53]

Today, the technique of negativity as a mode of critique is articulated with, but not reducible to, emergent problematics such as access to ICTS, ecological transmogrification, the uneven development of informational economies, and so on. To be sure, these are problems associated with the myriad ways in which new ICTS play an ever-increasing role in the mediation of social-technical relations. To this end, negativity has not so much disappeared or been made redundant; rather, it operates within a different social-technical historical constellation. The condition of post-negativity is one in which social-technical and ethico-aesthetic tensions are no longer articulated through the logic or episteme of dialectical negation, but instead through a multiplicity of differences that are immanent to the scalar dimensions and temporal modalities of states, networks and social-political formations.

The problem of conceiving informational technologies and network societies in terms of a supposed erasure of the outside can be usefully addressed through the logic of immanence. A notion of the outside plays an important role in Deleuze's understanding of immanence. This is a point frequently overlooked in recent work by Hardt and Negri, Lash, Buck-Morss, and Wark, among others. Contrary to these thinkers, I would maintain that a notion of the outside plays a central role in any political theory of network societies and informationalism. Combining a notion of the outside with that of immanence introduces a basis upon which to begin understanding the complexity of politics within informationalism, network societies and the Internet. Such a theoretical correspondence invokes the uneven, differentiated and pluralistic nature of social-technical systems. One is then able to combat the still very much pervasive sense of a 'global village' that is so often attributed to the Net, most particularly within popular, business and scientific discourses.

Essentially, Lash deploys the concept of immanence as a metaphor to loosely reinforce his claim that informationalism has no outside. At a conceptual level, we will see that this is plainly wrong. This is also the case at a material level. The brutal phenomenon of 'illegal immigrants' again is a good case in point: At a certain moment in time (the media-political event of an election and beyond[54]) 'they' at once condition the possibility of what it means to be an Australian citizen, what it means to maintain national sovereignty and so forth, while at the very same time precarious refugees are excluded from the rights and ways of life that are associated with existing within the rule of the sovereign power as a citizen-subject, or, for the 'legitimate' immigrant, as a global cosmopolitan subject. In this sense, 'we' do not so much cling to the outside in order to reject it, but are intimately bound with the outside as it is constituted – for the most part – within the spectral dimensions (the media imaginary) of our everyday life.

The phenomenon of flexible production by transnational corporations and the exploitation of sweatshop labour in both developing and developed countries are surely material and symbolic instances of an incommensurable, constitutive outside that conditions the possibility of high living standards, practices of consumption, and material wealth within advanced economies that adopt a neoliberal mode of governance. While labour within the 'invisible' zones of production is not directly part of informational economies in terms of belonging to those sectors identified as part of the creative industries, it is nevertheless a condition of possibility for social relations, consumer dispositions and labour practices within advanced economies. Even those workers located within informationalism are positioned in relation to IPRS in such a manner as to be 'outside' processes of power, authority, and decision-making, and hence occupy an illegitimate and structurally disabled position vis-à-vis a sovereignty of the self and social collectives. Paradoxical as it may seem, outsides of this sort play a constitutive role in terms of what it means to be within the immanent relations of informationalism.

Drawing primarily on Nietzsche, Bergson, Hume and Spinoza, Deleuze maintains that life can be practiced as an experiment, experience and thought process in radical empiricism. In dialogue with Guattari, Parnet, Foucault and 'an image of thought' that subsists within the present as 'coordinates, dynamics, orientations' for philosophy,[55] Deleuze invents a 'prephilosophical' plan – a chaosmosis of virtuality, a plane of immanence, a force of potentiality – in which 'relations are external to their terms' and from which transcendent organization is possible.[56] The 'instituted' plane of immanence constructs a network of relations of force that condition the possibility of concepts.[57] Yet concepts are not 'deduced from the plane'.[58] Concepts subsist within or 'populate' the plane of immanence as 'virtualities, events, singularities'.[59] As Deleuze and Guattari write, 'Concepts pave, occupy, or populate the plane bit by bit, whereas the plane itself is the indivisible milieu in which concepts are distributed without breaking up its continuity or integrity'.[60] Concepts are created in response to specific problems; the relationship between the two is one of immanence. The force of a constitutive outside, a univocity, makes possible the singular relationship between problems and concepts.

Deleuze and Guattari provide two conceptions of the plan(e),[61] one in opposition to the other: a plan(e) of organization and development as distinct from a plane of consistency or of composition or of immanence. The former comprises a structural and genetic order, the latter consists of rhythms and resonances in which 'there are only relations of movement and rest, speed and slowness between unformed elements.... There are only haecceities, affects, subjectless individuations that constitute collective assemblages'.[62] The plane of organization, on the other hand, is engaged in capturing and momentarily containing the pure potential of the plane of immanence. The plane of organization consists of 'rigid segmentarity, all the lines of rigid segmentarity, [that] enclose a certain plane, which concerns both forms and their development, subjects and their formation. A plane of organization which always has at its disposal a supplementary dimension (overcoding)'.[63] Moreover,

> Organization and development concern form and substance: at once the development of form and the formation of substance or a subject. But the plane of consistency knows nothing of substance and form:

haecceities [singularities], which are inscribed on this plane, are precisely modes of individuation proceeding neither by form nor by the subject.[64]

As discussed in chapter 5, the plane of immanence and the plane of transcendent organization are coextensive with the relational force of movement between the conditions of possibility and the grid of meanings, codes, signs. A processual force subsists in the movement between these two planes. This model may seem to be nothing more than a crude attempt to cunningly reappropriate the classical Marxist notions of base and superstructure. The differences with that model, however, are considerable. First, the base/superstructure consists of a dialectical relationship in which the social relations that define the economic base and mode of production determine the superstructure. As Massumi writes, 'When everything is served up in founding terms of determination – "of" or "by" – by design or by default – change can only be understood as a negation of determination: as the simply indeterminate'.[65] The logic of immanence is not one of determination or the indeterminate; it is not One or the Other. Neither total order, nor absolute chaos. Immanence communicates the force of movement that subsists within relations between determination and indeterminacy. Second, the plane of immanence, unlike the Marxian notion of the base, does not privilege the category of 'class' as the transcendent principle or motivation for political change; indeed, the category of class subsists in the plane of organization – or that which has emerged from and is in a mobile relationship with the plane of immanence. Moreover, the relation between the two planes is a multiplicity of 'interleaved' planes. Think of a cross-section diagram of a geological formation – there is no single layer, but rather a complex distribution and interpenetration of layers that in themselves are composed of a complex interleaving of materials, properties, qualities. 'Every plane of immanence is a One-All', write Deleuze and Guattari, 'it is not partial like a scientific system, or fragmentary like concepts, but distributive – it is in "each". *The* plane of immanence is *interleaved*'.[66] In other words, the plane of immanence does not function as a foundation or determining instance; it functions as a pure potential of virtuality. Agamben describes this process as one of 'virtual indetermination'.[67] Massumi elaborates the operation of the virtuality of the field of immanence in terms of superempiricism: 'Although inseparable from the empirical elements of whose contingent mixing it is an effect, the field of immanence is superempirical – in excess over the substantiality of already-constituted terms'.[68]

Deleuze most clearly establishes the operation of the outside within the plane of immanence in his book on Foucault. In the interests of clarity, I wish to focus briefly on this work. Deleuze reads Foucault as a cartographer of relations comprised of forces, strategies, foldings, forms of expression and forms of content that constitute the social field. Deleuze's Foucault offers a diagram of sociality, an abstract machine, with which to think the act of mapping projects as a multiplicity of relations. Such an approach holds a radical difference to the numerous mapping projects undertaken within the creative industries that seek to delimit the field of creativity *and* at the same time ignore the policy, theoretical, political and practical implications of intellectual property regimes. This is paradoxical to say the least, since it is supposedly the generation and exploitation of IP that distinguishes the creative industries from others. Danny Butt elaborates on this problematic within common approaches to creative industries' mapping projects as follows:

> They basically work on aggregating output in unreconstructed industry sector definitions ('Publishing' + 'TV' + '...' = 'Creative Industries') that they acknowledge are inadequate in their own footnotes! My view is that most 'mapping' is a political exercise to secure resources from governments, and impressive-sounding figures go down better than 'We still don't know how IP generates macroeconomic wealth, but we know your existing classifications will need to be changed'. There's a huge, relatively untheorised disjuncture between the attempt to theoretically delimit the 'creative industries' through their special relationship to IP (which has merit), the practical problems of capitalist accumulation within these industries (which are characterised by IP struggles), and the regional mapping projects which basically ignore this process of IP-intensive accumulation.[69]

Registering the complex of relations between different actants, forces, discourses and practices that constitute the transformative potential of creative labour is a process, I am suggesting, that can benefit from a Deleuzo-Foucauldian cartography of immanence. Deleuze distinguishes between a notion of 'the exterior' and that of 'the outside'. The latter 'exists as an unformed element of forces'.[70] Force is a relation: 'It is never singular but essentially exists with other forces'.[71] Force subsists, then, within the plane of immanence. Force is a potential; it is a multiplicity of relations that possess the power to affect, to shape, to create. Force thus functions as a constitutive outside. The exterior, by contrast, is 'the area of concrete assemblages, where relations between forces are realized'.[72] The actualization of forces takes on what Deleuze terms 'forms of exteriority' – these may share the same concrete assemblage, but will differ from one another.

Within systems theory and cybernetics, 'noise' functions as a constitutive outside for the system. However, there is a significant difference in the terms of reference between systems theory and a Deleuzian logic of immanence that are worth briefly noting. Luhmann does not speak exactly of the outside, of the external, whereas Deleuze distinguishes between externality or exteriority and the outside. For Luhmann, if something that is external to the system can be described and thus observed, then it is part of the system. Luhmann calls this kind of process 'paradoxical circularity', as William Rasch explains: 'Paradoxical circularity cannot be avoided by appeals to the outside; what escapes the system can be observed, and therefore communicated, only from within the system, and what can be communicated is, by definition, part of the system'.[73]

Well, politics isn't that straightforward. One can describe the condition of exploitation for creative workers. In so doing, a description is being made of activities that are located 'outside' the discourse of creative industries. But such an observation in itself doesn't change the system, at least not in terribly meaningful ways. In the case of the creative industries, the outside understood in terms of a logic of immanence functions in different ways than if it were understood in terms of systems theory. On the one hand, this chapter is attempting to do exactly what systems theory does: map the network of relations that constitute the system of 'creative labour' within the creative industries. But in thinking of the outside as a force that is 'a difference which can make a difference' (Bateson), the composition of the creative industries is opened to the potential of what Deleuze and Guattari term 'deterritorialization', 'reterritorializing' or recomposing as differently situated arrangement of forces, interests, possibilities. The process of immanent critique probably doesn't mean changing the way the creative industries go about empire building; it may slightly change the terms of reference within the creative industries, but probably not. In my view the best thing such a difference (of critical creative labour) could do is invent new institutions forms. The conditioning force for this form of creative expression rests precisely in the ways that labour is situated as a constitutive outside to the creative industries, understood as those activities, discourses and institutional practices inscribed as intellectual property. Deleuze's distinction between exteriority and the outside helps clarify how I understand the relation between creative labour and the creative industries.

Drawing on Foucault's *Archaeology of Knowledge*,[74] Deleuze gives the example of the keyboard and its letters and their relationship to a statement. The keyboard and the letters are a 'visibility', yet they are not a statement: 'They are external to the statement but do not constitute its outside'.[75] The keyboard is a 'concrete assemblage' which realizes 'relations between forces'. The keyboard, in a sense, awaits the force of the outside. The keyboard, as we know, is a component within various communications media – typically the typewriter or computer. Statements that may emerge from the typewriter are conditioned by an articulation with other forms of exteriority, both human and non-human: a desk, a chair, a human, a burning cigarette, an empty cup of coffee, etcetera. The articulation between these singular entities holds no essential relationship. Rather, the concrete assemblage – the articulation of parts – is an actualization of 'relations that are external to their terms'.

The articulation between the human and the machine – what Jünger termed an 'organic construction', Benjamin a 'mimetic correspondence', and McLuhan 'the extensions of man' – also holds the potential to create, to compose. The force of the outside creates what Deleuze calls a 'diagram' of 'topological' relations in which 'the inside is constituted by the folding of the outside'.[76] The fold consists of a 'doubling' of relations of force between inside and outside.[77] The fold constitutes a zone of life ('subjectivation'), 'inventing new "possibilities of life"' and new capacities of expression.[78] Media and cultural theorists who speak of 'global capital, global production, global labor migrations, and global penetration by technologies of communications' in terms of a 'global immanence' that has 'no outside' are taking, at best, a lazy shortcut to a mode of critique that dispenses with the ethico-political diagram of power and reflexivity that makes possible the very objects of study they wish to critique.[79]

Comparative Media Theory and the Constitutive Outside

Just as language has an outside – the limit *of* language, as noted in the epigraph by Deleuze – so too does the creative industries have an outside. To paraphrase Deleuze: creative industries' outside is not *outside* the creative industries, it is the outside *of* creative industries. The outside of the creative industries is the limit of critique from within. The limit of creative industries is defined by critique from the outside, which is at once a part of the constitutive dimension of the creative industries. The kind of critique I am proposing is one that addresses the multiplicity of outsides of the creative industries: these include the situation of creative labour in new media industries. This is living labour whose function, at least within the discourse of the creative industries, is to generate IP in order that it can be exploited. It is labour's internal outsides that operate on lines of class, ethnicity, age and gender.[80] Each of the components that constitute the plane of creative industries – academics, students, government, local business, service staff, new media workers, along with various media of communication and techniques of expression – has its own plane or logic of operation. Each of these components populates the plane of creative industries, and the relations between them are external to their terms. That is, each component or element functions within its own universe of sensibility, its own horizon of reference, its own system of communication.

It is useful to think of the operation of these components in terms of paradigms that are located on a larger plane of organization. While each paradigm has its own distinctive features, they hold the potential to interleave with each other. Within Marxian negativity, the potential for correspondence is predicated on an underlying socio-aesthetic antagonism. Within the Deleuzian logic of immanence, the interrelationship between component parts can be understood as the affirmation of difference. And within comparative media theory, the communication or articulation between different actors is constituted through an 'internally generative' process that is situated within an external context.[81] In each case, the point of intersection is a combination of antagonism, affirmation and constitution. What brings these three processes together is a notion of the outside. Such an assemblage signals the limits of critique from within.

In order to illustrate these points, I detour through the work of Canadian political economist and communications theorist, Harold A. Innis.[82] In his essay 'Orality in the Twilight of Humanism', Ian Angus describes Innis's method as one of 'micrology': 'He focuses on characteristic events within a society. He doesn't begin by characterizing the whole but from specific events, giving us a plurality of glimpses of these specific events, creating a montage effect that implies the nature of the whole'.[83] Explaining the relation between institutions, knowledge monopolies, and communications media in Innis's interpretation of society, Angus writes: 'Institutions are based on a medium of communication that is the most significant within that institution, which "monopolizes" knowledge through monopolizing access to, and use of, that medium of communication'.[84] Clearly, the creative industries are not a communications medium *per se*; they are, nevertheless, a cluster of institutional forms and discursive practices articulated with various media of communication (film and TV, digital technologies, architecture, photography, the arts and crafts, and so forth). Thus the creative industries do not utilize any single medium, but a combination of media forms, each with its own rules and capacities of expression. What bridges these communications media and their attendant practices is a combination of the juridical and economic architecture of intellectual property (primarily copyright) and the labour-power which it subsumes. As long as media corporations, government departments and university programmes see the exploitation of intellectual property as the means of wealth creation, the institutional effect is a monopoly of knowledge and a disregard of the desires of creative labour for self-sustaining work practices – technics of labour that are not subject to the vagaries of the politically motivated inequality of free trade agreements or fluctuating currency rates that determine the transnational movement of film and TV drama production, for example.

What Innis calls the 'bias' of communication can be understood in terms of a constitutive outside. Innis's central thesis is encapsulated in his book, *The Bias of Communication*: the duration and expansion of empires can be understood in terms of communications media and transport technologies peculiar to any culture, location, and epoch, and the attendant 'bias' towards either time or space that such media and technologies invariably have.[85] In his survey of the rise and fall of the city-states of ancient civilizations and the economies of modern nation-states, Innis considers a bias toward space or time as a defining feature of 'the monopoly of knowledge', and hence control, by the hegemon. At the end of his book *Empire and Communications*, Innis summarizes the operation and characteristics of communications media in terms of the monopoly of knowledge, or bias, they enable:

> Monopolies of knowledge had developed and declined partly in relation to the medium of communication on which they were built, and tended to alternate as they emphasized religion, decentralization, and time; or force, centralization, and space.[86]

Innis also charts the ways in which colonial empires and nation-states in the industrial era were defined by the dependency of the metropole on the capacity of the colonies to supply staple products that can then be processed into commodity objects and energy resources in the metropole, distributed back out to the colonies, and traded across empires. This relationship created its own peculiar structural dynamic of power. As Ian Angus and Brian Shoesmith put it, 'These conditions of production meant, in fact, that the margins continually subsidised the centre'.[87] Dependency theory is based on the logic, then, of a core/periphery model of geopolitics and political economy.

Despite the extensive critique dependency theory has attracted, particularly by postcolonial theorists preoccupied with identifying instances of liminality, hybridity and ambivalence, and hence resistance within colonial discourse, Innisian dependency theory continues to hold importance with regard to issues of power and politics as they relate to communications media and the organization of social relations. Unlike dependency models developed in world-systems theory and area studies, within Innis's framework a dependency relationship is not automatically a unilinear one where the ruling colonial power exerts unmitigated control over its colonial territories. Such a relationship assumes that the margins of empire are always subject to the economic, political and cultural influences, authority and support of the centre. Moreover, it overlooks the ways in which 'centres are as much dependent on their margins as margins are on the centres'.[88] Innis paid attention to the multilayered dynamic and the interrelationships between centres and margins, and his concepts of space, time and technological bias provided the basis upon which to locate the pivotal role played by communications media in the constitution of social relations. As Angus has noted, it is a mistake to see such a 'method of investigation' as one of technological determination:

> It is not the claim that the media of communication determine the form of the society, but rather the suggestion that investigation of the constitutive elements of a society as media of communication, shows that the micrological organisation prefigures and articulates the macrological structure.[89]

At first glance, the spatial or temporal 'bias' of different media, the relationship between 'centres' and 'margins', and the 'efficiency' or 'inefficiency' of communication in conditioning the success of empires are characteristics that can be explicated through the logic of negative dialectics. As Judith Stamps has argued, Innis's method of analysis proceeds by a series of juxtapositions 'in a manner comparable to the constellations created by Adorno, Benjamin, and McLuhan'.[90] Innis's approach departed, however, from his Frankfurt School counterparts in ways that signalled his attention to the problems of his own geopolitical and cultural situation. 'Unlike them', writes Jody Berland, 'Innis found himself poised between two conflicting dispositions: the bleak, post-totalitarian, anti-scientistic and post-enlightenment vision exemplified by Adorno's "negative dialectics" versus the more pragmatic nation-building culturalist modernity of his own milieu'.[91]

In foregrounding the 'positive' and 'negative' attributes of different communications media and their capacity to engender time or space-binding societies, Innis read the sensory imbalance of Western civilization against those premodern civilizations that had flourished due to a 'balance' between oral and aural media and visual media of print and the written word. A balance or 'efficiency' in communication determined the efficacy and longevity of an empire. Innis was especially attentive to the spatial bias of Western modernity, which, since the invention of the printing press, had consolidated a monopoly of 'sensory life', resulting in a visual bias that corresponded 'with the hegemony of modern science'.[92] In the event of one medium of communication dominating others, a stasis will prevail that prevents an 'openness' to creativity and thought. Print media, for example, have a spatial bias that emphasizes a preoccupation with administration, law and immediacy, neglecting aspects of continuity, tradition and systems of belief – features of media that are durable over time.[93] Innis's interest, then, was to study the material characteristics of different media of communication in order to 'appraise its influence in its cultural setting'.[94] His concern was for a 'co-existence of different media of communication', so that the bias of one may be 'checked' against the bias of another, creating 'conditions favourable to an interest in cultural activity'.[95]

Innis's insight was to point to the ways in which a technological bias towards time, for instance, results in a weakness or vulnerability with respect to the capacity to effectively control space. In one example, Innis describes how the art of horsemanship, the cross-breeding of horses, and the technology of the stirrup and chariot made successful invasion possible by the Hittites, and later the Assyrians, of ancient Babylonia, whose primary technology was the clay tablet: a medium of writing made possible by the discovery of rich deposits of alluvial clay.[96] The stirrup and chariot are technologies of space and speed, since they enable the rapid transport of cavalry and fighting units across territories. The clay tablet, on the other hand, is a technology of time, and played a key role in establishing the durability of the city-state of Babylon as one characterized by a centralized system of religious governance whose monopoly of knowledge extended over time.[97] Irrespective of whether the resulting bias of a medium of communication is a temporal or spatial one, certain monopolies of knowledge constituted in institutional form will follow in its wake. This is precisely what happened in the case of the Hittite and Assyrian invaders, whose initial successes were conditioned by the weakness in the Babylonian's attention to space and its attendant military problems as a result of their monopoly of knowledge over time. Interestingly, the Hittite and Assyrian empires were to prove relatively short lived due to their inefficient means of communication: 'Their attempts to build up new organizations of space in relation to an organization of time were defeated by the entrenched organizations of time in Babylon and Thebes'.[98] That is, the Hittite and Assyrian periods of rule were ultimately unstable since they were unable to achieve an effective balance in communication. This was matched by insufficient institutional infrastructures that facilitate the organization and control of social relations. In this sense, the Hittites and Assyrians do not qualify as proper empires in Innis's terms.

Within Innis's notions of 'bias' and 'dependency', one can detect the operation of a constitutive outside. To go back to the example of the Hittites with their innovations in iron and use of horse-drawn chariots, and the Babylonians and their clay tablets: the bias toward time of the Babylonian city-state is only made apparent when it is 'checked' against the bias toward space of the Hittites. The communicative bias articulated by each of these cultures is a virtual one of pure potential, subsisting within a plane of immanence until it is actualized through a plane of organization. 'The plane is not a principle of organization', write Deleuze and Guattari, 'but a means of transportation'.[99] The relations between these two planes are variously antagonistic, affirmative and constitutive. The 'external form' of one communicative arrangement 'interleaves' with another, and in so doing their respective bias toward time or space is expressed in material ways via the constitutive force of the outside. As Innis writes: 'Without a consistently efficient system of writing and the stabilizing conservative influence of religion, the Hittite Empire was exposed to difficulties from within and without'.[100] Angus explains how a comparative media theory is derived from the interrelationships between immanence, outside, inside and the expressive capacities of communications media as follows:

> [W]hile there is an immanent history of media forms, there is also a transcendental history of the constitution of media forms themselves.... Through this doubling, immanent history is turned 'outside' toward a wonder at the phenomenon of expression itself.[101]

Through the force of the outside, we can see how the transformation of the city-state of Babylon is conditioned by a plurality of 'relations [that] are external and irreducible to their terms', as Deleuze deduces in his study of Hume's empiricism. Radical empiricism, as a diagrammatic philosophy of relations, tells us something about the potential habitus of a communications medium: it too 'defines itself through the position of a precise problem, and through the presentation of the conditions of this problem'.[102] There is nothing intrinsic about the medium of the clay tablet that predisposes it toward a temporal bias. Certainly, as far as its material properties go, clay was heavier and less transportable than the substance of papyrus, as used by the ancient Egyptians. The reproduction of clay tablets is also less efficient than a substance like paper, especially once paper became articulated with the printing press and the political-economic need to administer mobile populations within the external form of the nation-state at the onset of modernity in the West. But there is nothing inherent about the material properties and expressive capacities of alluvial clay deposits that determines its transformation into the communications medium of the clay writing tablet. Such a development is contingent upon the alignment of political, economic and cultural forces that coalesce to address the problem at hand.

Conclusion

In this chapter I have sought to derive an understanding of the constitutive force of the outside as it figures in relation to the creative industries, cultural criticism and comparative media theory. I have argued that the force of the constitutive outside is what links these three approaches as social-technical idioms. Moreover, the constitutive outside manifests in material ways and holds expressive capacities. In this sense, the outside is not an impossibility, but a condition of possibility. Furthermore, the outside is not a position, but rather a force of distributed power within social relations. This chapter has not been so interested in the ontological question of the outside (how can one be outside?), but rather the political question (how can change be made within the dominant order?). In the case of the creative industries, the constitutive outside is a force of relations characterized by two key features: antagonism in the form of the exploitation of creative labour as it subsists within a juridico-political architecture of intellectual property regimes; and the affirmation of creative labour that holds the potential for self-organization in the form of networks.

As far as negative critique goes, the lineage between Adorno and Deleuze stems from the notion of 'immanent critique'. In a moment of seeming optimism, Adorno considers the limit of immanent critique as that which is embodied in the instant of the 'leap', though according to Adorno, this is only made possible by the undertaking of negative dialectics.[103] Following Deleuze, my interest has been in how immanent critique can be read as an affirmative force that retains the act of critique. The limit of critique from within is not a closure or negation, but rather an opening of possibilities. As Deleuze writes, 'the outside is always an opening on to a future ...'.[104] It is in this sense that the affirmation of living labour, for instance, conditions the possibility of creative industries. But this transformative force of the outside is one that institutes a substantially different form of creative industries to the kind that passes as dominant culture today.

Communications media play a vital role in securing the creative potential of labour-power as a transformative force. As Angus reminds us: 'Communication media thus constitute, through human labour, the limits of what is experienceable and the *manner* in which it is experienced in a social formation'.[105] The spatial bias of the creative industries as they currently stand is clearly apparent in their cartography of power that seeks to exploit the IP generated by creative labour. Such empire building is done at the expense of nurturing creative development over time.

4 Creative Labour

and the Role of Intellectual Property

This chapter reports on the survey I conducted for a session on 'Intellectual Property – Intellectual Possibilities' organized by Kate Crawford and Esther Milne for the fibreculture network of new media research and culture meeting in 2003.[1] I wanted to explore in some empirical fashion the relationship between intellectual property (IP) and creative labour. Such a relationship is the basis for defining what is meant by creative industries, according to the seminal and much cited mapping document produced by Blair's Creative Industries Task Force (CITF). Despite the role IP plays in defining and providing a financial and regulatory architecture for the creative and other informational or knowledge industries, there is remarkably little attention given by researchers and commentators to the implications of IP in further elaborating conceptual, political and economic models for the creative industries. There is even greater indifference towards addressing the impact of exploiting the IP of those whose labour-power has been captured: young people, for the most part, working in the creative and culture industries. Angela McRobbie's work is one of the few exceptions.[2]

At a different level, I was curious to see how a mailing list might contribute in a collaborative fashion to the formation of a research inquiry in which the object of study – creative labour and IP – is partially determined by the list itself. Finally, after levelling critiques at various times and occasions against what Terry Flew identifies as the 'new media empirics',[3] I thought it necessary to engage in a more direct way with this nemesis-object: what, after all, can a new media empirics do and become when it is driven through a processual model of media and communications? I will address this question in the concluding section of this chapter.

As I noted in the previous chapter: The list of sectors identified as holding creative capacities in the CITF Mapping Document include: film, music, television and radio, publishing, software, interactive leisure software, design, designer fashion, architecture, performing arts, crafts, arts and antique markets, architecture and advertising. The Mapping

Document seeks to demonstrate how these sectors consist of 'activities which have their origin in individual creativity, skill and talent and which have the potential for wealth and job creation through generation and exploitation of intellectual property'.[4] The CITF's identification of intellectual property as central to the creation of jobs and wealth firmly places the creative industries within informational and knowledge economies.

In posting the survey questionnaire to the list, I was interested in ascertaining the following:

1. The extent to which respondents perceived their primary activities (activities other than eating, sleeping, watching TV, having sex, substance abuse, etcetera – though I guess many would argue that they are indeed primary activities, and perhaps also creative ones!) to correspond with 'creativity', however that term might be understood (the survey synopsis clearly framed creativity in relation to the creative industries discourse, so the latitude for interpreting the term creativity was relatively circumscribed).

2. Whether a very partial mapping of the fibreculture network produced results similar to the sectors identified in the CITF Mapping Document. Whatever the results, I was interested in what they might then say about national, regional or state manifestations of the creative industries: are Australia's creative industries the same as the UK? Is there a temporal factor at work? That is, given the time of development, incubation, and so forth, would a mapping exercise produce different results depending of when and how it was conducted? In other words, how does the stability of the empirical object – creative labour – relate to the contingencies of time? This is as much a methodological question as it is a question of politics and ethics.

3. To establish whether respondents perceived or understood an extant relationship between their labour and intellectual property.

4. To find out whether IP in the workplace is considered a political issue.

At the time of the survey, the fibreculture mailing list had just over 700 subscribers (June, 2003). All responses were posted on the same day

I posted the survey, most within a few hours of it appearing on list. This in itself perhaps says something interesting about the 'attention economy' of email lists and the time in which any posting may receive a response – while the Stones could sing about the redundancy of newspapers after a day, do list postings have a life of three or so hours? Not so bad actually, though it's probably much less – more like seconds, depending on whether a post is read or not.

Of the 700 or so subscribers, then, I received seven responses. That's 1 per cent of all list subscribers, a lovely sample to be sure. One of the respondents provided a follow-up response as well. There was one other query from someone asking whether they could do the survey even though they thought they weren't a creative worker; they were a copyright lawyer – a category Richard Florida assigns to 'creative professionals' – 'business and finance, law, health care and related fields', as distinct from the core Creative Class: 'People in science and engineering, architecture and design, education, art, music and entertainment, whose economic function is to create new ideas, new technology and/or new creative content'.[5] Curiously, there is no mention – at least in this initial definition – of the role intellectual property plays in constituting a 'creative class'.[6] No doubt there are national-cultural and social-political explanations for the differences between how creative workers are perceived and constituted in the UK and North America. To my knowledge, there is yet to be a study that inquires into the different national and regional formations of creative industries, classes, economies and cultures. One could argue that OECD research papers and reports along with those by neo-conservative, libertarian think-tanks such as Demos and the Cato Institute do such work; however, while they certainly compile statistics and bring a dual mode of commentary and hyperbole to such figures, they do very little by way of historical, political, economic and cultural analysis of the variable conditions that have led to the emergence of creative labour and its attendant industries across these geopolitical regions.

Reflexivity and Empirical Research

While the sample I am drawing on is most certainly small, it is not insignificant. Indeed, I think its minutiae correspond to larger patterns of creative labour in Australia, and most probably elsewhere, as I extrapolate below. Much of the current, more reflexive literature on quantitative, empirical research argues that the fuss over sample sizes (for instance the need to have a large sample if the claims and results are to have any scholastic purchase on the phantasm of veridicality) is problematic in all sorts of ways. For instance, at what point can one say a sample is representative of the community, user-consumers, demographic or social-technical network under analysis? As Pierre Bourdieu argued so acutely and with such verve, public opinion does not exist.[7] What exists, for Bourdieu, is the discursive form of the survey or opinion poll, the interests that drive it, and the ends to which it is put. Of course my own survey is not immune from the sort of critical, theoretical and political interests I bring to the analysis of responses.

Then there is the whole pseudo-scientific language of 'observation', as though there might have ever been some sort of impartiality underpinning the process of enacting the survey. Lash associates such a paradigm with 'reflective modernization' and the work of Giddens, Habermas and Parsonian structural functionalism and linear systems theory: 'The idea of reflective belongs to the philosophy of consciousness of the first modernity. . . . To reflect is to somehow subsume the object under the subject of knowledge. Reflection presumes apodictic knowledge and certainty. It presumes a dualism, a scientific attitude in which the subject is in one realm, the object of knowledge in another'.[8] In contrast to a reflective first modernity, Lash posits a reflexive second modernity and non-linear systems of communication and risk comprised of quasi-objects and quasi-subjects and their theorization by the likes of Luhmann, Beck and Latour, along with Castells' network logic of flows:

> Second modernity reflexivity is about the emergent *demise* of the distinction between structure and agency altogether. . . . Second-modernity reflexivity presumes a move towards immanence that breaks with the [ontological] dualisms of structure and agency. . . .
> The reflexivity of the second modernity presumes the existence of non-linear systems. Here system dis-equilibrium and change are produced internally to the system through feedback loops. These are open systems. Reflexivity now is at the same time system *de*-stabilization.[9]

The extent to which reflexive non-linear systems wholly dispense with or depart from a constitutive outside in favour of a logic of immanence is a problematic I have begun to question with other fibreculture members in a posting to the list of an early version of this chapter.[10] Like the question of and tension between new media empirics and processual media theory, it is a problematic I will return to in my concluding remarks.

I think one reason I received even seven responses had much to do with prior knowledge and trust established between myself as 'observer' and the 'participants' in this survey: that is, I had either met or knew very well six of the seven respondents. Here, it is worth turning again to Bourdieu, who frames the concept of reflexivity in particularly succinct terms: 'What distresses me when I read some works by sociologists is that people whose profession is to objectivize the social world prove so rarely able to objectivize themselves, and fail so often to realize that what their apparently scientific discourse talks about is not the object but their relation to the object'.[11] Put in terms of non-linear systems theory, the on- and off-line relationships, trust and symbolic economy I had established largely through an online network operated as a feedback loop into the call for interest in and responses to this current survey. Obvious as it may sound, this very historical and social dimension to a communicative present actively destabilizes any rhetorical claims that I might attempt in the name of conducting a survey that follows the scientific principles of objectivity and impartiality and methodologies befitting quantitative research. The only thing that is remotely impartial about this survey is the anonymity of the respondents as I present them here.

Feedback loops further destabilize the very object-ness of this report as a discrete posting to a mailing list in so far as anyone who responded to this report breaks up components of the report by way of selective quoting or paraphrasing and interjecting their own critiques or comments.[12] Many of us do this when we reply to an email, separating the sender's text from our own; in so doing, we are translating or mimicking the effect of dialogue. Such a process is also registered in a material, symbolic form in the partially dissipative, non-linear structure of discussion threads as the user recombines and shifts between postings, disrupting what otherwise appears as a condition of equilibrium within the linear organization of the archive. Further registration of feedback loops are made in the 'Googlization' of this combinatory knowledge and information formation, where any particular posting has the potential to move up the vertical scale of 'hits' depending on the key words used in the user's search, the online links made to the posting, and the popularity of the posting: in short, the coding of the Google software program plays a determining role in the hierarchization of information that is then further shaped by the interests and habits of users. The economy and architecture of the Google search engine has been subject to considerable debate and discussion in mailing lists such as fibreculture and nettime, along with many other online fora, print and electronic media. If the posting of this report, for example, were made on any number of web conferencing systems, collaborative text filtering sites or blogs, such as slashdot.org, indymedia.org, makeworld.org or discordia.us, then a very different information architecture of feedback loops would prevail. I will now engage the findings of the survey.

Creativity – What's in a Name?

When I asked respondents what creative activities they engaged in, a list of 4-6 fields, practices or sectors of creativity by any one person was compiled. These included writing, performing and producing music; writing academic and policy papers (considered by one respondent and assumed by others as 'creative endeavours'); photography; design (interactive, information, education); publishing and editing; new media arts (dv, net.art, print, electronic music); painting; and creative writing. Three things stand out for me here:

1. Irrespective of whether or not respondents went on to identify themselves as part of the creative industries project, however that might be understood, the range of creative activities any single person might undertake suggests that diversity rather than specialization is a defining feature of creative workers. This isn't to say that specialization doesn't occur in any particular idiom of creativity – I think it's safe to assume that it would, but rather that respondents were not limited to one particular set of creative skills, trainings, or passions. Thus these respondents are clear exemplars of the so-called fragmented postmodern sub-

ject, traversing a range of institutional locations and socio-cultural dispositions.

2. Most of the respondents are engaged in academic work either on a
full-time, continuing basis or as sessional, casual teachers. In both cases,
university related activities and non-university related activities were
understood as holding creative dimensions. If nothing else, the diversity
of creative activities identified by respondents indicates the complexity
of labour in the contemporary university, further suggesting that: (a)
the university cannot accommodate the diverse interests and economic
necessities of its constituent labour-power, and/or (b) that individuals
wish to distinguish between the kind of work they do at university and
its concomitant values and the kind of work they do outside the university, or (c) that there is zone of indistinction, if you will, between the
university and its so-called outside, given that all sectors of cultural production and intellectual labour are today subject to market economies.
The extent to which tensions exist between these realms, or whether
they are better characterized as a sort of zone of indistinction that cannot be reduced in such a manner, varies, I suspect, according to the contingencies of time, interests, values, labour conditions, age, class, and
gender of individuals as they are located in different institutional settings. Each of the above possibilities corresponds with the economic
and labour conditions peculiar to the creative industries operating in
the UK, as McRobbie explains:

> Those working in the creative sector cannot simply rely on old work-
> ing patterns associated with art worlds, they have to find new ways
> of 'working' the new cultural economy, which increasingly means
> holding down three or even four 'projects' at once. In addition, since
> these projects are usually short term, there have to be other jobs to
> cover the short-fall when the project ends. The individual becomes
> his or her own enterprise, sometimes presiding over two separate
> companies at the same time.[13]

3. There is much overlap between this list of creative activities and the
CITF's list of creative sectors, with the exception that traditional arts and
crafts and antiques do not figure in the former; this comes as no sur-

prise, given that the survey was conducted on a listserv for critical Internet research and culture. As for how this list relates to Richard Florida's composition of the Creative Class in the USA, there is an obvious absence in my survey of engineers and scientists. Again, you might say this should come as no surprise; one could, however, describe software programmers, 'codeworkers' and game designers as computer scientists or information engineers – though no doubt there would be some disciplinary and perhaps ontological dispute over this.

Having established that they all are engaged in creative activities of one kind or another, there were then considerable differences among respondents as to whether they perceived themselves as engaged in the creative industries. Two respondents said they didn't – one being a bit hesitant as to whether they did or not, the other indifferent, implying the term was no more than a 'tag' associated with 'official places' and 'certain faculties'. Four respondents stated that they did associate their activities with the creative industries, some more emphatically so than others. One of those responded by writing 'Yeah, but I'm a special case :)', indicating that creativity, at least for this person, comes with a sense of individuality, difference and exception. Yet such subjectivities carry more baggage than this. As McRobbie notes, 'Individualization is not about individuals *per se*, as about new, more fluid, less permanent social relations seemingly marked by choice or options. However, this convergence has to be understood as one of contestation and antagonism'.[14] Much of this chapter seeks to unravel various tensions that underpin labour practices within the creative industries.

A seventh respondent took a more reflexive, Marxian and historically informed position, choosing to problematize and open up the question in the following way: 'All industry is creative; all human activity creates something; and nearly all human activity is subsumed under industrial imperatives (including the consumption of media and other products). Therefore I think this is probably a question whose answer is presupposed in the historical facts of its own terms'. On these grounds, then, irrespective of whether respondents did or didn't identify their creative activities with the creative industries, there is a sense among these respondents that there is an 'idea' of what constitutes the creative industries, and any particular respondent's identification with those industries is based, perhaps, on whether one meets the criteria or fits into the discursive boundaries, categories, or ethos of the creative industries, as established in part in the survey's preamble.

Intellectual Property and Creativity

The importance of intellectual property (copyrights, patents, trademarks) as a source of income was met with a mixed response. For one person it was important, for the rest it wasn't, at least in an exclusive sense: labour was paid for on an hourly basis or ip was assigned to the company or publisher commissioning the work; in other instances remuneration from ip contributed to a respondent's income, but wasn't relied upon as a primary source of income. Creative workers were thus primarily alienated from their intellectual property in one form or another. Such responses clearly signal a tension and power relationship between creative workers and their employers with regard to the citf definition of creative industries as those activities that have 'the potential for wealth and job creation through generation and exploitation of intellectual property'. Thus despite all the rhetoric around informational and creative labour consisting of 'horizontal' and 'fluid' modes of production, distribution and exchange, clearly there remain vertical, hierarchical dimensions within the 'New Economy'. If ip is to function as the mainstay of capital accumulation within informational economies, it doesn't take much imagination to foresee industrial, legal and political dispute focussing on the juridico-political architecture of ip. The extent to which workers are able to mobilize their potential power in an effective manner (that is, in a way that protects and secures their interests while inventing new political information architectures) depends, I would suggest, on their capacity to organize themselves as a social-political force. I will address this issue in relation to the problem of immaterial labour in more detail below.

Respondents found ip a source of tension not only at the level of financial remuneration; a tension prevailed around the concept of ip as well. In response to the question of whether intellectual property is important as a principle – that is, as a system or framework consisting of rules and beliefs that enables the transformation of labour into legal, moral and potentially economic values – one person stated that they found it of no importance at all. All others found it was, though the response, as expected, was mixed: 'Yes, but in a negative sense. The whole structure of IP has turned into a perversion of its intended principles: namely, that alienation rather than one's inalienable rights in one's own work is the guiding principle of IP law. Put differently, rights are seen to exist only so that they can be sold. That is a function of capital, long since dead. I would prefer a rights structure that existed to ensure the free flow of ideas'. In a similar vein, though without the libertarian overtone, another respondent writes: 'It is important to me as a principle to be critiqued, developed and (in some cases) rejected. The arm of IP is extending in several directions and in many industries – and it's that reach that needs to be reviewed with some urgency'.

A third respondent strongly rejected the idea that IP might be understood in terms of principles: 'No', they write, 'It's important to me as a discursive field!' By my reading, such a statement suggests that the respondent understands principles as holding some kind of unchanging, transcendental and universal status, while a discursive field is historically and culturally mutable and holds the potential for local intervention by actors endowed with such capacities. (A similar distinction is often made in philosophy between the universality of morals and the contingencies of ethics.) The idea of IP as a discursive field rather than a principle is also interesting in relation to the second response tabled above, which implies that limits need to be established with regard to IP and the extent to which it governs areas of life previously outside a market economy. Current debates around patenting the human genome, database access to DNA information on sperm and embryo composition and their relationship to insurance premiums and future employment possibilities (see *Gattica* for the filmic version of this scenario), and the pressure on developing countries to import GM food coupled with uneven, neo-colonial trade agreements along with clientelistic conditions imposed by the World Bank and IMF's structural adjustment and debt management policies are the most obvious examples that come to mind here.[15] These are issues I discussed in chapter 1.

Intellectual Property and the Labour Contract

The tensions associated with IP was further extended to the workplace, with all but one of the respondents noting that they had heard of and in some instances personally experienced conflicts over IP issues.

If such accounts are the norm rather than the exception, this clearly
signals a need for much greater attention to be given to the role of IP in
the workplace, and the status it holds as a legal and social architecture
governing the conditions of creative production, job satisfaction,
employer-employee relations and thus life in general. While only two
respondents reported losing a job or contract for refusing to assign IP to
their employer, many commented on the problems of such a condition
– as one person noted: 'This is common in film music now: if you don't
sell your rights to the film maker, you are not given the contract'. Could
this be a point at which to engage 'the refusal of work' – a political
concept and strategy developed by radical workers' movements of the
1960s in Italy?

The Italian autonomists of the 1960s and '70s sought to liberate work
from relations of waged labour and the capitalist State, to unleash 'a
mass defection or exodus' and in so doing subtract the labour-power
which sustains the capitalist system, affirming the 'creative potential of
our practical capacities' in the process.[16] There's a bit of a different rub,
however, in a capitalist logic of post-Fordist flexible accumulation,
whose modes of social and political regulation set the scene for our current informational paradigm. While the worker within Fordist systems
of assembly-line mass production and mass consumption conditions
the possibility of, to refer to the classic example, the assemblage of
motor vehicles that, ideally, are then sold to the leisurely consumer
who built the vehicle in their eight hour working day, the case of IP and
creative labour operates in substantially different ways.

Within an informational paradigm, the appropriation of labour-
power by capitalists does not result in a product so much as a potential.
This potential takes the 'immaterial' form of intellectual property
whose value is largely unquantifiable and is subject to the vagaries of
speculative finance markets, 'New Economy' style. Thus, in the case of
government institutions that don't recognize an individual's IP rights,
there is nothing to 'hand over' in the first instance. That is, the right to a
refusal of work is not possible; or put differently, the creative potential
of work, as registered in and transformed into the juridico-political
form of IP, is undermined by the fact that such a social relation – the
hegemonic form of legitimacy – is not recognized. As noted by another
respondent: 'I don't think you "lose" a contract for refusing to sign IP

over … it's more like you never had it in the first place if you do work for hire'. Instead, one does not so much refuse to work as decline to provide a service, whose economic value as wage labour – that is, labour separated from its product – bears no relationship to the potential economic value generated by the exploitation of IP. In effect, then, 'creativity' goes right under the radar. Prostitution functions in a similar manner. One does not buy 'love' from the prostitute, one acquires a 'service' in the form of an orgasm, or 'little death', with no value in and of itself. The prostitute's love does not figure in the relationship; love is off the radar. Like intellectual property, the expression of the orgasm in a given form – sperm, for the male who appropriates the labour-power of the prostitute – nevertheless holds the potential to translate into economic, social, political and biological values if its eruption is arranged under different conditions – the normative ones peculiar to heterosexual couplings living in advanced economies, for example.

A couple of respondents, both now working in the higher education sector, had mixed responses to the kind of conditions such a setting enabled vis-à-vis labour and IP. Respondent 1: 'I would always give in [and sign over IP] when I was self-employed, now I only take jobs where I'm happy with the IP arrangements'. Such a position is possible when, as noted earlier, producing IP for others (that is, employers/clients) is not the primary source of income. Interestingly, the other respondent anticipates conflicts over the assignation of IP within university settings – Respondent 2: 'As I continue to collaborate in university settings, the problem will arise'. The problem of job security arises where IP policies can vary substantially from university to university and at an intra-university level, depending on the kind of contract an individual is able to negotiate with management as universities undergo increasingly deregulation toward a system that destroys the legal concept of collective wage agreements fought for by unions. For many working in the higher education sector, the course materials staff produce are the intellectual property of the university. These educational materials may often incorporate parts of articles or books they have written or are in the process of writing. They may also include lists of references to articles and debates located in open-access online repositories, as found in the fibreculture and nettime archives, for example. And here, a curious institutional tension over IP emerges: depending on the publisher, the IP of articles and books an individual writes will more often than not belong to the publisher. One of the respondents noted how this problem of proprietary rights of academic IP has been dealt at their university: 'The new IP rules (e.g. the one which came into effect on 14th March [2003]) gives the university ownership of all IP created by staff (with a "scholarly work" exception). This creates major problems – for example, academics moving to different universities who intend to use educational materials they have developed previously'. Thus the extent to which IP functions as an architecture of control is and has always been dubious at the level of the everyday. Just think of what happened with the appearance of the Xerox machine in university settings – in effect it became a free license to appropriate the property of writers, with myriad staff and students reproducing the pages of otherwise copyright-protected materials.

Even if the legal aspects of IP are frequently difficult if not impossible to regulate, there are important symbolic dimensions to IP that have implications and impacts at the level of subjectivities and their degree of legitimacy within institutional and national settings. Here I am thinking – yet again – of that rather chilling line in the CITF's definition of the creative industries in which IP is not only generated, but more significantly, it is *exploited.* Notwithstanding conventional use of the term 'exploitation' within legislative and juridical considerations of copyright, the exploitation of IP is not simply a matter of extracting the potential economic value from some inanimate thing. The exploitation of IP, let us never forget, is always already an exploitation of people, of the producers of that which is transformed from practice into property, which in its abstraction is then alienated from those who have produced it. While there are clear problems with such a system, IPRS are not necessarily a bad thing. As I argued in chapter 1, to simply oppose IPRS is not a political option. Individuals and communities must look for ways in which IPRS can be exploited for strategic ends. Such a political manoeuvre is possible, for instance, in efforts to advance indigenous sovereignty.[17]

Intellectual Property and (Dis)Organized Labour

Most of the respondents corrected the assumption in my question on the relationship between collaborative production and the difficulty of assigning IP rights to individuals or joint-authorship. Respondents noted that corporations own the creative efforts of both individuals and collaborations, since the corporation has paid for that work. This brings me to the final component of the survey – the relationship between IP and the problem of disorganized labour. It seems to me that unions are among the best placed actors to contest the seemingly foregone conclusion that corporations have an *a priori* hold on the appropriation of labour-power. As Castells has noted:

> [W]ith the acceleration of the work process [enabled by new ICTS], worker's defense continues to be a fundamental issue: they cannot count on their employers. The problem is that the individualization of management/worker relationships makes the use of traditional forms of defense, in terms of collective bargaining and trade union-led struggles, very difficult except in the public sector. Unions are realizing this and finding new forms of pressure, sometimes in the form of consumer boycotts to press for social justice and human rights. Also, individual explosions of violence by defenseless workers could be considered forms of resistance.[18]

However, there is an impasse of paradigmatic proportion to the potential for unions to assist workers – particularly younger workers – within creative industries or knowledge and information economies. The so-called strategy of consumer sovereignty is a relatively weak one, and only further entrenches the problem of individualization inasmuch as the potential for a coalition among workers is sidelined in favour of that mantra urged on us by our politicians who are so keen to protect 'the national interest' – yes, the national economy is fragile, so enjoy yourself and go out and shop! There is a general perception that unions and their capacity to organize labour in politically effective and socially appealing ways are a thing of the past. To address this issue I will first table comments from respondents. I will then move on to the thesis of 'immaterial labour', as presented by Maurizio Lazzarato, Hardt and Negri, and argue why the condition of 'disorganized labour' more accurately describes the circumstances in which labour finds itself within an informational paradigm.

Three of the respondents stated they did not belong to a union, one with perhaps a degree of ironic self-affirmation characteristic of what

Lash and Urry term 'reflexive individualization':[19] 'Nope', writes one person, 'I'm a manager and self-employed :7'. In his book on globalization, Beck identifies a nexus between those who work for themselves – a mode of coordination he attributes to 'life-aesthetes' in particular – and their desire for 'self-development'. He goes on to suggest that such dispositions lend themselves to 'self-exploitation': 'People are prepared to do a great deal for very little money, precisely because economic advantage is individualistically refracted and even assigned an opposite value. If an activity has greater value in terms of identity and self-fulfilment, this makes up for and even exalts a lower level of income'.[20] Voluntary and service labour by many artists within the cultural sector would also fit this condition of self-exploitation.

Richard Caves prefers to explain the condition of non-union labour in more economic terms. Citing the example of independent filmmaking, Caves notes that '30 to 35 per cent of production costs [can be saved] by operating a nonunion project'.[21] In productions involving union labour, most of these additional costs are a result, so Caves claims, of inefficient and interventionist management practices and regulations by unions, which sees workers being paid for standing around doing nothing. Caves casts unions as manipulative entities who have a propensity to 'hold-up' production unless their wage demands are met.[22] Certainly, the militancy of unions has long been a staple of news narratives structured around a binary logic that has little time for articulating larger contextual forces and values that give rise to particular actions. Irrespective of whether the political form is union or non-union, issues of creative governance are always going to have local or national peculiarities, and will vary from industry to industry. In every case, however, the challenge for creative workers is, it seems to me, to create work that holds not only the maximum potential for self-fulfilment and group cooperation on a project, but just as importantly, creative workers need to situate themselves in ways that close down the possibility of exploitation.

The other respondents belonged to various unions or professional organizations: National Tertiary Education Union (NTEU) [2], Media, Entertainment and Arts Alliance (MEAA)/Australian Journalists' Association (AJA) [2], the College Arts Association (USA) and Australasian Performing Rights Association (APRA), 'which is not really a union, but is primarily concerned with IP'. All these respondents were aware of their union's policy on IP issues, though one respondent held a high level of cynicism: 'I've never heard a union take a credible position on IP'. The follow-up question on the efficacy of unions in instances of dispute with management over IP elicited further cynicism from another respondent: 'Unions are too stupid to do this properly. They are as much a part of the problem since they agree to perverse work relations. Unions are corporations'. Others noted that disputes of this nature were 'an ongoing battle on many fronts' and that 'the MEAA/AJA newsletter often has such stories. Most of it is so thoroughly covered in case law that the major players don't bother to buck the system. The case of US freelance journos seeking payment for new media republication of their stories is seminal'. The *New York Times v Tasini* case which this second respondent refers to is notable for the successful class action filed in 1993 by the National Writers Union (NWU) on behalf of freelance journalists against *The New York Times*, which had resold and republished articles electronically from their print archive and were refusing to pay freelance journalists for republication on the grounds that there was no difference in form between a print, microfilm or microfiche archive and new archival and storage media such as online newspapers or magazines, electronic databases such as LexisNexis or CD-ROMS.[23] Despite the US Supreme Court ruling in favour of Tasini in 2001, *The New York Times* refused to compensate journalists and decided instead to delete all freelance written articles from their electronic archival media.

The *New York Times v Tasini* case prompts two key issues that I will only flag here: firstly, material previously part of common repositories of knowledge such as public libraries becomes subject to litigious society within the political economy of a digital age, resulting in the erasure of what would otherwise be a digital commons;[24] and secondly, while freelance journalists – that is, those who belong to the class of creative labourers – obtained some success in this instance, *New York Times v Tasini* foregrounds the continued importance the nation-state and its domestic legal regimes hold for any analysis of information societies. While digitally encoded information has the capacity to transcend the borders of the nation-state, we are again reminded of the social-political forces which shape our understanding of and relationship to media technologies. Further, the social-technical condition of all communications media is always already situated within specific discourse networks; the media situation in turn gives rise to the problematic of translation for media culture and its attendant labour practices and modes of creation. To put it simply, while *New York Times v Tasini* set a legal precedent for how media corporations are to go about republishing the work of commissioned freelance journalists, such a ruling has no legal bearing outside the USA in terms of how some of the very same transnational media conglomerates conduct their business practices in other countries.

To summarize: while the majority of respondents did belong to one or more unions, a good proportion of these respondents did not seem satisfied with or have any great faith in the efforts of unions to negotiate disputes over IP in the workplace.

Multitudes and the Exploitation of Network Sociality

The final question in the survey asked respondents if they thought there was a need for workers in their field to become more organized, particularly around the impact that IP has on their potential income. One person said 'yes', and two others didn't know. The remaining four respondents took the opportunity to register more developed responses. One person stated that 'Musicians need a militant union. That said, the old divisions of labour in what are generally considered "the creative industries" (really the cultural industries) have broken down because of technological changes'. Interestingly, this respondent correlates the convergence of different media technologies with the demise of the previous markers of class distinction premised on the vertical organization of labour within the culture industries. It has been commonplace since the late 1990s to hear stories of musical entrepreneurs who simultaneously engage in the previously separated activities of production, distribution and consumption. Yet such horizontal organization isn't without its own class distinctions that continue to operate in symbolic, economic and political dimensions.

While the old divisions of labour may have been cast away, at least within the advanced economies, this isn't to say that new divisions of labour haven't taken their place. Indeed, the task of identifying new divisions of labour within the creative industries and informational economies has been one of the key underlying interests and motivations behind this chapter. Such divisions are invoked by another respondent:

> I think the issue is broader than the impact on our 'potential income' as individual workers – perhaps this is already too close to the commodity rhetoric that has permeated the creative industries. Part of the problem is that we are taught to respond to our projects as personally-owned intellectual products that must be protected, so that we can drain the maximum profit from their use. This disguises several processes that go into creative work. Open source programming networks, for example, reveal other ways to interpret and develop our intellectual labours.

Here we have it then, the return to the classic debate over closed regulation versus open flows within a field of new ICTs. But there is more to it in this instance. This respondent rightly observes that creativity is irreducible to the generation and exploitation of IP. Herein lies a key tension that proponents of the creative industries face with a potential constituency that in the majority of instances resides outside the institutional borders of the university or a government department of creative industries. This tension concerns the relationship between discourse and identity formation. Just as the success of governments operating within liberal democracies depends upon getting the right spin, so too does the capacity for the creative industries project to obtain a purchase with a variety of actors that include politicians and government departments, university officials, students, academics, industry managers and creative producers. In other words, within a discursive regime of neoliberalism that grants hegemony to those with greater institutional, political and economic purchase – for instance industry managers, government departments, and university professors – there remains a constitutive outside of creative and service workers with little or no political representation.

Such a condition of 'invisibility' is symptomatic of the dependency of capital on the commodity value of labour-power. It was on the basis of this relationship between capital and labour-power that Italian radical leftists in the 1960s and '70s such as Mario Tronti would observe that '*Labour is the measure of value because the working class is the condition of capital*.[25] Within the workers' movements of the 1960s, the class function to supply capital with labour-power and produce surplus value was seen as the condition for dismantling and disarticulating the reproduction of capital.[26] As noted earlier, the technique for undertaking this action was referred to as the 'refusal of work' – a radical intervention which unleashed the creative capacities of workers and affirmed their 'right to nonwork'.[27]

Recognizing the political limitations of the unitary concept of class within a post-industrial, post-colonial era, Hardt and Negri have spearheaded the internationalization of the Italian autonomist concept of 'the multitude' – the movement of movements that goes beyond the traditional working classes who established political representation within the institutional structures of trade unions and social-democratic parties.[28] Developed out of the activities Negri and others have with *officine precarie* (non-unionized precarious, unpaid workers), the multitude is a political, 'post-representational' and in some instances ethico-aesthetic expression of those seeking to actualize another possible world – ethnic and social minorities, women, exploited workers, activists, leftist intellectuals, and so forth. Virno locates the multitude in opposition to the Hobbesian concept of 'the people', which 'is tightly correlated to the existence of the State and is in fact a reverberation of it'.[29] Against the political unity and will of the 'the people', the multitude's 'virtuosic' heterogeneity – or 'ensemble of "acting minorities"' – 'obstructs and dismantles the mechanisms of political representation'.[30] Redefining the position of the multitude, Negri's oral intervention at a meeting of *officine precarie* in Pisa, 2003, is apposite on the correlation between exploitation and creative labour, though in ways that contradict his earlier thesis with Hardt that Empire has no outside:

> The concept of the multitude can only emerge when the key foundation of this process (the exploitation of labour and its maximal abstraction) becomes something else: when labour starts being regarded, by the subjects in this continuous exchange of exploitation, as something that can no longer enter the relation of exploitation. When labour starts being regarded as something that can no longer be directly exploited. What is this labour that is no longer directly exploited? *Unexploited labour is creative labour*, immaterial, concrete

labour that is expressed as such. Of course exploitation is still there, but exploitation is of the ensemble of this creation, it is exploitation that has broken the common [that is, abstract labour in a wage relation] and no longer recognises the common as a substance that is divided, produced by abstract labour, and that is divided between capitalist and worker in the structures of command and exploitation. Today capital can no longer exploit the worker; it can only exploit cooperation amongst workers, amongst labourers. Today capital has no longer that internal function for which it became the soul of common labour, which produced that abstraction within which progress was made. *Today capital is parasitical because it is no longer inside; it is outside of the creative capacity of the multitude.*[31]

Now this a lengthy quotation to be sure, and I elect it at this particular moment for its immense richness. I will attend to Negri and Hardt's work on immaterial labour in more detail shortly. At this stage, however, it is worth spending a little time unpacking some of Negri's key points, since they are commensurate with my larger critique of creative industries and the role of intellectual property. It strikes me that Negri is decidedly dialectical in his thinking of the relationship between capital and the multitude. What we read here is not talk of indeterminacy, flows and zones of indistinction – the primary conceptual metaphors used to describe the biopolitical operation of Empire; rather, there is a return to the bad old language of dialectics, albeit without the full force of its logic. If capital is no longer inside but outside the creative capacity of the multitude, such a condition is made possible by the fact of its relation with the inside of the multitude. Capital, then, operates as the constitutive outside of the multitude, a social-technical body that, according to Negri, has somehow escaped or transcended abstract labour in a wage relation *yet* at the same time continues to exist in an immanent relation with capital: 'Exploitation is of the ensemble of this creation'. So exploitation persists, but it is no longer the 'direct' exploitation of abstract labour. Rather, it is exploitation of 'cooperation among workers'; that is, it is an *indirect* exploitation of that which has become 'creative labour'. What does Negri mean by this? As I read him, Negri is suggesting that capital – which supposedly is no longer inside – exploits creative labour inasmuch as creative labour constitutes (provides the enabling conditions for) capital's new location *outside* 'the creative capacity of the multitude'. What Negri is saying, then, is that nothing less than a revolution has taken place!

To speak of a revolution of our time – of a dramatic rupture from a prior order, a transformation that historically has been characterized by excessive violence and bloodshed – is a mistake. There has not been a revolution. Rather, capital has transmogrified into an informational mode of connections and relations, a mode that does not so much come *after* industrial and post-industrial modes of production as incorporate such modes within an ongoing logic of flexible accumulation. Within an informational mode of connection, the creative capacity of the multitude comprises a self-generating system in which abstract labour as a wage relation is not so much replaced – for such a social-political relation is in fact very much a reality – as it is given a secondary role in favour of what Andreas Wittel terms a 'network sociality' consisting 'of fleeting and transient, yet iterative social relations; of ephemeral but intense encounters'. Further:

> In network sociality the social bond at work is not bureaucratic but informational; it is created on a project-by-project basis, by the movement of ideas, the establishment of only ever temporary standards and protocols, and the creation and protection of proprietary information. Network sociality is not characterized by a separation but by a combination of both work and play. It is constructed on the grounds of communication and transport technology.[32]

The conditions of work described here by Wittel join the refrain of characteristics attributed to labour in the creative industries as seen in studies by leftist academics such as McRobbie, Andrew Ross, and Castells as well as their libertarian counterparts like Caves, Florida, Leadbeater, Howkins and Brooks. While these scholars and commentators do not all use the term 'creative industries', they all describe similar patterns of labour. This isn't to say that creative labour is universally the same. Earlier I suggested that we are yet to see a study that comparatively maps the national characteristics of creative labour. Perhaps one reason such a study is still to emerge has to do with the mistaken view often propagated by creative industries' commentators, policy-makers, new media critics, and global theorists alike that the nation-state is obsolete. One thing a comparative study of creative labour in their national locales would reveal is the role IP law has at the level of the nation-state within an informational era. In accordance with the TRIPS Agreement (1995), member states are responsible for administering and governing IP law within their respective territories. This is just one layer that distinguishes the manifestation of creative labour in one country from the next. Other layers, or rather systems of arrangements, are defined by the social-political, cultural, institutional and economic peculiarities of locales, nation-states and regions and the multiple contingencies that articulate creative labour in singular ways.

As I have been arguing, there are two key issues at stake for workers undertaking creative labour within informational economies:

1. The mode and form of exploitation. For proponents of the creative industries, this consists of the exploitation of IP. Wittel also alludes to such a condition, noting that network sociality involves 'the creation and protection of proprietary information', but he refrains from engaging the political dimensions that underpin such activities. To the extent that the respondents to my survey provide an index of abstract labour in the creative industries, then one can contest Negri's claim that creative labour has transcended modern and postmodern forms of capitalism that function through the exploitation of labour as a wage relation.
2. However different the articulations of creative labour may be, they hold one thing in common: disorganization. The history of workers' movements is a testament to the force of organization in contesting the exploitation of labour by capital. The question is, can creative labour organize itself within an informational mode of connection?

In describing the circumstances from which the multitude emerges, Negri comes close to suggesting that creative labour is in fact organized: Capital 'can only exploit *cooperation* amongst workers, amongst labourers'.[33] Hardt strikes a similar tone in his earlier work on Deleuze: 'Spinozian democracy, the absolute rule of the multitude through the equality of its constituent members, is founded on the "art of organizing encounters"'.[34] As I have suggested, Wittel's notion of 'network sociality' may be a more useful description of Hardt and Negri's multitude: such a social-technical formation is not so much *directly* exploited, as it is *indirectly* exploited. 'Content is not king', as one Silicon Alley PR brochure in 1999 declared, 'the user is'.[35] Capital thus continues to exploit creative labour, since its social mode is one of cooperation. If the various studies of creative industries have got it right, then such cooperation takes the form of emphemerality, fleeting, project-by-project engagements and value adding personal relationships designed to enhance network capital. The function of the creative worker is not to produce, but to set new trends in consumption.[36]

Such activities are depicted well in the documentary film *The Merchants of Cool* (2001), where Douglas Rushkoff narrates the busy lives of 'trend-spotters' and 'cool-hunters' who track down youth whose vanguard sensibility for hip-consumerism is packaged and choreographed through symbolic affiliations with major brands and their vehicles: Sony, Pepsi-Cola, MTV, etcetera. 'Cool' youths, with their predilection for creative-consumption, function as underpaid and exploited cultural intermediaries for their less imaginative compatriots in consumerism. As Tiziana Terranova notes, this kind of operation or process is not about capital 'incorporating' some authentic, subcultural form that somehow resides outside of capitalism's media-entertainment complex. Instead, it is a 'more immanent process of channeling collective labor (even as cultural labor) into monetary flows and its structuration within capitalist business practices'.[37]

However, the social-political organization of creative labour requires a radically different impetus that is yet to emerge. As one respondent soberly puts it: 'That organization is not going to take the role of unions as we currently know them, who for the most part have no clue'. The respondent elaborates this observation, or perhaps it was a perception, with the following example: 'I do know a young woman trying to effect change in the union movement in nz [New Zealand] and organise cinema workers ... but finds the entrenched movement incredibly uninterested in understanding the desires and motivations of the young people working in these fields ... which is a prereq [sic] for representing them adequately'.

Immaterial or Disorganized Labour?

Lazzarato defines the emergent and simultaneously hegemonic form of immaterial labour 'as the labour that produces the informational and cultural content of the commodity'.[38] Lazzarato discerns 'two different aspects' within immaterial labour:

> On the one hand, as regards the 'informational content' of the commodity, it refers directly to the changes taking place in workers' labor processes in big companies in the industrial and tertiary sectors, where the skills involved in direct labor are increasingly skills involving cybernetics and computer control (and horizontal and vertical communication). On the other hand, as regards the activity that produces the 'cultural content' of the commodity, immaterial labor involves a series of activities that are not normally recognized as 'work' – in other words, the kinds of activities involved in defining and fixing cultural and artistic standards, fashions, tastes, consumer norms, and, more strategically, public opinion.[39]

It is this second aspect of immaterial labour that most readily corresponds with the types of work engaged in by those in the creative industries. Note that the 'content' of the commodity is not the sound of music, the image repertoire of the screen, the flash of animation, etcetera. As with Wittel, the content for Lazzarato is a social relationship: 'Immaterial labor produces first and foremost a "social relationship" (a relationship of innovation, production, and consumption)'.[40]

Hardt and Negri expand upon this definition to include affective forms of labour, as found in domestic and service work that involves the care of others. Importantly, the concept of immaterial labour is not to be confused as labour that somehow has eclipsed its material dimension. Hardt and Negri note that affective labour, for instance, 'requires (virtual or actual) human contact, labor in the bodily mode'.[41] However, 'the affects it produces are nonetheless immaterial. What affective labor produces are social networks, forms of community, biopower'.[42] I have no idea how such products are immaterial. Moreover, such an understanding of affect obviates an inquiry into the more nuanced concept of affect as found in the work of Deleuze and Guattari, as well as Massumi. For these thinkers, affect consists of the sensing of sensation. A material dimension is apparent here in so far as the sensing of sensation assumes that a process of corporeal transformation and de-subjectification is under way. Thus the 'product' of immaterial labour in its affective mode is precisely this transformation, which is also a change in materiality and the relationship between various actants.

Lazzarato, Hardt and Negri are concerned, then, with defining immaterial labour in terms of the *product* of labour that is immaterial (knowledge, communication, affect-care, etcetera) as distinct from its actual undertaking.[43] It is true that one does not sell care as a material product, but rather the image or sound of care. One may also sell the memory of care, but this operation depends upon a medium which still, nonetheless, communicates such memories in the form of an image or sound. Memory is thus predicated on what could be termed a sonic image. And such constellations, as we know, saturate the marketplace. Or as Lefebvre once observed, 'We are surrounded by emptiness, but it is an emptiness filled with signs'.[44] All sonic image forms are encoded by communications media, and as such they possess a material dimension. Palpable as an image or sound may be, care, in its commercial form, is not something that one holds or drives down the street, but a service one acquires. Yet the immaterial labour that produces the service of care holds a material dimension. The material dimension of this operation of exchange value tells us something of great significance vis-à-vis the commodity object. What, in fact, is occurring in this relation of exchange is nothing less than the de-ontologization and deterritorialization of the commodity object itself. I am speaking here of a question of boundaries and a question of time; in short, a question of the limits of capital. It is a category mistake to understand the commodity object as a 'thing in itself'. When the commodity object is situated, as it is, within a system of social relations, the extent to which it becomes intelligible is only possible in terms of a social relation. That is, the commodity object is simultaneously constituted by and conditions the possibility of the contingencies of a social system. It is impossible, then, for the commodity object to be extricated from this system. To do so is to speak of a utopia, the utopia of post-capitalism. Were such a world to actualize, it would not feature a role for the commodity object.

Because the concept of immaterial labour is open to various abuses, misunderstandings (my own included), and complex intellectual filiations, I suggest that it be dropped within critical Internet, cultural and information theory in favour of a concept of disorganized labour. Creative and informational modes of labour as they currently exist are better understood as disorganized; by conceiving work in this manner, the political dimension of labour is retained in so far as opposition and revolution have in modern times required workers to either self-organize or form a compact alliance with intellectuals, who have formed the symbolic spearhead of political change. Granted, our times consist of post-Fordist modes of production, exchange and accumulation integrated with informational modes of connection, all of which have seen the steady erosion of organized labour. Even so, there persists an ineradicable class dimension to labour and the uneven distribution of capital. From these conditions, the reorganization of labour is possible. And while the failures of revolution are well documented and acutely experienced by many, and the problems of political and symbolic representation clearly theorized in the work of Baudrillard, Spivak, Balibar, Mouffe and others, there remains the need – perhaps greater than ever before – to retain a sense of the importance, a sense of the urgency, for labour to have the means and the potential to organize itself.

The distinction between conceiving labour as immaterial or disorganized has implications not only at the level of political theory. While Hardt and Negri's book *Empire* has without question captured a latent structure of feeling simmering within many leftist movements, it is now time to extend that political momentum in ways that go beyond the partisan interests of 'the multitude' and engage workers at the local level of their everyday institutional circumstances. The condition of disorganized labour corresponds, of course, with the disorganized technics of capitalism, as discussed by Lash and Urry.[45] However, these two arrangements are not equivalent. The disorganized technics of capital – flexible accumulation, transnational labour mobility, risk societies, etcetera – are simply another mode by which capitalism is managed in a 'postnational', globalized setting. Disorganized labour, on the other hand, is symptomatic of the demise of union power, the deinstitutionalization of labour, and the consolidation of individualization within a neoliberal paradigm.

Lash and Urry suppose that the different temporal modes by which organizations and technologies operate, conditions the possibility of disorganized capitalism. They associate a decline in national institutions and their capacity to regulate flows of subjects and objects within a national frame with the end of organized capitalism. While they seek to go beyond a dualistic mode of thinking, they in fact reproduce such a mode: 'Disorganized capitalism disorganizes everything'.[46] As rhetorically appealing as this slogan may be, such a blanket approach to the complexity of contemporary capitalism precludes the possibility of labour organizing itself in multi-temporal ways through various media of communication in conjunction with the cultural peculiarities of socio-institutional locations and networks. Crucially, the exploitation of creative labour continues as what the autonomists have called 'a theft of time'. The possession of time by any kind of worker is the condition of possibility for the organization of labour.

The failure of Negri, Lazzarato and others who gather around the concept of immaterial labour is, quite remarkably given their respective intensely political life experiences, a failure to understand the nature of 'the political'. The concept of immaterial labour, in its refusal to locate itself in specific discourse networks, communications media and material situations, refuses also to address the antagonistic underpinnings of social relations. As Marx so clearly understood, capital is first and foremost a social relation (this, the autonomists know well). This remains just as true today for those engaged in creative, intellectual and service industries – tiers of labour that, in their state of disorganization, of course hold intimate connections with other sectors of work no matter how abstracted they may be from one another in geographical, class, cultural, economic and communicative terms.

There is a remarkable correspondence between Hardt and Negri and other 'radical' Italians on immaterial labour and the disorganized multitude, and the kinds of views put forward by many proponents of the creative industries such as Florida, Caves, Leadbeater, Brooks, Howkins, the National Research Council of the National Academies (USA) and their Australian counterparts. If there is a perception that Hardt and Negri offer a structure of feeling for the renewal of left politics and activism and that creative industries are, broadly speaking, an extension of Third Way ideology and neoliberalism with a softer face, then the similarities between these two camps are in some respects greater than their differences. The variegated system of disorganized labour within

creative industries and informational economies is homologous,
I would suggest, with Hardt and Negri's multitude; organized labour is
seen by Hardt and Negri as an obsolete, politically limited vestige of a
socialism constituted by industrial capitalism.[47] The promotion by the
creative industries of 'individual creativity and skill' at the expense of
the social relations that make both individual and collective activities
possible corresponds at a discursive level with neoliberalism's 'customization' and atomization of the subject, or what Brian Holmes co-
gently diagnoses as 'the flexible personality'.[48] Furthermore, in isolating
the networked individual as the unit of creative production there is an
implicit hostility within the creative industries to the concept of organized labour, the practice of which has historically placed demands on
capitalists for fairer and more equitable working conditions. Creative
industries are far from alone here. As Justin Clemens argues, the affirmation of bricolage, mobility, and heterogeneous subcultural styles so
typical within many Cultural Studies 'accounts unfold on the basis of a
prior covert *identification* of organization with authority, and authority
with oppression'.[49] Surely it is time to get over such hostility toward the
dark phantasm of organization?

Unions today not only have increasingly limited purchase on governments with neoliberal dispositions, they also have limited appeal for
younger workers whose political ideologies have emerged within a
neoliberal paradigm and whose social experiences are not, for the most
part, formed within the institutional cultures offered by union movements, as has been the case for older generations. Just as Hardt and
Negri dismiss 1980s and '90s postmodernism for its collusion with corporate culture (and there is much merit in this thesis, as documented
more succinctly by Thomas Frank), so too their own multitude is en-
twined within the arguably more accentuated managerialism of the
creative industries, where labour continues its transformation into surplus value, only this time in the form of intellectual property – a socio-
juridical form that lends itself more readily to the technical system of
electronic stock markets and financial speculation than it does to a
radical politics. Though here, of course, one finds the counterforms of
p2p file-sharing, tactical media and open source movements; digital
piracy of software, music and new release cinema; clones of drug, technical and GM food patents, etcetera. The extent to which these counter-

practices can be called a politics in the sense of an organized intervention into hegemonic regimes is, however, questionable and needs to be assessed on a case by case basis. Is digital piracy, for example, a political act or just a business strategy by less powerful economic actors in their efforts to circumvent transnational corporate monopolies and the legal regimes and trade agreements that advance corporate interests?

Conclusion

At the start of this chapter I drew a distinction between a processual media empirics and the new media empirics. The former is concerned with analysing and being a part of the movements and modulations between the conditions of possibility and that which has emerged as an object, code or meaning within the grid of the present. The latter is primarily interested in delimiting the field of movement, and stabilizing the object of study as an end in itself. Processual media theory does not dispense with the empirical, rather it is superempirical. But its mode of empiricism does not conform to the logic of immanence as expounded by Lash in his book *Critique of Information*: 'The global information society has an immanentist culture, fully a one and flat world culture. As such, its regime of culture is radically empiricist'.[50] The world Lash describes is not one that contains the wonders, difficulties and complexities of life. Nor for that matter is the world Hardt and Negri call Empire: 'In this new historical formation it is thus no longer possible to identify a sign, a subject, a value, or a practice that is "outside"'.[51] Today's media-information cultures – the situation of creative labour – are indeed characterized by reflexive non-linear systems; they do not, however, eschew their constitutive outsides.

In his essay on Blanchot, Foucault notes that 'Any reflexive discourse runs the risk of leading the experience of the outside back to the dimension of interiority; reflection tends irresistibly to repatriate it to the side of consciousness and to develop it into a description of living that depicts the "outside" as the experience of the body, space, the limits of the will, and ineffaceable presence of the other'.[52] Further: 'It risks setting down ready-made meanings that stitch the old fabric of interiority back together in the form of an imagined outside'. Such a mode of reflexivity is one that Lash and Beck attribute to 'first modernity'. It is a mode of reflexivity that is anterior to a processual understanding of communication, where transformation, agonism and change are integral to the operation of reflexivity.

Processual reflexivity is the operative mode peculiar to quasi-subjects and quasi-objects situated in social-technical arrangements and conditioned by the accumulation of knowledge, experience and social-political and economic forces. It is a reflexive mode that 'must not be directed toward any inner confirmation – not toward a kind of central, unshakable [sic] certitude – but toward an outer bound where it must continually contest itself'.[53] The non-discursive dimensions of creative labour operate as the constitutive outside of the creative industries; the invisible plurality of creativity cannot be generated in order to be exploited in the form of IP, yet the lives in which creativity subsists certainly can be exploited. For this reason, the antagonism intrinsic to 'the political' will persist as a social-technical potential of labour-power. The trick is to work out ways in which the antagonisms underpinning creative labour within a system of intellectual property regimes might be translated otherwise.

So how, we might ask, can a para-radical, all-too-social politics be created as organized labour within informational media ecologies? Žižek is only partly right when he declares with typical impudent brio that 'the key Leninist lesson today is that politics without the organizational *form* of the party is politics without politics'.[54] The time for parties is over! Go to your next creative industries bonding session if you want to play with cherry-flavoured vodka. It is now time for modest, pragmatic engagements with localized networked politics. This amounts to finding a form or modality of political organization that appeals to those working within the creative industries. In doing so, one is also attending to the question of how we think the relationship between communications media and the new institutional possibilities they enable.

Given the reluctance by unions to organize their constituencies within the logic of what Régis Debray terms 'mediology',[55] and what we translated in the fibreculture reader as the mediation of politics within a digital present,[56] it is unlikely that the organizational habitus of union culture will provide the institutional framework for creative labour. Or as Danny Butt notes in his response to an earlier draft of this chapter, 'The union that should represent the interests of my colleagues remains monist, masculinist, and mired in a basic inability to simply listen and understand the motivations and experiences of its constituency'.[57] This is but one instantiation of the antagonism of 'the political' as it figures in the complex of relations between the institution of unions and the informational-material situation of creative labour. Tensions of this order do not, however, preclude the possibility of translating some of the fundamental values peculiar to union culture (collective bargaining, equality and democracy, safe and healthy working conditions, etcetera) into the political form of *organized networks*: a conceptual technics in which networks rather than the organization or institution *per se* are the condition of possibility for labour articulated within new media terrains.[58] Ultimately the challenge of political organization is a challenge for all critical creative workers as they subsist in the form of networks, not the party.

Part III

5 Processual Media Theory

> Sense-perception happens without our awareness: whatever we
> become conscious of is a perception that has already been
> processed.
> Friedrich Nietzsche, *Writings from the Late Notebooks*, 2003.

'Process as such', writes Michel Serres, 'remains to be conceived...'.[1]
Furthermore, if we take Gilles Deleuze and Félix Guattari at their word
(something they warn us not to do!), then all concepts are connected to
problems.[2] The relationship between concepts and their problems constitutes a situation. For the purpose of this chapter, the formation of intelligibility is a system consisting of concepts, problems and situations.
Process is something ongoing in nature, an emergent quality whose
expression is shaped by the contingencies and field of forces of any particular situation. In this respect, process can never be conceived in itself.
Given this immediate predicament, this chapter investigates the possibility of at once conceiving a processual theory for media studies while
locating the emergent concept of process alongside a series of problems.
Or rather, the concept of process emerges through the encounter with a
series of problems, which in turn can be understood as situations of possibility or 'a continuum of variation'.[3] The central problems addressed
in this chapter include those of aesthetics, new media empirics, time
and movement. Of course this series of problems, this continuum of
variation, in no way outlines the totality of the field of new media
studies.[4] That would be absurd, or just plain stupid. These problems
emerge as instances of encounter, as framing devices, in thinking the
concept of process.

The term aesthetics (*aesthesis*) is used in this chapter to speak of the
organization and management of sensation and perception. My interest
is in the way sensory affect and an aesthetic regime, as distinct from representation (*mimesis*), can be discussed in relation to new communications media. The aesthetic dimension of new media resides in the
processes – the ways of doing, the recombination of relations, the figural dismantling of action – that constitute the abstraction of the social.
Herein lies the unconscious code of new media empirics. That is to say,

new media empirics can become something other than what it predominantly is at the current conjuncture. It is the potential for a superempirics of new media that this chapter seeks to translate through the concept of process. A super- or renewed empiricism is coextensive with the processual as a diagramming of different layers and registers of relations and regimes of value that constitute the possibility of the event where 'affect [is] expressed as pure potentiality'.[5] Following Massumi, a Deleuzian superempiricism comprises a mode of encounter that articulates the field of forces, the sensing of sensation, which traverses the movement between that which has emerged as an object, code, or meaning and their conditions of possibility.[6] It is by paying attention to these very local instances, which are of course bound up and tangled with larger structural forces, that the political and ethical work of a renewed empiricism might proceed.

A processual aesthetics of media culture enables things not usually associated with each other to be brought together into a system of relations. The combination of art, commerce and the routine practice of stock market day trading constitutes such a system, as I will go on to discuss. Far too frequently the representation, understanding or view of art practice divorces the artwork or artist from the actually existing economic forces that shape and affect art practice. With such oversights, one could be excused for thinking the modernist project was well and truly intact. Michael Goldberg's installation *catchingafallingknife.com* instantiates the ways in which aesthetic forces are not simply underpinned by economic relations; aesthetics, as the sensing of sensation, also plays an important substantive role in shaping economic outcomes. There is a vital lesson at work here, namely that art does indeed have effects that go beyond the typically self-aggrandizing ghetto of spot-lit obscurity and cyclical fashions of the culture industries. Art is part of a process of *'difference which makes a difference'*, as the anthropologist Gregory Bateson neatly put it.[7]

A processual media theory describes situations as they are constituted within and across spatio-temporal networks of relations, of which the communications medium is but one part, or actor. As with any approach, processual media theory itself is implicated in the systems of relations it describes; as such, it too operates in a reflexive mode that contributes to change within the system. Aesthetic production is defined by transformative iterations, rather than supposedly discrete objects in commodity form. Processual aesthetics is related to the notion of the sublime, which is 'witness to indeterminacy'.[8] The media sublime unravels the security presupposed by the political economy of empirical research on new media.

Political economy has a tendency to treat the media as a set of objects and, accordingly, objectivizes media technologies or media content as 'products', such as advertisements. Political economy and functionalist sociology of the media cannot understand the locus of social-technical transformations that are relational and have sensory effects whose operation is not determined by a positivist empirics of the media as seen, for example, in traditional media impacts/effects analysis, content analysis and 'uses and gratifications' functionalist research.[9] Then there is the political economy *of* new media empirics. That is, the political, economic and institutional conditions which shape neo-empirics as the emergent paradigm in the field of new media studies.[10] While new media empirics is useful for cataloguing observable trends and phenomena, this paradigm is not so adept at reflecting upon the dominant interests and questions of power that condition its own legitimacy.[11]

The political dimension of aesthetics is manifest in the power relations that attend processual systems. In order to undertake an analysis of the social-technical assemblages that constitute the processual, attention would need to be paid to the institutional settings of new media and their uses, be they in the office, at home, or in networked gaming arcades, for example, and the conditions of cultural production. A processual aesthetics of the socio-technics of these arrangements attests to the politics of post-representation. The articulation of various elements that constitute a network can be thought of in terms of duration (a mode of temporality that is antithetical to instrumental time), which might also be termed the processual aesthetics of new media. So, a processual aesthetics of new media is related to and constituted within the time and space of the media event.[12] Networked gaming, online opinion polling, web petitions and blogs are all instances of new media that incorporate an aesthetic regime defined by non-linearity, interactivity and real-time processing that constitutes everyday media events.

A processual media theory can enhance existing approaches within the field of new media studies, registering the movement between that which has emerged as an empirical object, meaning or code, and the various conditions of possibility. Processual media theory inquires into that which is otherwise rendered as invisible, yet is fundamental to the world as we sense it. Thus, processual media theory could be considered as a task engaged in the process of translation.[13] To this end, this chapter addresses the problematic of a renewed empirical mode that has come to dominate intellectual practice within media studies; indeed this predominant mode extends beyond any single discipline and prevails across the humanities and technosciences. As we saw in the previous chapter, new media empirics has found itself enlisted in the mission of neoliberalism, which subordinates the practice of life to the demands of a market economy. Building on the argument set out in chapter 4, this chapter develops a processual model of media theory as an alternative to, and mode of critique of, empirical research. Further, this chapter contends that a processual model of communications is useful in addressing the politics of information societies. As Deleuze has written, 'Concepts, with their zones of presence, should intervene to resolve local situations'.[14] This chapter begins its correspondence between concepts and problems with a discussion of 'new media empirics'.

New Media Empirics

Over the past few years, one is increasingly able to detect the emergence of empirical approaches to the study of new media as the current dominant paradigm. An empirics of new media describes the various forms, objects, experiences and artworks that constitute new media. The empiricist desire to fix all that is virtual into concrete is coextensive with a certain weariness, boredom or distrust of the excesses of 'postmodern theory' that came to characterize much work going on in media and cultural studies and contemporary art during the 1980s and '90s.

These fields all share a desire to ground their objects of study, to retrieve them from the ravages of 'speculative theory', and in so doing, perhaps begin a process of reconstructing or securing disciplinary identities. Arguably, all of this coincides with the perceived displacement of national and local communities wrought by communications media such as satellite TV, the Internet and the mobile phone. Very real displacement across social scales accompanies the structural transformations of national and regional economies in a post-Soviet era in which populations have become increasingly mobile at transnational levels as professional or unskilled labour, as refugees, or as tourists.

It is the task of empirical studies to describe and analyse these various transformations, yet to delimit such work to the scholastic mode of production is to overlook the ways in which such research corroborates the interests of capital which, in the corporatization of universities, finds the current empirical paradigm as the new frontier of instrumental reason. Much research on the Internet is quantitative and commercially driven, measuring, for example, the number of hits and counting users on web pages. Researchers, or information workers, in many instances are providing data analysis that has commercial applications in ascertaining consumer habits and, in the case of new media studies, there is an attempt to foreclose the myriad ways in which users engage with media forms and content. It's all quite desperate. And it's all related to a quest to capture markets.

A non-reflexive and non-reflective new media empirics assumes that the various uses of new media forms, or the practices constituted by media forms, define the horizon of intelligibility of new media. Different uses, different meanings. But is that all there is to it? Are the arrangements or networks of new media confined to their uses, whether it's by human or non-human actors? And at what point does one say the field of actors has been identified? When does the list of actors end? Upon what plane of abstraction does use manifest? Are there registers of use that are overlooked because the multidimensional planes of abstraction are not identified? These are all questions which begin to problematize the security, even arrogance, presupposed by a method which seeks to quantify the semiotics of new media in terms of the uses made of particular new communications media.

Empirical research typically proceeds by securing what is otherwise a fluid, contingent and partially unstable process constituting a system of interrelations. While there are significant distinctions between the two, empirical research across a range of disciplines is often based on principles found in positivist empiricism. Louis Althusser locates the problem of empiricism as a method in terms of its assumption of having captured the essence of an object through the process of abstraction. As he wrote over thirty years ago in *Reading Capital*: 'Empiricist abstraction, which abstracts from the given *real* object its essence, is a *real ab-*

straction, leaving the subject in possession of the *real* essence'.[15] In order to extract the real essence from the object, empiricism undertakes an operation that eliminates the object's constitutive outside. This procedure serves as an epistemological validation of empiricism, since 'To know is to abstract from the real object its essence, the possession of which by the subject is then called knowledge'.[16] Hence a relationship based on presence-absence is produced between that which is revealed as real (the objects of knowledge) and the procedural mode that has enabled this operation (the form of knowledge and its structural forces). For Althusser, empiricist knowledge is part of a larger hegemonic episteme or 'apparatus of thought' that grants primacy to vision, seeking to make visible the invisible.[17] The fundamental error of such abstraction is that it fails to reflect critically upon the conditions of possibility for such a procedure.

As a methodological practice, empiricism is captured by a delirium in which there is an assumption that the essence of the object can be revealed. Due to an incapacity to reflexively engage with the field of forces that condition its methodology, empiricism eliminates the processual dimension that underpins the emergence of the supposed essence of the object, revealed as a form whose meaning is stable. In contrast to empiricism, Marx and Engels write in *The German Ideology* that 'Empirical observation must in each instance bring out empirically, and without any mystification and speculation, the connection of the social and political structure with production'.[18] And: 'As soon as this active life-process is described, history ceases to be a collection of dead facts, as it is with the empiricists (themselves still abstract), or an imagined activity of imagined subjects, as with the idealists'.[19] As a result of these sorts of oversights, empiricism offers nothing by way of political critique. Indeed, to do so would endanger the very legitimacy of empiricism as a method. Further, as David Holmes has noted, 'The more it [empiricism] establishes the visibility of what it sees, the more it establishes knowledge, the better able it is to guarantee itself'.[20] Since the social relations of production that condition the space and time of 'the political' are part of the constitutive outside that the empiricist problematic excludes, empiricism attributes, according to Althusser, an 'inessential' value to social-political and historical conditions of formation.[21]

While Althusser is one of the principal theorists of ideology critique responsible for thumping positivist variants of empiricism, as outlined above, I would suggest that Althusser's work holds a useful enough foundation, actually, for empirical – as distinct from empiricist – research. Ideology, for Althusser, is associated with the imaginary. This image repertoire, most importantly, is reproduced in material practices located in institutional settings, from which subject formation occurs (through, admittedly, the flawed notion of interpellation). In order to begin talking about the processes of ideology and its attendant power relations, one needs to start identifying, in an empirical manner of the kind argued by Marx and Engels, the very local practices within which ideology is reproduced.

In the case of new media empirics, which reproduces the methodological procedure of empiricism, a reflexive encounter with its techniques of operation would begin to take into account the plurality of forces, including those of institutional interests, which condition the formation of a practice, code or meaning. In doing so, the multidimensional pluralism that functions as empiricism's constitutive outside would come to bear. Moreover, the politics that attends such an operation could be situated in an 'agonistic' framework in which pluralistic discourses, practices, forces and interests procure a legitimacy that is otherwise denigrated by empiricism's claim to have abstracted the essence of the object from the real.

The shift in media studies and other disciplines to a non-reflective and non-reflexive empirical mode is perhaps best accounted for by paying attention to the shift that has occurred in the conditions of production associated with intellectual labour within a neoliberal paradigm. Within this mode is a pressure for intellectual practices to become accountable. This pressure is not motivated by ethical considerations, which include the delivery of knowledge and engagement with teaching and research in ways that are responsive both to their own disciplinary circumstances and to those who are subjects within a particular institution and its disciplinary formations. Rather, there is a managerialist demand for the products of intellectual labour – knowledge coded as intellectual property, which makes possible the commodity object – to be accountable to the logic of exchange value and market mechanisms.

The neoliberal imaginary seeks to subject all socio-cultural practices to the laws of the market, which are one manifestation, albeit limited, of the logic of capital. As such, a technique of verification is required, and the humanities have turned to the sciences for such a tool. This is hardly surprising, since the sciences have long held a relationship with industry, which sees the output of labour within the sciences as holding commercial and industrial application. A perception dominates within the managerial culture of academe that assumes vulgar empirics to be the technique that best enables intellectual labour to be measured, quantified and reported in terms of stasis or stability.

The key problem of an empirics of new media aesthetics resides in its failure, in a number of instances, to understand that the aesthetics of artworks, software applications and technologies are conditioned by social relations as well as the theoretical paradigms through which analysis proceeds. Technology, as understood by Raymond Williams, is found in the processual dimension of articulation, where the media is but one contingent element that undergoes transformation upon every re-articulation.[22] This presents a challenge to the empirical turn in Net studies, which seeks in vain to pin down a terrain that is made historically redundant prior to its emergence. By way of an alternative, Lash proposes that 'Empirical meaning is neither logical (as in classification) nor ontological, but everyday and contingent'.[23] Empirical approaches to the Net, if nothing else, need to work in a reflexive mode that is constantly aware of the conditions attached to funded research, to critique them, to describe the institutional cultures that shape the emergent third paradigm of Net studies, and to see the seemingly secure ground of any empirical moment as something which is always interpenetrating with something else.

Processual Aesthetics as Radical Empiricism

With the invention of the telegraph came the genre, form or style of telegraphic writing, of news wires. Think of Ernest Hemingway, with his telegraphic, machine-gun writing style – a mode of writing within and through media of communication. Moreover, a zone of indistinction between the human and non-human emerges with the advent of new communications media. As Friedrich Kittler suggestively notes of Nietzsche upon his use in 1882 of a Malling Hansen typewriter: 'Our writing tool not only works on our thoughts, it "is a thing like me"'.[24] With failing eyesight, the 'mechanized philosopher' undergoes a transformation of expression: Nietzsche 'changed from arguments to aphorisms, from thoughts to puns, from rhetoric to telegram style'.[25]

The Malling Hansen model initiates a kinaesthetics based on touch, since its 'semi-circular arrangement of the keys itself prevented a view of the paper'.[26] The shift from visual control and linearity associated with the pen and paper to the blind activity of typing constitutes a feminization of philosophy, argues Kittler.[27] The primacy of the classical author corresponds with a closed system predicated on social-technical distinctions associated with the 'phallogocentrism of classical slate pencils' and 'the sexually closed feedback loop' of the Gutenberg Galaxy.[28] The machinic philosopher, by contrast, is part of a combinatory system that brings together philosopher, typewriter, a 'delicacy' of touch, and women, who dominated the ranks of secretaries in printing houses in the late nineteenth century. Piano fingers turn out to be good typing fingers.

With the Internet, we have seen hypertext, listservs, net.art, and so forth. With the mobile phone, short-text messaging (sms) has emerged as one the most popular social-technical forms of communication. These could all be talked about in terms of media aesthetics. However, I think it is more interesting for an aesthetics of new media to consider the ways in which social and cultural formations not immediately attributable to the media with which they are contemporary might also be included in the pantheon of media aesthetics. Such articulations might constitute the unthought of media aesthetics: social and cultural forms that are not determined by media technologies, but are potentialities that coincide with or are parallel to contemporaneous communications media.

A processual aesthetics of new media goes beyond what is simply seen or represented on the screen. It seeks to identify how online practices are always conditioned by and articulated with seemingly invisible forces, institutional desires and regimes of practice. Furthermore, a processual aesthetics recognizes the material and embodied dimensions of Net cultures. When you engage with a virtual or online environment, are you simply doing the same thing as you would in a non-virtual environment, where you might be looking at objects, communicating, using your senses – vision, sound, etcetera? In other words, if the chief argument of the new media empirics lies in the idea that we simply ought to pay close attention to what people 'do' on the Net and ignore any grander claims about virtual technologies, is this adequate? Is there anything in this 'do-ing' which deserves greater analysis?

Do virtual environments simply extend our senses and our actions across space and time, or do they reconstitute them differently? There is a strong argument to be made for the latter. In the same way that visual culture – especially the cinema – legitimized a certain way of looking at things through techniques such as standardized camera work and continuous camera editing, then virtual technologies reorganize and manage the senses and our modes of perception in similar ways. As Kafka once noted: 'Cinema involves putting the eye into uniform'.

Software design, virtual environments, games, and search engines all generate and naturalize certain ways of knowing and apprehending the world. We can find examples of this with database retrieval over linear narrative, hypertext, 3D movement through space as the means to knowledge, and editing and selection rather than simple acquisition. So if empirics can record that we have virtual conversations, look up certain sites, and so forth, it doesn't consider *the technics of combining visual and tactile perceptions* in certain ways and in certain contexts to allow for distinct modes of understanding the world. Nor does a new media empirics inquire into the specific techniques by which sensation and perception are managed. This is the task of processual aesthetics.

The repetition of technics of sensation and perception are partially distinguished by the regimes of value (economic, legal, political and cultural) which are inscribed upon such ways of doing. A processual aesthetics of media theory seeks to identify the various methods that typify empirical research on the Internet, and to follow this up with a critique of the empirical mode by considering the institutional desires and regimes of practice that condition the types and methods of research undertaken on new ICTs at the current conjuncture within informational societies. While recognizing that the Internet does make our social and cultural transactions more 'abstract' – that is, reconstituted from place-bound relations into the 'space of flows'[29] – this of course does not mean that everyone uses the Net in the same way, or that the Net has the same significance for everyone. Instead, an emphasis is placed on process, on the organization and management of sensation and perception, which are understood here as the basis of aesthetics. The experience of time, space, others and embodiment cannot be encompassed by a new media empirics which simply lists and categorizes what an actor does, overlooking the forces and contexts that allow action to occur.

In *The Language of New Media*, media theorist and artist Lev Manovich undertakes a media archaeology of post-media or software theory.[30] He focuses on a very particular idea about what constitutes the materiality of new media, and hence aesthetics. In excavating a history of the present for new media, Manovich's work is important in that it maps out recent design applications, animation practices and compositing techniques, for example, that operate in discrete or historically continuous modes. However, Manovich's approach is one that assumes form as a given, yet forgets the social-political arrangements that media forms are necessarily embedded in, and which imbue any visual (not to mention sonic) taxonomy or typology with a code: that is, a language whose precondition is the possibility for meaning to be produced.

The aesthetic that constitutes a code is only possible through a process of articulation with modes of practice, of interpenetrative moments, of duration. In Niklas Luhmann's terms, a code is integral to the reproduction of structural difference within a functional system.[31] As Luhmann writes: 'Codes are distinctions, forms that serve as observational devices. They are mobile structures that are applied differently from situation to situation'.[32] Structural determination is thus dependent on the code, whose function is to symbolize. Such an operation enables self-organization within a system, as I discuss below. In Gregory Bateson's terms, codes are the 'difference which makes a difference'. These are all processes that new media empirics eliminates.

The network is not 'decomposable into constituent points'.[33] That is what a non-reflective and non-reflexive empirics of new media, of informational economies and network societies in its reified institutional mode, attempts to do. The network is not a 'measurable, divisible space'. Rather, it holds a 'nondecomposable' dimension that always exceeds – or better, subsists within – what in the name of non-reflexive empirics are predetermined regimes of quantification, which, as Massumi has it, 'is an emergent quality of movement'.[34] This is not to say that things never occupy a concrete space. An analytics of space (and time), if it is to acknowledge the complexity of things, cannot take as its point of departure the state of arrest of things. Instead, attention needs to take a step back (or perhaps a step sideways, and then back within), and inquire into the preconditions of stasis. And this does not mean occupying a teleological position, which seeks to identify outcomes based on causes. Or as Massumi puts it, the 'emphasis is on process before signification or coding'.[35]

That is, there is a multidimensionality to socio-aesthetic experiences. They are not bound or contained by any particular communications medium or transport technology. Thus we can say, on precisely these sorts of grounds, that the 'virtual' and the 'material' are always intimately and complexly intertwined. And to overlook this fundamental principle is to impoverish, among other things, the practice of research on new media. What Massumi terms a 'superempirics' would register this multidimensionality of socio-aesthetics: a complex of practices that is constituted within and across pathways, passages and vectors of mediality.

In formulating a processual model for media theory, this chapter does not dispense with empirical work. Far from it. A processual media theory registers the ways in which communications media – any medium of expression – are bound in a system of relations, a singularity of expression, that consists of a field of forces in which things are defined or registered as a concrete stable form, which in turn becomes a condition for transformation and change. Massumi describes this process in terms of the *movement* between that which has emerged and the conditions of potentiality or 'the virtual', understood in a Deleuzian sense of radical empiricism.[36] Time for new media empirics, which is not to be confused with radical empiricism, consists of the present, where things are manifest in concrete form. This kind of presupposition cannot account for the multiplicity of time immanent to the operation of the virtual and the actual, which Massumi explains in the following way: 'The virtual is the future-past of the present: a thing's destiny and condition of existence.... A thing's actuality is its duration as a process...'.[37] Similarly, as Deleuze notes, 'Movement always relates to a change, migration to a seasonal variation'.[38] Thus a processual media theory examines the tensions and torques between that which has emerged and conditions of possibility; it is an approach that inquires into the potentiality of motion that underpins the existence and formation of a system.[39] Herein lies the practice of a radical transcendental empiricism. New media studies has yet to express this particular encounter.

If anything, the dominant mode of empirical research unwittingly defines 'the axis of escape along which the differential object ... [slips] quietly away from its own growing objectivity'.[40] With regard to encountering the empirical, Massumi notes:

> If by 'empirical' is meant 'pertaining to predictable interactions between isolatable elements, formulatable as deterministic laws', then the conditions of emergence of vision are superempirical. They actively *include* the constancy of empirical conditions. The superempirical conditions of experience complexly include the empirical in the mode of responsive accompaniment. As experience takes off, its empirical conditions fall away.[41]

The superempirical is immanent to the concept of the processual, which questions the logic of the grid, of categories, of codings and positions.[42] Those things which precede these orders of distinction are in fact bound together on a continuum of relations as partial zones of indistinction. Categories are only ever provisional, and emerge to suit specific ends, functions, interests, disciplinary regimes and institutional realities. To this end, the mode of empirical research that predominates in the humanities and sciences – and in particular current research on new media – needs to be considered in terms of not what categories say about their objects, but rather, in terms of what categories say about the *movement* between that which has emerged and the conditions of possibility. Herein lie the contingencies of process.

As the sensing of sensation, of the experience of pre-linguistic attributes, superempiricism corresponds with that other pre-linguistic category – the imaginary.[43] Within Marxist-Lacanian psychoanalytic theory, an imaginary construction signals that there can be no essence, but multiple imaginary terrains that contest, support or ignore one another. Each imaginary formation is articulated with a series of material preconditions. A genealogy of any imaginary formation would involve examining the constellation of material forms and practices and symbolic dimensions that distinguish one imaginary formation from another. So, the imaginary does not forego the possibility of the real, but actively inculcates the real or non-discursive entity as a necessary condition of its own formation. If there is a fundamental lesson to be gained from Althusser's seminal essay 'Ideology and Ideological State Apparatuses', it was this: ideology consists of lived relations or social practices organized in part by a logic of sensibility found in symbolic realms.[44] The imaginary, as such, is constituted by material practices located within institutional settings. The work of cultural industries, which circulate images of celebrities in abundance, evinces the relationship between the imaginary and materiality. The latter, it must be noted, is not to be confused with 'the real', whose surplus resists integration into the symbolic order.[45]

Unlike the Classical Marxist view of the superstructure as a reflection of the economic base/mode of production, Althusser's advance on Marxist theory was to explain how the ISAs displayed a 'relative autonomy' from the determining influences of the economic base, except 'in the last instance'. Many critics over the years have taken the opportunity to attribute this seeming contradiction and regression to a vulgar Marxian orthodoxy as evidence of the failure of a Althusser's model of ideology. Further, the overdetermining role of the economic base on the realm of ideology suggests a point of finitude whereby a distinction of mutual exclusion or incommensurability exists between the realm of the imaginary and that of the real. However, as John Frow has argued:

There is no 'determination in the last instance by the economic' because the last instance never comes. Rather, determination is exercised by 'permutations, displacements and condensations', and this means that the social formation is characterized by the uneven and nonteleological play of its elements, since the invariant structure of the complex whole exists only through discrete variations for which it is a precondition. This is not a pluralism, but it allows an understanding of the effect of a plurality of determinations within a structure where one instance is dominant as a necessary condition of complexity.[46]

One key relationship of determining forces, then, is found in the relationship between the imaginary and the real. Indeed, the imaginary is intricately linked with and plays an active role in both constructing and being constructed by the real. In other words, while the imaginary may appear to be violated by the presence of the real, this does not mean the real resides irrevocably in a space of alterity, impossible to locate within either the imaginary or the symbolic order. For Žižek's Marxian reading of Lacanian psychoanalytic theory, 'the real' is inscribed within spectral dimensions. As Žižek argues, the 'resistant kernel' of 'the real' is always 'present *within* the symbolic process itself',[47] often in the form of some antagonism that is played out in the cultural domain. In this respect there is a materiality that attends the interplay between the real, the imaginary and the symbolic.

A superempiricism that registers the interplay of forces in the constitution of the event can be found in much of media theorist McKenzie Wark's work on 'weird global media events': those media imaginaries that implode, or better, exceed, the logic of discourse, the symbolic order of things, and constitute the event as that which escapes, momentarily, the restrictive confines, conventions and representative structures of news narratives.[48] Such events – the September 11 terrorist attacks on New York City being the most obvious recent example – consist of signs, certainly, but they perhaps are better understood as 'a-signifying' semiotic systems.[49] Such systems involve what Guattari calls an 'aesthetic processual paradigm', 'autopoietic machines', and 'processual assemblages' in which expression is 'extra-linguistic' and semiotic substance is 'relatively untranslatable'.[50] That is, such media events are irreducible to a semiotic encoding/decoding model, as seen in the early work of Stuart Hall and adopted by many within cultural studies. While the encoding/decoding model of ideology played a key role in opening up new questions pertaining to the cultural and political dimensions of meaning that were not being addressed by uses-and-gratifications and effects schools of empirical research in mass communications, the model remains very much one concerned with structuralist understandings of the sign, representation and language.[51]

By contrast, a-signifying semiotics only partially relies on semiologies of signification as a substrate in as much as the prior semiotic order of content/form (for instance the redundancy of news narratives) is radically torn apart (deterritorialized) and rendered anew as a different con-figuration.[52] The constitutive operation of a-signifying semiotics is a process of 'escaping coding and redundancy'.[53] In such cases, empiri-cism, maybe at its best, can diagram the transversal coordinates beyond the space and time of the relatively contained instance of news instal-ments. This includes the externality of relations, namely percepts, con-cepts, affects and their habits.[54] One of Wark's techniques for register-ing this interrelationship between the mediatized event and its move-ment within the event of the social-technical assemblage or arrange-ment is to incorporate the everyday into, and as part of, the singularity of the event.[55] The key point, as noted by Gary Genosko, is that 'semi-otic-machinic or sign-matter fluxes are unmediated by representa-tion'.[56] Experience, on the other hand, is mediated or governed by prop-erties, forces, rules, habits and relations that constitute the event. To this extent, a translation has occurred. Most basically, I see a renewed empiricism or superempiricism as coextensive with the processual, where a diagramming of different layers and registers of relations and regimes of value constitute the possibility of the event in which, as Deleuze puts it, 'affect [is] expressed as pure potentiality'. I will address this dimension of affect after I locate the emergence of processuality as a concept within cybernetics theory.

Feedback Loops and Dissipative Structures

> [C]ybernetics, the theory of self-guidance and feedback loops, is a the-ory of the Second World War.
> Kittler[57]

A processual media theory can be related back to cybernetics and sys-tems theory and early models of communication developed by mathe-matician and electrical engineer Claude Shannon in the 1940s. Howev-er, there is no single originary point of development of cybernetics. As Gregory Bateson notes, 'The ideas were developed in many places: in Vienna by Bertalanffy, in Harvard by Wiener, in Princeton by von Neumann, in Bell Telephone labs by Shannon, in Cambridge by Craik and so on'.[58] Shannon's model is often referred to as the transmission model, or sender-message-receiver model. It is a process model of communication, and for the most part it rightly deserves its place within an introduction to communications programme since it enables a historical trajectory of communications to be established.

However, it quickly becomes clear that this model holds considerable problems because it advances a linear model of communication flows, from sender to receiver. And this of course just isn't the way communication proceeds – there's always a bunch of noise out there that is going to interfere with the message, both in material and immaterial ways, and in terms of audiences simply doing different things with messages and technologies than the inventors or producers might have intended. The polyvocal, multilayered character of communication, culture and the production of meaning was indeed one of the key tasks Hall's encoding/decoding model set out to establish in response to the assumption of transparent, unilinear communication flows by traditional empirical, positivistic research in mass communications.[59] As Katherine Hayles puts it, 'Claude Shannon defined information as a probability function with no dimensions, no materiality, and no necessary connection with meaning'.[60] Such a model has limited uses in calculating choice, probability, behavioural patterns and risk – and hence holds an appeal for determining likely economic outcomes, as the young Rupert Murdoch was to discover in his encounter with games theory[61] – but it flounders when conditions are not stable but contingent, variable, and embedded in social-technical and biological forms.

The point to take from this process model is that it later developed to acknowledge factors of noise or entropy (disorder and deterioration), once in the hands of anthropologists such as Gregory Bateson. Central to second-order cybernetic theory is the problem of change and relationships. As Bateson notes of self-referential relationships, 'Cybernetics is, at any rate, a contribution to change – not simply a change in attitude, but even a change in the understanding of what an attitude is'.[62] As distinct from understanding information as a homeostatic thing in itself, Bateson, by Paul Virilio's account, 'who was one of the first to think of information as a general process, added that "Information is a difference that makes a difference"'.[63]

Second-order cybernetics shifted from a closed system to an open system of communication. Or, more correctly, it shifted from a linear system to one that took feedback loops into account. This becomes interesting for a model of processual media and cultural theory, which is interested in mutually determining relationships between that which has emerged and the conditions of possibility. The notion of feedback loops is homologous with the concept of 'organizational closure' in second-order cybernetics, as found in the work on neurophysiology and biological systems by Humberto Maturana and Francisco Varela, for example.[64] The central feature of Maturana and Varela's autopoietic systems consists of the organization of organization. Difference inter-mingles with the operations of a system in order to maintain a dynamic equilibrium.

Organizational closure acknowledges the role of the observer in the functioning of a system, and hence introduces the concept of reflexivity where the observer constitutes a node within the scene or operation of observation. In this respect, second-order cybernetics shares something with post-structuralist critiques of the subject: both are concerned with questioning the primacy of the individual and the autonomy of the sub-ject/consciousness from the environment in which it is embedded. Even a summary as cursory as this suggests the implications such a model has for political and ethical considerations: at issue is the status and limits of boundaries understood as constructed, and hence open to change. On the question of a system and its context, Hayles notes that 'For Bateson, decontextualization is not a necessary scientific move but a systematic distortion'.[65]

A significant extension of the cybernetic model is necessary in order to recast the limits of 'organizational closure'. In so doing, it becomes possible to acknowledge the ways in which networks of communica-tion flows operate in autopoietic ways where media ecologies develop as self-generating, distributed informational systems. Within the theory of social systems developed by Niklas Luhmann, a system is a set of possibilities whose relations are regulated, organized and distinguished by combinatory forces of interpenetration-penetration, indeterminacy-determination and contingency-stasis.[66] Together, these features consti-tute the conditions of possibility for change within a self-referential or autopoietic system. For Luhmann, 'In the self-referential mode of opera-tion, closure is a form of broadening possible environmental contacts; closure increases, by constituting elements more capable of being deter-mined, the complexity of the environment that is possible for the system'.[67] Thus closure is temporary in the sense that closure offers a distinction or boundary that feeds back into the system, making change and transformation possible.

Time is an important operation within any system. The multidimensionality of time corresponds with the varying planes of abstraction within which the movement between that which has emerged and the conditions of possibility occur. Luhmann expresses the organizational closure afforded by time and change within a system as follows: '"Time" symbolizes the fact that whenever anything determinate occurs, something else also happens, so that no single operation can ever gain complete control over its circumstances'.[68] There is a seemingly paradoxical aspect to the notion of organizational closure within autopoietic systems whereby the ongoing process of feedback in the form of incorporating entropy and perturbations conditions the future of the system. Keith Ansell Pearson explains it like this:

> The claim that autopoietic systems are organizationally 'closed' can be misleading if it is taken to imply that these systems do not interact with their environment. Such systems are simply closed in the sense that the product of their organization is the organization itself.[69]

Just as autopoiesis is understood as self-referentiality within the organization of organization, processual aesthetics can be understood as the resonance of the sensation of sensation.[70] Resonance is a feedback loop. Moreover, processual aesthetics of new media occupy what philosophers of science Ilya Prigogine and Isabelle Stengers call a 'dissipative structure' that organizes and incorporates contingencies, non-linearities and fluctuations into a dynamic state in 'far-from-equilibrium conditions'.[71] A temporal dimension is reintroduced into the equation here, since 'dissipative structures seem to prolong indefinitely the fertile instant of the genesis of structures'.[72] Elsewhere, Stengers enticingly proposes the following: 'The contingent process invites us to "follow" it, each effect being both a prolongation and a reinvention'.[73] Put another way, if a continuum of variation ceases to be, so too does communication within a system.

184

The Art of Day Trading

We are yet to see what capital can become. So goes the 'New Economy' mantra as its proponents go about laying claim to the future, which is synonymous with the 'free market'. Mastery of the latter supposedly determines the former.[74] Bubble economies – exemplified in our time most spectacularly by dotcom mania and the tech-wreck of 2000[75] – are perhaps one index of the future-present where the accumulation of profit proceeds by capturing what is otherwise a continuous flow of information.[76] Information flows are shaped by myriad forces that in themselves are immaterial and invisible in so far as they do not register in the flow of information itself. The condition of motion nevertheless indelibly inscribes information with a speculative potential, enabling it to momentarily be captured in the form of trading indices.

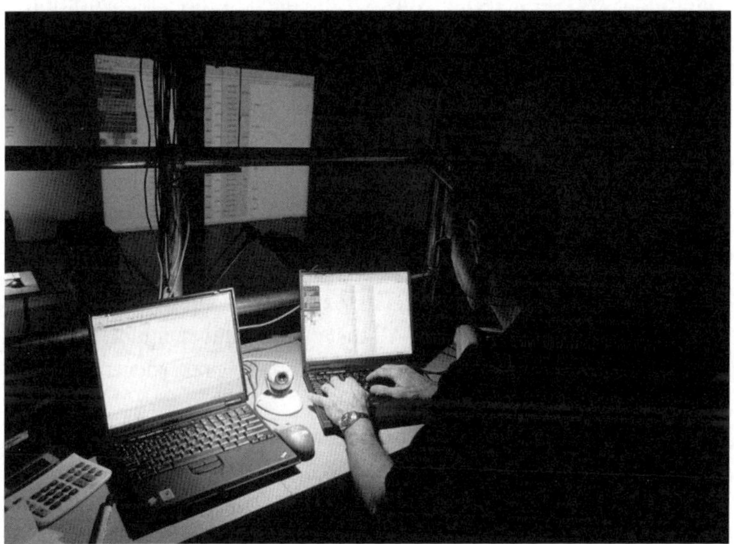

2. *Artist at work and catchingafallingknife.com installation, Artspace, Sydney, 2002 Courtesy of Michael Goldberg.*

Michael Goldberg's installation at Sydney's Artspace – *catchingafallingknife.com* – nicely encapsulates aspects of a processual media theory.[77] The installation combines various software interfaces peculiar to the information exchanges of day traders gathered around electronic cash flows afforded by the buying and selling of shares in Murdoch's News Corporation. With $50,000 backing from an anonymous consortium of stock market speculators cobbled together from an online discussion list of day traders, Goldberg set himself the task of buying and selling News Corp shares over a three week period in October-November, 2002.

Information flows are at once inside and outside the logic of commodification. The software design of market charts constitutes an interface between what Felix Stalder describes as informational 'nodes' and 'flows'.[78] The interface functions to capture and contain – and indeed make intelligible – what are otherwise quite out of control finance flows. But not totally out of control: finance flows, when understood as a self-generating system, occupy a space of tension between 'absolute stability' and 'total randomness'.[79] Too much emphasis upon either condition leaves the actor-network system open to collapse. Evolution or multiplication of the system depends upon a constant movement or feedback loops between actors and networks, nodes and flows.

Referring to the early work of political installation artist Hans Haacke, Goldberg explains this process in terms of a 'real-time system': 'The artwork comprises a number of components and active agents combining to form a volatile yet stable system. Well, that may also serve as a concise description of the stock market.... Whether or not the company's books are in the black or in the red is of no concern – the trader plays a stock as it works its way up to its highs and plays it as the lows are plumbed as well. All that's important is liquidity and movement. "Chance" and "probability" become the real adversaries and allies'.[80]

Trading or charting software can be understood as stabilizing technical actors that gather informational flows, codifying such flows in the form of 'moving average histograms, stochastics, and momentum and volatility markers' (Goldberg). Indicators of this sort provide the basis for 'technical analysis', which is concerned with discerning the movement of prices according to the supply and demand of particular shares. While simplistic, the attention paid to supply and demand as basic concerns of financial management can be seen to correspond with the focus cultural studies and new media empirics places on the conditions of possibility and that which has emerged. In both instances a processual dimension is overlooked: that is, the very movement within and between these variables, which acts to continuously refigure both conditions, challenging the assumption that the world exists in a state of arrest.

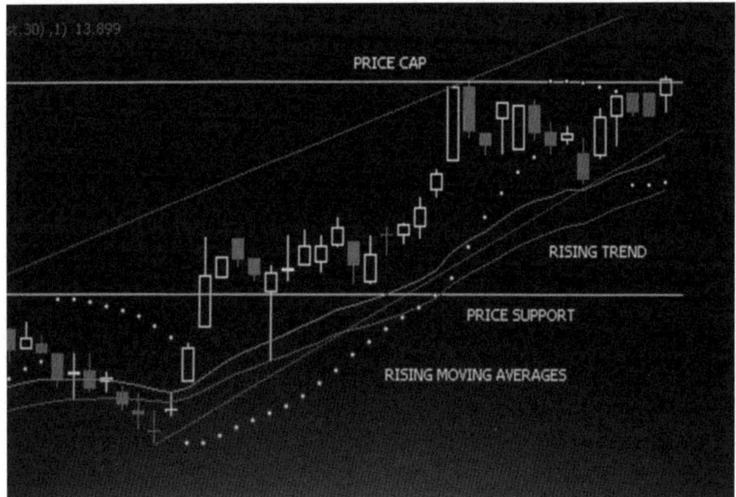

3. *'Technical analysis' ('candle-stick') trading chart, catchingafallingknife.com installation, Artspace, Sydney, 2002 Courtesy of Michael Goldberg.*

Lash claims that 'The feedback loop is the locus of the critique of information'.[81] Software trading charts operate as a closed self-referential and self-generating system: movement up or down the trajectory of a graph is determined at one level by inputs of information that register the value of a particular share. Yet at another level, the stochastic chart is an interpenetrative system. That is, the movement of the graph is contingent on a wider field of forces. For example, Goldberg notes in his diary that he was unable to make a trade on a particular day. The Australian Stock Exchange had gone down. Not only does this impact upon the flow of information that enables the possibility of economic exchange, it also suggests the stability of a system interpenetrates with a wider political economy that articulates with technical standards. In this instance the maintenance of finance networks is subject to the vulnerability that attends concentrations of IT infrastructures. Herein lies a political and economic argument for distributed informational systems.

Chart-analysis software simulates the market situation, computing the movement and value of stocks. However, chart analysis by a modelling program alone is insufficient. While the system is dynamic – in so far as the reaction of the user manifests as the sale or purchase of stock, which in turn feeds back into the system – the system is necessarily a closed one. Parameters have to be defined that represent the effect various data inputs have on likely market outcomes. Any simulation model is thus based upon a principle of inclusion/exclusion. In his essay on breakdowns within international stock market systems, Wulf Halbach explains the construction of a simulation model as follows:

> In order to create a model for any reality in question, as many details and parameters must be taken into consideration as possible (also a question of costs). The details and parameters chosen are the most relevant – maximum parameters – and those that are left out are the least influential – minimal parameters.[82]

By design, the simulation model reduces the complex field of forces that shape the perception one might have of the market value of a particular stock. That is, there is *something more* that comes to bear to shape the perception and actualization of value. As Genosko writes, 'The output values feed back through the possible parameters, which re-engage the minimal parameters, causing a crash in as much as the minimal parameters could not become maximal'.[83] In other words, 'the simulation is unresponsive to its own terms!' The field of emergence is comprised of distributions of chaos, 'not to mention fear, momentum, noise, caffeine-induced phantasms, etc.'.[84]

The surfeit of force that escapes the parameters of chart-analysis software is augmented by 'fundamental analysis'. Fundamental analysis looks 'at the realities underlying price movements – broad economic developments, government policies, demography, corporate strategies'.[85] Such market indicators are then rearticulated or translated in the form of online chatrooms, financial news media, and mobile phone links to stockbrokers, eventually culminating in the trade. In capturing and modelling finance flows, trading software expresses various regimes of quantification that enable a value-adding process through the exchange of information within the immediacy of an interactive real-time system.

Such a process is distinct from 'ideal time', in which 'the aesthetic contemplation of beauty occurs in theoretical isolation from the temporal contingencies of value'.[86]

The *something more* that escapes both the parameters of chart-analysis software and fundamental analysis can be understood as 'the question of the constitutive gap between "reality" and simulations'.[87] The aesthetic figure for this constitutive gap consists of the power of affect. An affective dimension of aesthetics is registered in the excitement and rush of the trade; biochemical sensations in the body modulate the flow of information, and are expressed in the form of a trade. As Goldberg puts it in a report to the consortium midway through the project after a series of poor trades based on a combination of technical and fundamental analysis: 'It's becoming clearer to me that in trading this stock one often has to defy logic and instead give in, coining a well-worn phrase, to irrational exuberance'.[88] Here, the indeterminacy of affect subsists within the realm of the processual, where a continuum of relations defines the event of the trade. A continuity of movement prevails. Yet paradoxically, such an affective dimension is coupled with an intensity of presence where each moment counts; the art of day trading is constituted as an economy of precision within a partially enclosed universe or system.

Wark makes a similar point in his analysis of the stock market crash on Wall Street in October 1987. Drawing on Serres' notion (or was it an intuition?) of 'noise as a "third man" present in the exchange of information', Wark employs the metaphor of noise to explain the 'competing and contradictory interests', irrationality, feedback loops and unconventional techniques used by traders arguably more attuned to the informational patterns and flows in global finance markets.[89] As Wark puts it:

> Noise becomes a tool among others in what Donald Trump christened 'the art of the deal'. Profiting from noise becomes equivalent to profiting from information, and in the short term, possibly more profitable. The volume of movement caused by noise in the short term may be more profitable than the tendency of movement in the long run. Which is bad news for the fortunes of the firms that make and sell things on the terrain of second nature. One can indeed make

'cash from chaos', as the self-styled pop svengali Malcolm McLaren proposed. The third nature of global finance, like the third nature of global style, admits the *false move* as a profitable option.[90]

The borders of a processual system are also open to the needs and interests of extrinsic institutional realities. The node of the gallery presents what is otherwise a routine operation of a day trader as a minor event, one that registers the growing indistinction between art and commerce. Interestingly, the event-space of the gallery expresses the regularity of day trading with a difference that submits to the spatio-temporal dependency news media has on the categories of 'news worthiness'. A finance reporter for Murdoch's *The Australian* newspaper gives Goldberg's installation a write-up. Despite the press package which details otherwise, the journalist attempts to associate Goldberg's trading capital with an Australia Council grant (which financed the installation costs) as further evidence of the moral and political corruption among the 'chattering classes'. In this instance of populist rhetoric, the distinction between quality and tabloid newspapers is brought into question. The self-referentiality that defines the mode of organization and production within the mediasphere prompts a journalist from Murdoch's local Sydney tabloid, the *Daily Telegraph*, to submit copy on the event. Unlike the dismissive account in *The Australian* and the general absence of attention to the project by arts commentators, Goldberg notes how the *Daily Telegraph* report made the front page of the Business section (rather than the News or Entertainment pages), in full colour, with his picture alongside the banner headline 'Profit rise lifts News'. The headline for Goldberg's installation was smaller: 'Murdoch media the latest canvas for artist trader'.

Here, the system of relations between art and commerce also indicates the importance narrative or storytelling has in an age of information economies. Whether the price of stocks go up or down, profit value is shaped not, of course, by the kind of political critique art might offer, but rather by the kind of spin a particular stock can generate. Or, as Neil Chenoweth puts it in his book *Virtual Murdoch*, 'Markets work on appearances'.[91] Goldberg's installation discloses various operations peculiar to the aesthetics of day trading, clearly establishing a link between narrative, economy, time and risk, performance or routine practice and the mediating role of design and software aesthetics. *catchingafallingknife.com* demonstrates that it is the latter – a theory of software – that still requires much critical attention. And unlike most players in the new economy, Goldberg's installation is a model in accountability and transparency.

There is a process at work in all this, part of which involves a linear narrative of stabilization by structural forces. Massumi explains it this way: 'The life cycle of the object is from active indeterminacy, to vague determination, to useful definition (tending toward the ideal limit of full determination)'.[92] Yet this seemingly linear narrative or trajectory, if that's what it can be termed, is in no way a linear process. Quite the opposite. It is distributed or is constituted through and within a process of feedback where the technical object, in its nominated form, feeds back and transforms its conditions of possibility, which can be understood as 'the field of the emergence'.[93]

Given that the production of art has been ensconced within the cultural industries throughout the twentieth-century – and most particularly since the end of the Second World War – it really is remarkable how little attention is given by artists and critics to the basic economic conditions of production which make possible their very existence. Certainly, there are exceptions, as evidenced in the case of Goldberg's installation. But for the most part, artists have failed to inquire into the role of the economy as a constitutive force *within* and not outside of aesthetics. Yet strangely, both artists and critics seem to think the object or process of art is somehow immune to or autonomous from prevailing economic conditions. That strikes me as a hopelessly naïve and incredibly self-undermining position to adopt.

Don't get me wrong, I'm not suggesting artists return to some kind of social realist portrayal of workers in the factory and peasants in the field. Nor am I calling on critics to revert back to vulgar Marxist ideology critique. Let's not bore ourselves with regressive pastiche that's incapable of addressing the situation of contemporary media cultures. By engaging in a post-representational way with the economy, critical artists have a key role to play in redistributing the contingency of relations between economic conditions and aesthetic sensibilities. Now is the time to set a new aesthetic intelligence into play by creating new institutions of possibility, by organizing networks of sustainability, and by asserting a relationship between aesthetics and the economy in a way that does not resign the artist to the role of yet another self-governing entrepreneur within a 'creative economy'.

Towards a Politics of Processual Time

> Media cross one another in time, which is no longer history.
> Kittler[94]

> I speak once more in the language of history, processual time and its multiple circumstances pass through the cramped network of their own monuments.
> Serres[95]

The processual locates the temporal modes that operate within the information age. This is precisely why a processual model facilitates a political critique of network societies and information economies. Processes, after all, *take* time. That is, processes abstract time. A politics of legitimacy coextends with the instantiation of abstraction. Further, the fundamental problem with Lash's thesis in his book *Critique of Information* is his failure to engage with 'the political' by reducing the complexities of time.[96] Time is not simply 'long duration' that corresponds with old media and its mode of representation, as distinct from the 'short duration' or immediacy that supposedly defines the new media as ephemeral presentations.[97] Time consists of a multiplicity of modes: rhythmic, instrumental, scalar, biological, compressed, flexible, and so forth. Each temporal mode has a different function in the regulation, control and organization of entropy. Irrespective of its encoding mode, time is an agent of translation between stability and randomness. In this respect, time corresponds to the processual.

Modalities of time are also central to the constitutive framework within which politics happens. In the case of new media, a tension is played out across the temporal modes that distinguish new media forms and their concomitant uses and conditions of production. Each temporal mode is socially inscribed with varying degrees of legitimacy. For this reason, one can speak of a politics of time. New communications media consist of various temporal modes: mobile phones and instant short-text messaging, the web and real-time video and audio files, the interactive real-time of day trading, 24/7 and net-time,[98] and as Wark notes, 'many kinds of time intersect'.[99] Whatever the operative mode may be, time's multiplicity is internally situational to self-organizational closures or limits in social-technical complexity.[100] The contest over such closures thus constitutes the politics of technological time.

On the question of time and space, there are two key points to make. First, new media are characterized by their 'remediation' of the spatio-temporal aspects of old media.[101] The form, content, meaning and techniques of use peculiar to old media such as cinema and the novel are re-fashioned and reformed within new media technologies. New media technologies are thus better characterized in terms of the multidimensional layers of space and modalities of time; there is a continuum of relations, albeit reconfigured, rather than strict rupture between old media and new media. Referring to McLuhan, Kittler explains the media continuum as 'partially connected media links' in the following way:

> [O]ne medium's content is always other media: film and radio constitute the content of television; records and tapes the content of radio; silent films and audiotape that cinema; text, telephone, and telegram that of the semi-media monopoly of the postal system.[102]

Second, within a capitalist system, time determines exchange value in as much as the smaller and more flexible the increment of time the higher the exchange value. This operation also makes possible what Marx termed the 'annihilation of space through time', where more intensive cycles of production and consumption are required to speed up capital circuits, as Harvey has analysed.[103] And as Holmes has noted, 'If capital can't get the cycle speeds it needs, it lobbies for war – the exchange-value of armaments will go up as others deflate; capital flows to war according to the law of equalization of value, until the war's over'.[104] A processual model investigates the multiple, competing dimensions of time that condition the instance of exchange. Exchange value itself is processual, yet it appears as a simple linear instance of exchange. This feature is symptomatic of the politics of labour-power and the ways in which the process of abstraction within a technologically enriched capitalist system subsumes the field of forces that condition the instance of exchange. The processual model attempts to register the complexity of forces and non-linearity of communications systems. What is at stake, finally, is the question of the legitimacy of existence that is irreducible to the techniques of instrumental time promulgated by new media empirics.

Conclusion

More than anything, processuality is best understood as a mode of communicating. For this reason, the processual is integral to media theory. Communication is based upon relationships. Processual media theory attempts to identify the diagram of relations peculiar to particular media-information situations and events. Such a task inevitably addresses the operation of power as a constitutive force. Inquiries into power relationships can happen in two key ways: first, under the delusion of the detached, disinterested observer. Such an option is a false one. And it is one this book resists in chapter 1, where I stage a critique of non-governmental organizations and their relationship with developing states and supranational entities. The issues outlined in that chapter fold into a larger inquiry that underpins much of this book – namely, how political activists might best organize themselves in ways immanent to the media of communication as it articulates with the network of social relations.

In its own modest way, this chapter, and indeed the remainder of this book, engages with what Paul D Miller, a.k.a. DJ Spooky that Subliminal Kid, identifies as *the* problematic of our time: '[T]wenty-first-century aesthetics needs to focus on how to cope with the immersion we experience on a daily level'.[105] This brings me to the second option in analyses of power relations: immanent critique. Strange as it might sound, such a mode of critique within this book is informed by the histories of colonialism and the ravages and violence that attends epistemological and ontological frameworks that assume one can be detached or separate from a communicative situation. As the discussion in this chapter of day trading makes clear, a rationalist approach to the problem of communication systems is simply never going to work. While a direct engagement with the histories and literature of colonialism is not present in this book beyond a passing reference here and there, the lessons from colonialism can be detected in the reflexive empiricism adopted within this book. Immanent critique, as developed most explicitly over the previous two chapters, occupies a situation of reflexivity in terms of the interrelationships between institutional settings, epistemological frameworks and the media of communication.

These sorts of elements operate as constitutive forces in the development of the case studies and objects of critique. The mode of critique within a processual situation is never negative in the sense of negativity being that which subtracts something from something else. Since processuality consists of systems of relations that are mutually constitutive, the immanent critique or radical empiricism of processual media theory is an affirmative operation. This book has been motivated by a curiosity and passion for the potentiality of transformation within and intervention by networks of critical Internet researchers. Process, in this sense, involves modes of experimentation as far as techniques of critique and research go. I'm speaking here of something that Negri calls a 'tendential' method, one that 'consists of anticipating the value of things that form an evolving system of tendencies, or trends, which is to say things one thinks will end up coming to pass in the future'.[106] The reason a degree of experimentation, chance and potential 'defeat' attend such a mode of inquiry has to do with the inescapable contingencies of life as it subsists within media-information systems. Similarly, processuality, as a mode of communication, is coextensive with what Negri calls 'forms of life' that constitute the common.[107] Life as it resides within relations immanent to media of communication constitutes the common of this book.

6 Virtuosity, Processual Democracy
and Organized Networks

Language presupposes and, at the same time, *institutes* once again
the 'publicly organized space'.
Paolo Virno

I am a Stalinist – everyone should do as I say and think; I have no idea
what I am – I don't exist . . . . The contradiction between these two statements signals a tension between identity politics and the politics of
desubjectification. Identity operates within a regime of coding; desubjectification is a process of subjectivization and transversality in which
'relations are external to their terms'.[1] There is nothing essential about a
particular object, subject or thing that determines its relations. The externality of relations to their terms is what makes change possible. The
identity of the Stalinist emerges from a milieu of radical contingencies.
The individuation of the Stalinist is thus a potentiality that subsists
within the plane of immanence. The logic of coding is part and parcel
of the unforeseen capacities that define the outside of immanence.

The relationship between the overcoded subject and the process of
subjectivization is one of movement, and the movement between the
two comprises the force of processuality, and a politics of contingency
and potentiality. Stalinist subjects are everywhere – we are all Stalinists,
and we also don't exist. The force of relations external to their terms operate in a manner that continuously destabilizes the authoritarianism
of the Stalinist subject. The process of desubjectification corresponds
with the plane of immanence. This is the common from which exodus,
flight and exit subsist as potentialities – potentialities that can also be
found in the exploitation of cooperation that is the common of labour-
power.[2]

The analysis of these relations is a practice of radical empiricism.
Such an approach registers the ways in which the formation of coded
subjects (identity) is an internally generative operation within the distributed plane of subjectivization. As Antonio Negri has noted, 'From
the standpoint of the body, there is only relation and process'.[3] Such

196

a diagram of relations can be transfigured upon organized networks, whose capacity to develop new institutional formations is immanent to the workings of situated social-technical systems.[4] In both cases, there is a danger of identitarianism (the Stalinist subject) or what Gary Genosko calls 'bureaucratic sclerosis' (technicist institutions) overdetermining the unforeseen creative capacity of the plane of immanence.[5] I don't think it is too much a case of conceptual promiscuity to say that such an event is kept in check through the hegemonic operation between the coded subject and the constitutive force of the plane of immanence. A continuum of negotiation and re-manoeuvring characterizes the tension between the desire for rule on the part of the coded entity (be it a particular subject or institutional habitus) and the potentiality of difference and proliferation peculiar to the plane of immanence.

Summarizing the encounters between Félix Guattari and Italian autonomous thinkers in the late 1970s, Franco 'Bifo' Berardi explains the process of 'subjectivation' (or what I am terming subjectivization) as a displacing of the historical legacy of the Hegalian subject.[6] Berardi sees the autonomist political concept and strategy of 'refusal of work' in terms of processes of subjectivation. He considers the *operaismo* (workers) movements in Italy during the 1960s and '70s as an instantiation of the larger international transition from Fordism to post-Fordism:

> Refusal of work does not mean so much the obvious fact that workers do not like to be exploited, but something more. It means that the capitalist restructuring, the technological change, and the general transformation of social institutions are produced by the daily action of withdrawal from exploitation, of rejection of the obligation to produce surplus value, and to increase the value of capital, reducing the value of life.

Berardi is resolute that it was the process of autonomization among workers that 'provoked' the capitalist response of institutional and market deregulation. As much as workers may have escaped the industrial time of the factory, capital was awakened to new possibilities of managing time. The flexibilization of labour coupled with advances in information and communication technologies enabled capital to intensify the process of economic globalization. For Berardi, the transformation in the socio-technics of labour and production amounts to a 'capitalist takeover of social desire', resulting in an 'alliance between recombinant capital and cognitive work'. As labour-power has become integrated with the deterritorializing capacities of information technologies, the effectiveness of political organizations such as unions has, in many instances, declined. The result of this has been a tendency toward what I called 'disorganized labour' as distinct from 'immaterial labour'.

It is within such post-Fordist, informationized settings that the problematic of democracy has become renewed. Following the thesis advanced by Paolo Virno, I start with the premise that the decoupling of the state from civil society and the reassertion of the multitudes over the unitary figure of 'the people' coincides with a vacuum in political institutions of the state.[7] Against Mouffe's promotion of an 'agonistic democracy', I argue that the emergent idiom of democracy within networked, informational settings is a non- or post-representative one that can be understood in terms of processuality.[8] I maintain that a non-representative, processual democracy corresponds with new institutional formations peculiar to organized networks that subsist within informationality. In contrast, Mouffe has a faith that is still too deeply invested in political institutions of the modern state form and her agonistic democracy depends heavily on the institutional legitimacy of the state. As states across Western liberal democracies have increasingly disengaged from discourses of political and social citizenship in favour of the oxymoronic notion of individualized 'shareholder-democracy', the legitimacy of the state as a complex of representative institutions is only brought into greater question.

More significant for this book, which seeks to advance a political and media philosophy of processuality, is Mouffe's failure to recognize how media forms and institutions and their attendant practices have interpenetrated the ordinary lives of people, most especially since the creeping departure from the early 1980s onwards of the welfare state and its social-political institutions. As I have argued elsewhere in this book, it is important not to confuse the seeming disappearance of the state with its transformation.[9] We are witnessing the ongoing structural transformation of state apparatuses in ways that reproduce the patterns of change seen in a plethora of corporate, cultural and not-for-profit institutions. The gestures and protocols of transparency once associated with and expected from public institutions have given way to a corporate culture of secrecy. The privacy that once, quite paradoxically, 'deprived'[10] individuals of a voice and public presence has now become inverted: life within a reality-media complex voraciously extracts people from under the radar, extending the social-technical capacities of the mediasphere as the definitive organ of social and cultural legitimation and value formation.[11] Similarly, it has become routine practice for the state to tender its social services and fiscal management to firms that provide the best post-political packages for career politicians while, more insidiously, retaining the right of privacy common to corporate law – the 'confidentiality agreement' – that serves the interests of protecting corporate-state negotiations. Whereas privacy within an era of the bourgeois public sphere deprived the individual of a public presence, perversely, privacy in an epoch of neoliberalism functions to enhance the security of the corporate-state nexus.

Such changes in the way social relations are organized have not advanced toward some more enlightened, rational stage of social-political development. Instead, on the one hand, they have resulted in capital extending its destructive capacity with a massive intensification in environmental degradation associated with new techniques in agricultural and industrial production, the expansion of urban infrastructures and the demands by consumers for greater diversity of the same; in generations of people being left to live in poverty; and in technological advancements in the military-entertainment complex, which have fuelled the political economy of corporate governments as they impose their domestic agendas on minor states. Yet, on the other hand, the transformation of social relations and the techniques of organization more generally have coincided in recent years with a re-emergence and reassertion of the multitudes – a mutable movement of movements whose tactics of social-political intervention and cultural production have been greatly facilitated by the widespread availability of relatively cheap new media technologies associated with the Internet. Mailing lists, web campaigns, real-time audio-streaming, the mobile phone and blogs have played key roles in shaping the actions of tactical media. And, it should be said, such technologies have also benefited the interests of global capital. The difference between these two endeavours is one that runs along the lines of values, interests, constituencies and desires.[12] Hope is reasserting its force. The re-emergence of the multitudes as the inventors of another possible world, along with the gradual dissolution of supranational governing agencies such as the WTO and the increasing incapacity of powerful states such as the USA and Britain to manage their pursuits of crisis, are all part of a proliferation of signals that indicate the hegemony of neoliberalism is on the wane.

Against this backdrop, this chapter seeks to resituate Mouffe's notion of agonistic democracy as a radical pluralism within networked media ecologies. Such a shift necessitates new models with which to think and enact the possibility of radical democracy within a digital terrain. I deploy the notion of media translation as the figurative passage that ushers in the conditions for a processual democracy within network societies. With reference to the limits of both tactical media and traditional institutional structures, the chapter argues how the persistence of organized networks as new institutional forms depends upon addressing two key problematics: sustainability and scale. This chapter advances an argument for political activists to make a strategic turn in order to raise the stakes of what it means to live – and, indeed, how we live – within informational societies. In as much as processuality corresponds with social-technical networks of media-in-translation, so too do the multitudes – as a mutable, proliferating social-technical expression of life – hold the potential to create polities that support the ongoing formation of life as an affirmative force.

Finally, the task of this chapter is to identify how and why an institutional turn is now required among media activists. Of course there can be no definitive programme for such a shift. Nevertheless, emergences can be detected. 'Movement', writes Deleuze, 'is translation in space. Now each time there is a translation of parts in space, there is also a qualitative change in the whole'.[13] Transformations register on the radar of this media-informational present and hold the capacity to translate across social-technical networks in unforeseen ways. Pure virtuality.

Virtuosity and Processual Democracy

Surplus value is based on excess – an excess of labour-power. With a surplus of labour-power (unemployment), the cost of production decreases and profit rises. Labour-power, however, is predicated on coop-

eration, and herein lies the potential for transformation, since cooperation subsists in the plane of immanence, the common. The capacity for
the articulation of other values, and the mobilization of other affects is
immanent to the surplus value of labour-power. Surplus value can also
be understood as an individuation transduced from the pre-individuali-
ty of cooperation, of the 'general intellect'. This is what Negri identifies
as the 'ontology of the multitudes'. The cooperation peculiar to the surplus value of labour-power grants what Hardt and Negri identify, and
had previously dismissed, as the class dimension of the emergent social-
technical form of the multitudes, since exploitation conditions the possibility of cooperation.[14] The multitudes are co-extensive with cooperation. Since the surplus value of capital is parasitic upon and conditioned by cooperation, so too can the multitudes (cooperation) be understood as a class concept.

The organized network is a potentiality co-extensive with the
process of becoming instituted. Virtuosity, as the absence of an 'extrinsic product', institutes the political potential of organized networks.[15]
The virtuosos 'activity without an end product' is at once ordinary and
exceptional: ordinary in the sense that 'the affinity between a pianist
and a waiter', as anticipated by Marx, comprises the common of wage
labour in so far as 'the product is inseparable from the act of producing';
exceptional in the sense of the potential that subsists within perform-
ances with no end product holds the capacity of individuation – of
transformation of the common – into singularities with their own distinct universes of sensibility, logics of sensation, regimes of codification.[16] Institutions (coded formations) consist of practices and affects,
techniques and sensations. Institutions emerge within the interplay
between the plane of immanence and the plan of organization. Within
the cooperation common to surplus value's exploitation of labour-
power resides the potential for new relations, new institutions, new
socialities.

Yet can we become democratic? Since – following Virno, a Deleuzo-
Foucauldian line, along with a strand within political philosophy and
international relations – the activities of the multitudes are exterior to
the idea of *representation*, which is the key procedure by which modern
democracy figures itself, how might democracy constitute itself within
contemporary social-technical networks? To ask this question is also to

ask whether the mobilization of capacities within social-technical networks – or processes of translation which might incorporate computer systems, software designers, cognitive workers, and so on – can produce political institutions, or arrangements of the social. Moreover, and following Mouffe, it is to ask whether the realm of networks consist of or are articulated with a material dimension, hence constituting a 'politics', which Mouffe defines in her book *The Democratic Paradox* as 'the ensemble of practices, discourses and institutions that seek to establish a certain order and organize human coexistence in conditions that are always potentially conflictual because they are affected by the dimension of "the political"'.[17]

In other words, to ask the question of democracy with respect to actors, networks, processes of translation and politics is, at a fundamental level, to inquire into the power relations that condition the formation of the social. If the modern is underpinned by processes of translation, which might also be understood as 'border wars', then it might be said that the multitudes, as 'an infinity of singularities' that brings boundaries into question, inhabit the abstracted spaces of the modern.[18] As I discuss below, part of this 'border work' of the multitudes corresponds with what Virno identifies as the re-emergence of the multitudes as a force with presence in a post-Fordist era of capitalism. First, however, it is helpful to further distinguish the political concept of the multitude from the logic of representation. As Negri explains:

> Most generically, the multitude is diffident to representation because it is an incommensurable multiplicity. The people is always represented as a unity, whilst the multitude is not representable, because it is monstrous vis-à-vis the teleological and transcendental rationalisms of modernity.[19]

Virno suggests that the communicative performance of the multitudes constitutes 'the feasibility of a *non-representational democracy*'.[20] Virno is elusive when it comes to developing that proposition. A non- or post-representational democracy is one that no longer operates within constitutive framework of the nation-state and its associated institutions and civil society organizations. This is something Mouffe's 'agonistic democracy' is not able to confront. While Mouffe correctly wishes to go beyond rational consensus, deliberative models of liberal democracy, her proposition that agonistic democracies negotiate the antagonisms that underpin sociality is nevertheless one that is predicated on the maintenance of the state as modern complex of institutions. Mouffe has not made the passage into the post-Fordist state and its connection with capital's modes of informatized production and flexible accumulation. The informatization of social relations is nowhere to be found in Mouffe's thesis on agonistic democracy. As such, Mouffe is unable to describe the new modes of sociality, labour and politics as they are organized within network societies and information economies. Even so, her notion of an agonistic democracy – like Virno's non-representational democracy – can be retained, but only, I would suggest, when they are recast in terms of what I call a *processual democracy*. How might the politics of networks as they operate within informationalized institutional settings be understood in terms of a processual democracy?

A processual model of social-technical operations inquires into the movement between the conditions of possibility and that which has emerged within the grid of signs, codes and meanings – or what Deleuze understands as the immanent relationship between the plane of consistency and the plan of organization.[21] Conditions of possibility are different in kind from that which comes to be conditioned. There is no resemblance or homology between the two. Think back to the difference between the process of subjectivization and the Stalinist identity. There are relations between the two, but they are not of the same. External forces are not grids whose stabilizing capacity assures the intelligibility of a problematic as it coalesces within a specific situation.

Yet despite these dissonances, networks are defined by – perhaps more than anything – their organization of relations between actors, information, practices, interests and social-technical systems. The relations between these terms may manifest at an entirely local level, or they may traverse a range of scales, from the local to the national to the regional to the global. Whatever the scale may be, these fields of association are the scene of politics and, once they are located within institutional settings, are the basis of democracy in all its variations. A processual democracy goes beyond the state-civil society relation. That relation no longer exists. Processual democracies necessarily involve institutions, since institutions function to organize social relations. This isn't to say that in and of themselves the modulation of networks some-how automatically results in democracy. But it is to suggest that the processes by which networks undergo a scalar transformation signal the emergence of new institutional forms that are shaping politics as a non-representational idiom.

The potential of processual democracies is underpinned by the in-formatization of social relations. Berardi's model of the infosphere and the psychosphere is a useful one to describe the complex settings with-in which new polities may emerge.[22] Berardi's conception of the infos-phere as a technical, digital coding of data whose unilinear flows 'inter-mingle' with the unstable, recombinatory filter of the psychosphere is, however, only partially right.[23] The infosphere is, of course, much more complex. Think of the uneven geography of information, the political economy of root servers and domain names, and the competing inter-ests surrounding Internet governance debates and policy-making. The infosphere thus not only 'intermingles' with the psychosphere, it is inseparable from it: put in different terms, the real is always inscribed or present within the symbolic as an antagonism or trauma. The infos-phere is shaped by background noise, which Michel Serres defines as the 'absence of code'.[24] Processuality – the relationship between coding and conditions of possibility – incorporates background noise as a con-stitutive outside.

A processual democracy unleashes the unforeseen potential of af-fects as they resonate from the common of labour-power. Processual democracies also continue to negotiate the ineradicability of antago-nisms. Their difference lies in the affirmation of values that are internal to the formation of new socialities, new technics of relations. Certainly, they go beyond the limits of resistance and opposition – the primary ac-tivity of tactical media and the 'anti-corporatization' movements. This is not to dispense with tactics of resistance and opposition. Indeed, such activities have in many ways shaped the emergence of civil society val-ues into the domain of supranational institutions and governance, as witnessed in the World Summit on the Information Society debates. A radical adaptation of the rules of the game is a helpful way of thinking the strategic dimension of processual democracies.

Organized Networks

My argument is that in order for networks to organize mobile information in strategic ways that address the issues of scale and sustainability, a degree of hierarchization, if not centralization, is required. Let's not forget that for all the anti-state rhetoric of anarchists, they, like many 'radical' outfits, are renowned for being organized in highly hierarchical ways – typically around the cult of the alpha male. The point is that such organization occurs within the media of communication. Herein lies the difference between the organized network and the networked organization.[25] The latter consists, quite simply, of networking traditional institutional settings. The architectural configuration of the building provides the skeletal framework within which electronic and social networking is negotiated. Certainly, this is not as entirely straightforward as bringing in the stooges to refit the shell, like we see in all those house renovation and lifestyle TV shows that appeal to our aspirational fantasies. No doubt many people have heard of, if not directly experienced, the difficulties faced by many workers who over the past couple of decades had to adjust to the computerization of work environments.[26] Such changes require the acquisition of new skills and a transformation of habits. And this affects many, from the cognitariat to those engaged in more menial forms of labour. Nonetheless, the distinction remains: the techniques of governance within the networked organization, unlike the organized network, do not place a primacy on the media of communication. Or rather, bricks and mortar prevail as the substrate within which communication and social-technical relations are managed.

Organized networks, on the other hand, hold an entirely different range of potentialities with regard to the orchestration of social-technical relations. While organized networks principally consist of online forms of communication such as mailing lists, IRCS or newsgroups, it would be a mistake to overlook the importance of face-to-face meetings – or 'fleshmeets' or 'meatspaces', as the 1990s style cyberspeak would have it. Such occasions are crucial if the network is to maintain momentum, revitalize energy, consolidate old friendships and discover new ones, recast ideas, undertake further planning activities, and so on. Different spaces, different temporalities, different media of communication, different mediations of sociality. This is mediology. Translation is the media logic that makes possible a continuum of relations between one social-technical form of mediation and another. There is no *a priori* smoothness that defines a continuum of relations.[27] Frequently enough tensions are going to prevail. Antagonisms may indeed be immanent to the process of translation. Any media translation involves an engagement with 'the political'. Such is the relationship between the plane of consistency and the plane of organization. Both coexist within a field of sociality. It helps, then, to invent a media theory of these kinds of relations as a way of making intelligible and actionable the politics of informationality.

It is time to make a return to and reinvestment in strategic concepts, practices and techniques of organization. Let's stop the obsession with tactics as the modus operandi of radical critique, most particularly in the gross parodies of de Certeau one finds in US-style cultural studies.[28] Don't get me wrong – I'm not suggesting that the time of tactical media is over. Clearly, tactical media play a fundamental role in contributing to the formation of radical media cultures and new social relations. If one starts with the principle that concepts and practices are immanent to prevailing media forms, and not somehow separate from them, it follows that with the mainstream purchase of new media forms such as the Internet come new ways in which relations of production, distribution and consumption are organized. An equivalence can be found in the shift from centralized Fordist modes of production to decentralized post-Fordist modes of flexible accumulation. Strategies within the spatio-temporal peculiarities of the Internet are different from strategies as they operate within broadcast communications media. The latter ultimately conceives the 'audience-as-consumer' as the end point in the food chain of media production, whereas the former enables the 'user' to have the capacity to sample, modify, repurpose and redirect the social life of the semiotic object. Moreover, there are going to be new ways in which institutions develop in relation to Internet-based media culture. How such institutions of organized networks actually develop in order to obtain a degree of sustainability and longevity that has typically escaped the endeavours of tactical media is something that is only beginning to become visible.

Ultimately, the networked organization is distinguished by its standing reserve of capital and its exploitation of the potentiality of labour-power. Such institutions are motivated by the need to organize social relations in the hope of maximizing 'creativity' and regenerating the design of commodity forms that have long reached market saturation.[29] Virno's observation that post-Fordist 'labor has acquired the traditional features of political action' – thus reversing Hannah Arendt's thesis that politics is subsumed into the experience of labour – is a forceful one evidenced within the informational industries by the migration of tactical media style practices into more traditional institutional settings of both capital and its substrate, the neoliberal state.[30] Virno notes that the previously distinct and traditionally indisputable boundaries between labour, action and intellect have now become indiscernible within post-Fordist modes of production.[31] As Virno writes: 'the world of so-called post-Fordist labour has absorbed into itself many of the typical characteristics of political action … this fusion between Politics and Labour constitutes a decisive physiognomic trait of the contemporary multitude'.[32] This move of the multitudes into the sphere of post-Fordist production clearly signals the operation of the constitutive outside. But there are vital issues at stake here: issues of how a life is to be constituted, how it is to be invented within the network of relations that populate the common of creative potentiality. The clear danger is that politics, as 'a difference which makes a difference', becomes nothing more than market strategies aimed at commodity differentiation.[33]

By contrast, the kind of emergent organized networks that I'm speaking of are notable for the ways in which information flows and social-technical relations are organized around site-specific projects that place an emphasis on process as the condition of outcomes. The needs, interests and problems of the organized network coincide with its emergence as a social-technical form, whereas the traditional modern institution has become networked in an attempt to recast itself while retaining its basic infrastructure and work practices, clunky as they so often are. Strangely enough the culture of neoliberalism conditions the emergence of the organized network. The logic of outsourcing has demonstrated that the state still requires institutions to service society. Scale and cost were the two key objections 'econorats' and servants to neoliberalism responded to. Forget about ideology. These bureaucrats are highly neurotic, obsessive-compulsive types. They hate any trace of disorder and inefficiency, and the welfare state embodied such irritations.

The organized network can take advantage of such instituted patholo-
gies by becoming an educational 'service provider', for instance. The key
is to work out what values, resources and capacities distinguish your
network from the MIT model of 'free courseware'.[34] The other factor is to
work out a plan for sustainability – a clear lesson from the dotcom era.
With the multitudes situated in post-Fordist modes of production, an
opportunity presents itself – the opportunity to mobilize what Virno
calls the 'pure potential' of labour-power as an ethico-aesthetic force
into the process of eradicating capital's predisposition to marshal the
mode of production toward 'effective labour' as a service provision.

Translation, Transduction and Individuation

Code is a language whose precondition is the possibility for meaning
to be produced. Similarly, and like the relationship between the plane
of immanence and the plane of organization, individuation consists of a
process that Deleuze, Virno and Mackenzie call a *pre-individual reality*:
'Something common, universal and undifferentiated'.[35] Singularities
emerge out of common capacities: of language, of perception, of production.[36] Transduction is the complex of forces through which the process
of individuation translates pre-individual realities – that which is common – into singularities. As Adrian Mackenzie explains:

> The main point is that transduction aids in tracking processes that
> come into being at the intersection of diverse realities. These diverse
> realities include corporeal, geographical, economic, conceptual,
> biopolitical, geopolitical and affective dimensions. They entail a
> knotting together of commodities, signs, diagrams, stories, practices,
> concepts, human and non-human bodies, images and places. They
> entail new capacities, relations and practices whose advent is not al-
> ways easy to recognize. . . . Every transduction is an individuation in
> process.[37]

The organized network as a new institutional formation is another example of the stabilizing capacity of transductive forces. The primary difference, however, is that organized networks are shaped by the power
of social-technical needs, interests, affects and passions that hold the
potential to translate into new institutional forms. All communication

is a process of translation. Networks are uneven, heterogeneous modulations and combinations of communication in and through which translation is intrinsic to the connectivity of information as it encounters technical, social, political, economic and cultural fields of articulation, negotiation and transference. Translation, then, is about making connections between seemingly incommensurate things and objects. Translation conditions the possibility of communication, transversality, transduction, intensity and individuation between different systems.[38] From the connection emerges a new logic, a new sensibility and new capacities. At a very basic level, the logic of networks is the process of connectivity.

Networks have the capacity of transduction, which Adrian Mackenzie, via Gilbert Simondon, describes as a process of ontogenesis 'in which a metastability emerges' within biological and social-technical systems.[39] Or as Andrew Murphie puts it, 'transduction translates intensities so that they can be brought into individuating systems'.[40] The form of organized networks provides a mutable architecture in which matter is temporarily arrested within a continuum of differentiation and individuation. Transductive forces subsist within the relation between form and matter. The organized network can be considered as a new institutional actant whose political, economic and expressive capacities are shaped and governed by the metastability of the network system. The intelligibility of such arrangements, relations and informational flows is thus most accurately summarized by a theory of translation which incorporates processes of transduction. Translation is truly a concept of praxis. It is part and parcel of every network. Transduction conditions the possibility of organized networks as emergent institutional entities.

At the start of this chapter I made passing reference to the way in which the 'citizen-subject' has been supplanted by the individual who engages not with a democratic state but a shareholder-democracy. It's important to carefully distinguish the sense of *individualization* evoked here from the Simondonian idea of *individuation.* The former has been addressed by sociologists such as Beck and Lash in terms of individual subjects engaged in the self-management of 'risk' peculiar to the era of 'second modernity', while the latter, as discussed by Deleuze, Mackenzie and Virno, is understood as a processual ethico-political cartography of potentiality. Individuation is a process by which a multitude of subjectivities emerge from that which is common: living labour, life, general intellect, cooperation, sociality, exploitation by capital, and so on. The organized network carries the potential for the individuation of subjectivities into new institutional forms. This process is one of political invention. Individuals become individuated, organizing as multitudes, creating the potential for the emergence of instituted singularities. Beck and Lash, on the other hand, reduce and thus dismiss the possibility of institutional life as specific to an industrial era of risk society, or 'first modernity', which has been surpassed by an era of 'second modernity' characterized by disorganization, informationization and networks.

Beck initiates his book *What is Globalization?* with a rendition of the bleak outlook held by 'postmodernists' and neoliberal ideologues alike, who, by Beck's reckoning, associate the crisis of democratic polities with the erosion of traditional institutional forms. This shift arises as a result of 'the secular trend of *individualization*', which effects a loosening of social bonds.[41] Accompanying this trend, according to Beck's summation of the general discourse on economic globalization, is a society that has lost its 'collective self-consciousness and therefore its capacity for political action'.[42] Beck dismisses this fatalistic scenario in which the totalizing effects of economic globalization debilitate political action, though he sees such a discourse as little more than the incapacity of people to advance out the imbroglio of some kind of false-consciousness.[43] Beck's faith in the possibility of an alternative political culture is evidenced by the political actions undertaken by global civil society movements, which operate within a different dimension or layer of what he refers to as the experience of 'globality' – or a 'world society' conceived of as a 'multiplicity without unity', as distinct from processes of economic 'globalization' and the neoliberal ideology of 'globalism'.[44]

Certainly, Beck is correct to observe that the remodelling of the state within a neoliberal ideology has seen a shift of the modern state form away from the social. Yet he is mistaken, I would maintain, to see the decoupling of sociality from politics as corresponding with a decline in institutional forms and their techniques of organizing social relations within political frameworks. Not only does Beck overlook the continued purchase the state has on the management of everyday lives – think, for example, of the legal authority institutions of the state have in both the movement of peoples and the flow of information (for example, the WTO's TRIPS Agreement in 1995 and the bond with member states, enhanced national security measures with regard to the movement of individuals, and free-trade agreements that determine the composition of cultural commodities) – but, more significantly, he greatly underestimates the fundamental importance that institutions in a general sense play in the organization of social relations. Moreover, in terms of how to begin both theorizing and undertaking political action in a sustained manner within an informational society, the futility of Beck's position, by my reading, lies in its failure to recognize and imagine the ways in which the multitudes incorporate a strategic potential that can manifest in the creation of new institutional forms.

Lash arrives at a similar conclusion to Beck. Lash considers the shift from 'first modernity' to 'second modernity' as paralleling the decline of organizations (such as the firm, the institution, unions and the family) and the emergence of disorganizations (such as youth subcultures, criminal gangs, computer designers and the 'neo-family').[45] There is an implicit assumption here that, firstly, 'disorganized capitalism' is indeed disorganized – capital, here, is much better understood in my view in terms of what Harvey calls 'flexible accumulation'.[46] The rise of transnational capital has not at all meant that the firm or institution loses its hegemony as an architectonic form involved in the management of social relations and economic production. Far from it. Disorganized capitalism simply means that capital is organized differently. The primary activity by capital of organizing labour-power in order to effect production, distribution and exchange has not disappeared. Rather, it is dispersed and relocated on the basis of currency exchange rates, the cost of labour, taxation rates, government incentives (or, more properly, corporate welfare), levels of technical infrastructure and supporting service industries. Herein lies the flexibility of capital. Secondly, Lash assumes precisely the linear model that he seeks to reject, claiming that disorganized capital results in disorganized sociality. Disorganized capital is capital organized by different means. Similarly, 'disorganized sociality', consists, at least within the logic of informationality, of social relations organized in ways that are immanent to prevailing communications media. Lash is correct on this point, albeit without comprehending the ways in which a constitutive outside operates within the plane

of immanence. The overdetermining binary system by which Lash
secures his logic of disorganizations is worth quoting at length:

> Organizations and the 'power resources' that reside in organizations
> stand thus in no way in contradiction to the individualization
> process of high modernity. Indeed, individualization is the comple-
> ment, the other side of this organizational power. Organizational
> power is the condition of existence of individualization, and individ-
> ualization is the condition of existence of organizations ... What I
> want to argue, however, is that organizations and their accompany-
> ing power, and indeed individualization as we know it, are decaying
> social forms ... What is emergent is not so much organizations as
> *dis*organization, not so much individualization as sociality, and not
> so much power as violence ... Disorganizations are not the absence
> of organization, but the decline of organizations. The decline of or-
> ganized capitalism does entail a decline in organization and a rise in
> individualism. But it also entails a rise in certain forms of sociation
> that are non-organizational, indeed often non-institutional. So disor-
> ganizations are not the absence of sociation, but particular forms of
> sociation. They are chaos, not chaotic ... Disorganizations presume a
> certain level and a particular mode – or should we say singular mode
> – of individualization, though they are somehow at the same time
> much more collective than are organizations. Disorganizations pre-
> sume a different mode of individualization than organizations, they
> presume a non-utilitarian, non-strategic, non-identical mode of indi-
> vidualization ... Disorganizations are perhaps less hierarchical than
> horizontal. They are anti-system – they are too open to interference
> and invasion from the environment to be systems.[47]

To dismiss the technics of organization enlisted by the new social
movements is to rob them of vitality, and of the great urgency that now
beckons the multitudes to register their political potential on another
scale, and with a capacity for sustainability that has hitherto evaded
this common plurality of living labour. Or as Paul Miller puts it, 'What
differentiates today from yesterday is the scale and scope of the paradigm'.[48] Just as the pre-individual is common to the process of individuation, whereby capacities are that which are shared and coextensive,

so too the organized network as a new institutional form corresponds with the pre-individual as that which is held in common. Let me unpack this. If political and corporate institutions within an industrial era of 'first modernity' typically functioned to de-individualize the worker in terms of a common unit to be managed, then such institutions reify the worker as a mass and incapacitate the individual through the conformist unity of 'effective labour', 'the people' or 'the citizen'. In other words, the potential of labour-power as a common set of capacities – what Hardt and Negri understand as 'linguistic, communicational and affective networks' – is subordinated to the mode of production.[49] Virno explains: 'The capitalist production relation is based on the difference between labor-power and effective labor. Labor-power, I repeat, is pure *potential*, quite distinct from its correspondent acts'.[50] Moreover, it is this potential of labour-power that is of primary value for the capitalist. Virno again:

> Potential is something non-present, non-real; but in the case of labour-power, this non-present something is subject to the laws of supply and demand. Capitalists buy the *capacity* for producing as such ('the sum of all physical and intellectual aptitudes which exist in the material world'), and not simply one or more specific services.[51]

Such a notion of labour-power suggests that the 1960s and '70s autonomist mantra and radical worker movement's political strategy of a 'refusal of work' is perhaps more clearly expressed in terms of 'a refusal of potentiality' as it is subsumed by capital. Thus the key strategy for the multitudes is to secure their production of potentiality and direct it toward self-generating ends. The pure potential of labour-power turns on an important distinction that Virno reads into the 'mode of production'. Not only is 'mode of production' to be understood as 'one particular economic configuration', writes Virno, 'but also [as] a composite unity of forms of life, a social, anthropological and ethical cluster'.[52] The process of individuation subsists within and emerges from this commons as a plurality of differences. A mode of producing. The combinations, arrangements and expressions of these relations constitutes an 'ethical cluster'. An event. To be in relation is to become ethical. A productive force is at work. Individuation is a process of becoming individual within a multiplicity of relations. Thus, 'the individual is not just a result, but an *environment* of individuation'.[53] Within the social-technical environment of informationality emerges the organized network as a potentiality coextensive with the process of becoming instituted.

Conclusion

While I have been arguing for the need for organized networks to create – or what Berardi calls the unforeseen capacity to invent – new institutional forms, let me emphasize that such activity is not some kind of end in itself.[54] 'It is not a question of "seizing power"', as Virno writes of the force of the multitude, 'of constructing a new State or a new monopoly of decision-making; rather, it has to do with defending plural experiences, forms of non-representative democracy, of non-governmental usages and customs'.[55] The invention by the multitudes of new institutional forms, and the persistence of their attendant practices, is part of a process that exists within a larger and more complex field of critical Internet cultures. Such developments can only occur when the networks are attentive to the technological composition of communications media as that which consists of social-technical relationships.[56]

In order for tactical media and the movements to organize as networks that have multiple institutional capacities, there has to be – first and foremost – an intellect, passion and commitment to invention. There has to be a desire for social-technical change and transformation. And there needs to be a curiosity and instinct for survival to shift finance capital to places, people, networks and activities that hitherto have been invisible. The combination of these forces mobilizes information in ways that hold an ethico-aesthetic capacity to create new institutional forms that persist over time and address the spectrum of social-political antagonisms of information societies in a situated fashion.

The concept of the multitudes is a seductive one. It presents the 'radical intellectual' with an image of passion, change and, yes, even unity, which corresponds with an image of 'radical politics' as seen in the news media. The terribly dull thing about the multitudes is that 'they' – as a plurality of differences, a movement of movements, a performance 'with no end-product' – are not composed of 'enlightened', 'ordinary' people who enact the fantasies of the radical intellectual. In many ways, the multitudes are a distribution of disorganized, individualized workers – in the sense that Beck and Lash mean by this term – who possess a potential to encounter the transductive force of individuation that shifts the individualization of labour-power into a singularity with networked capacities. My argument throughout much of this book has been that such a transformation is conditioned by a capacity to become organized.

Notes

Introduction

1   See Paul Di Maggio (ed.), *The Twenty-First Century Firm: Changing Economic Organization in International Perspective*, Princeton: Princeton University Press, 2001; Brett Neilson and Ned Rossiter, 'From Precarity to Precariousness and Back Again: Labour, Life and Unstable Networks', *Fibreculture Journal* 5 (2005), http://journal.fibreculture.org/issue5/neilson_rossiter.html.

2   See Ulrich Beck, *The Brave New World of Work*, trans. Patrick Camiller, Cambridge: Polity, 2000; David Harvey, *A Brief History of Neoliberalism*, Oxford: Oxford University Press, 2005; Nigel Thrift, *Knowing Capitalism*, London: Sage, 2005.

3   As I discuss at greater length below and in chapters 1 and 2, representation in its party-political sense is antithetical to the logic of networks. See also Paolo Virno, *A Grammar of the Multitude*, trans. James Cascaito, Isabella Bertoletti, and Andrea Casson, forw. Sylvère Lotringer, New York: Semiotext(e), 2004.

4   Andrew Murphie defines the term 'technics' 'as a combination of technologies, systematic processes and techniques, whether these are found in the organization of living or non-living matter'. I adopt this sense of technics throughout this book. See Andrew Murphie, 'The World as Clock: The Network Society and Experimental Ecologies', *Topia: A Canadian Journal of Cultural Studies* 11 (Spring, 2004): 136. See also Lewis Mumford, *Technics and Civilization*, London: Routledge & Kegan Paul, 1934; Bruno Latour, *We Have Never Been Modern*, trans. Catherine Porter, Cambridge, Mass.: Harvard University Press, 1993; Christopher May, *The Information Society: A Sceptical View*, Cambridge: Polity, 2002.

5   The collaborative political concept of organized networks is one I have developed with Geert Lovink, Brett Neilson and Soenke Zehle. See, for instance, Geert Lovink and Ned Rossiter, 'Dawn of the Organised Networks', *Fibreculture Journal* 5 (2005), http://journal.fibreculture.org/issue5/lovink_rossiter.html.

6   The characteristics of different forms of networks were the topic of debate on the Nettime mailing list. See the archive for April, 2006, http://www.nettime.org.

7   Neilson and Rossiter, 'From Precarity to Precariousness'.

8   Here, I differ from Phil Agre, who sees complentarities between what he calls the 'commodity model' and the 'community model' in the 'institutional design of the university'. While there is much with which I agree in Agre's essay, my position does not see an affinity between the concept of communities and that of organized networks. Agre tends to conceive communities and new institutions as spaces of consensus, whereas I would take an opposite line: the social-technical dimensions of organized networks are better understood in terms of dissensus. Both economic and institutional design implications follow on from this distinction, which I develop throughout this book. See Phil Agre, 'Commodity and Community: Institutional Design for the Networked University', in Kevin Robbins and Frank Webster (eds), *The Virtual University? Knowledge, Markets and Managment*, Oxford: Oxford University Press, 2001, pp. 210-223.

9   Mike Newnham, 'Foreword', in Paul Miller and Paul Skidmore, *Disorganisation: Why Future Organisations must 'Loosen Up'*, London: Demos, 2004, p. 9. Available at: http://www.demos.co.uk/files/Disorganisation.pdf. Founded in 1993 by Marxist journalists and then positioning itself as an organ of Blair's New Left government, Demos defines itself as a think-tank for 'everyday democracy'.

10   Richard Florida, *The Rise of the Creative Class: And How It's Transforming Work, Leisure, Community and Everyday Life*, New York: Basic Books, 2002.

11   Geert Lovink holds another view: 'in my experience the call for disorganization has to be read as an attempt to crack up the closed structures of the firm, due to IP regimes, but also firewalls and most of

216

all the knowledge management systems. These are the main obstacles to introducing blogs and social network tools within organizations, be it for profit or non-profit'. It's at this point that questions of technical systems and organizational form come into play. Geert Lovink, email correspondence, 20 July, 2006.

12   This is not to regress to the equally deluded position of social-democratic politics – an accusation enough so-called autonomist and anarchist activists have levelled against me in the past.

13   Mario Tronti, 'The Strategy of Refusal', trans. Red Notes, in Sylvère Lotringer and Christian Marazzi (eds), *Italy: Autonomia, Post-Political Politics*, New York: Semiotext(e), 1980, pp. 28-35. I am drawing from a longer version of the essay available at: http://www.libcom.org/library/strategy-refusal-mario-tronti.

14   This was a point raised by Soenke Zehle and others at the close of *Incommunicado.05: Information Technology for Everybody Else*, Amsterdam, 16-17 June, 2005, http://incommunicado.info/conference. Geert Lovink and Christoph Spehr discuss the topic further in their text 'Out-Cooperating Empire: Exchange on Creative Labour and the Hyrbid Work of Collaboration', 2006. Available at: http://www.networkcultures.org/geert/2006/07/08/out-cooperating-the-empire-exchange-with-christoph-spehr/.
Earlier incarnations of the topic can be found in the various texts associated with the *Free Cooperation* conference organized by Trebor Scholz and Geert Lovink, Buffalo, New York, April 24-25, 2004, http://freecooperation.org/. Collected papers from that event have been published in Geert Lovink and Trebor Scholz (eds), *The Art of Online Collaboration*, New York: Autonomedia, 2006. See also the Institute for Distributed Creativity, http://distributedcreativity.org/.

15   This process is discussed and analysed at length in Saskia Sassen, *Territory, Authority, Rights: From Medieval to Global Assemblages*, Princeton: Princeton University Press, 2006.

16   For a history of La Borde, see Gary Genosko, *Félix Guattari: An Aberrant Introduction*, London and New York: Continuum, 2002; Félix Guattari, 'La Borde: A Clinic Unlike Any Other', trans. D. L. Sweet, in *Chaosophy*, ed. Sylvère Lotringer, Semiotext(e): New York, 1995, pp. 187-208.

17   Gary Genosko, 'Félix Guattari: Towards a Transdisciplinary Metamethodology', *Angelaki* 8.1 (2003): 29.

18   Ibid., p. 35.

19   See the National Endowment for Science, Technology and the Arts (NESTA), UK, partnership programmes for 'Futurelab', 'FameLab' and 'Zero-to-Hero', http://www.nesta.org.uk/insidenesta/hwf_extend.html.

20   My gloss here is derived from Rolf Wiggershaus, *The Frankfurt School: Its History, Theories and Political Significance*, trans. Michael Robertson, Cambridge, Mass.: MIT Press, 1994. See also Martin Jay, *The Dialectical Imagination: A History of the Frankfurt School and the Institute of Social Research, 1923-1950*, Berkeley: University of California Press, 1996.

21   Max Horkheimer, 'The Present Situation of Social Philosophy', in *Between Philosophy and Social Science: Selected Early Writings*, trans. G Frederick Hunter, Matthew S. Kramer, and John Torpey, Cambridge, Mass: MIT Press, 1993, p. 9.

22   An interesting connection can perhaps be made here with Virno on the instituting of the multitude: 'Multitude is the form of social and political existence for the many, seen as being many: *a permanent form*, not an episodic or interstitial form'. *A Grammar of the Multitude*, p. 21. My emphasis.

23   See Wiggershaus, pp. 431-435.

24   Ibid., p. 434.

25   Slavoj Žižek, *The Ticklish Subject: the Absent Centre of Political Ontology*, London: Verso, 1999, p. 74.

26   Comment made by Holmes at the *Finnish Social Forum*, Helsinki, 1-2 April, 2006. See video recordings of talks by Brian Holmes, Carlos Fernández, Ned Rossiter and Stevphen Shukaitis and the follow-up discussions at: http://www.m2hz.net/uusityo/index.php?title=Kommunikaatio.

27   Angela Mitropoulos and Brett Neilson, 'Exceptional Times, Non-Governmental Spacings, and Impolitical Movements', *Vacarme* (January, 2006), http://www.vacarme.eu.org/article484.html.

28   Obviously there are exceptions – here I am thinking of the important work by researchers such as Angela McRobbie, Rosalind Gill, Toby Miller and George Yúdice. See also the special issue on creative industries and cultural policy in the *International Journal of Cultural Policy* 11.1 (2005), edited by David

Hesmondhalgh and Andy C. Pratt. Essays on creative industries in *Mute Magazine's* (February, 2005) special issue on precarity are a standout example of political critique, http://www.metamute.org/?q=en/taxonomy/term/178.

29 Creative Industry Task Force: Mapping Document, DCMS (Department of Culture, Media and Sport) (1998/2001), London, http://www.culture.gov.uk/global/publications/archive_2001/ci_mapping_doc_2001.htm?properties=archive%5F2001%2C%2Fcreative%5Findustries%2FQuickLinks%2Fpublications%2Fdefault%2C&month=.

30 Up until this point I have rendered the constitutive outside as a *constituent force*. I adopt the former throughout this book despite the appeal the notion of a *constituent outside* holds. My reference here is to Negri, who makes a distinction between the concept of 'constituent power' and 'constituted power'. In short, 'constituent power ... resists being constitutionalized'. And: 'To speak of constituent power is to speak of democracy.... constituent power has been considered not only as an all-powerful and expansive principle capable of producing the constitutional norms of any juridical system, but also as the subject of this production – an activity equally all-powerful and expansive. From this standpoint, constituent power tends to become identified with the very concept of politics as it is understood in a democratic society. To acknowledge constituent power as a constitutional and juridical principle, we must see it not simply as producing constitutional norms and structuring constituted powers but primarily as a subject that regulates democratic politics'. By my reading, this sketch of constituent power is consistent with my deployment of the concept of a constitutive outside. See Antonio Negri, *Insurgencies: Constituent Power and the Modern State*, trans. Maurizia Boscagli, Minneapolis: University of Minnesota Press, 1999, p. 1.

31 Branden W. Joseph and Paolo Virno, 'Interview with Paolo Virno', trans. Alessia Ricciardi, *Grey Room* 21 (Fall, 2005): 32, http://mitpress.mit.edu/journals/pdf/GR21_026-037_Jospeph.pdf.

32 See Neilson and Rossiter, 'From Precarity to Precarious and Back Again'.

33 Harold A. Innis, *The Bias of Communication*, Toronto: University of Toronto Press, 1951.

34 Robins and Webster, *The Virtual University?*, p. 5.

35 Of course the TRIPS Agreement does not inaugurate the international approach to copyright regulation and harmonization. The nineteenth century *Berne Convention* established the international standards to copyright to which the laws of member states must conform. As I note above, the WTO's TRIPS Agreement coincides with the informatization of the commodity object and labour-power, thus amplifying legal regimes and discourses as a biopolitical force.

36 See Simon Marginson and Mark Considine, *The Enterprise University: Power, Governance and Reinvention in Australia*, Cambridge: Cambridge University Press, 2000; David Noble, *Digital Diploma Mills: The Automation of Higher Education*, New York: Monthly Review Press, 2002; Robbins and Webster, *The Virtual University?*; Marc Bousquet, 'The "Informal Economy" of the Information University', *Workplace: A Journal for Academic Labour* 5.1 (2002), http://www.cust.educ.ubc.ca/workplace/issue5p1/bousquet-informal.html.

37 See Florian Schneider's documentary *Organizing the Unorganizables* (2002), downloadable at: http://wastun.org/organizing.

38 In this regard, sociality can be understood as the empty centre of neoliberalism in so far as neoliberalism disavows the social. Thatcher put this most explicitly in that much cited declaration of hers: 'There is no such thing as society' (and she then goes on to say that individuals and the family are fine). In a rhetorical sense, neoliberalism has no *sense* of the social, and what it passes off as social – individual relations of self-improvement, risk, responsibility, etcetera – are indeed empty. Yet we know that it is also impossible for anything to emerge without the constituent force of social relations, and this is where sociality operates as the constituent outside of neoliberalism – structurally, psychically, etcetera – that is going to come back and bite neoliberalism on the arse. That doesn't necessarily mean in any organized sense, but rather as a force of relations (a sociality of things in the broad sense such as pollution, contaminated foods and environmental degradation) that coalesce around a set of problematics expressed in terms other than neoliberalism.

39 An EU initiative since 1999 aimed at establishing uniform standards across European universities in order to encourage the movement of students, teachers and researchers.

40 Bologna Secretariat, http://www.dfes.gov.uk/bologna/.

41 Admissions Officers and Credential Evaluators' (ACE) professional section of the European Association for International Education (EAIE), http://www.aic.lv/ace/default.htm.

42 Of course NGOS and grass-roots organizations such as community networks have long histories of incorporation. But for some reason very few networks have done this. Thing.Net and xs4all are exceptions that come to mind. Yet these networks seem to have reached a plateau, and perhaps even stagnated, as just yet another option in the sea of ISPs to choose from, albeit with their own brand of special attractors.

43 Projects Schneider and Lang have either initiated or participated in include Borderline Academy, Makeworlds, Incommunicado, Was Tun?, Noborder Network, and V2V Video Syndication Network. A full listing can be found at: http://www.kein.org/projects.

44 Gregory Bateson, 'Form, Substance, and Difference', in *Steps to an Ecology of Mind*, New York: Ballantine Books, 1972, p. 453. Italics in original.

45 See Tiziana Terranova, 'Free Labor: Producing Culture for the Digital Economy', *Social Text* 18.2 (2000): 33-58.

46 Bousquet, 'The "Informal Economy" of the Information University'.

47 Julian Kücklich, 'Precarious Playbour: Modders and the Digital Games Industry', *Fibreculture Journal* 5 (2005), http://journal.fibreculture.org/issue5/kucklich.html.

48 World Commission on the Social Dimension of Globalization, *A Fair Globalization: Creating Opportunities for All*, Geneva: International Labour Organization: 2004, http://www.ilo.org/public/english/fairglobalization/report/index.htm.

49 OECD, *Governance in the 21st Century*, Paris: OECD, 2001, p. 4, http://www.oecd.org/dataoecd/41/42/35391582.pdf.

50 A point made in Spehr's contributions to Free Cooperation.

51 In fact one can simply view the history link in order to see the names and IP addresses that comprise the distribution of labour.

52 Joseph Reagle, 'Open Communities and Closed Law', Open Codex weblog, 13 June, 2006, http://reagle.org/joseph/blog/culture/wikipedia/open-discourse-closed-law?showcomments=yes.

53 Antonio Negri with Anne Dufourmantelle, *Negri on Negri*, trans. M. B. DeBevoise, London and New York: Routledge, 2004, p. 117.

54 In this sense, a medium theory of network cultures necessarily combines both social and technical dimensions of communication and cannot simply be reduced to notions of media as container devices of communication.

55 Having said this, I am inconsistent in my use of institutional forms over institutions. This is largely a matter of style and syntax. Where I connect institutions to networks, I am thinking of forms.

56 Manuela Bojadzijev and Isabelle Saint-Saëns, 'Borders, Citizenship, War, Class: A Discussion with Étienne Balibar and Sandro Mezzadra', *New Formations* 58 (2006): 22-24.

57 Angela Mitropoulos and Brett Neilson, 'Cutting Democracy's Knot', *Culture Machine* 8 (2006), http://culturemachine.tees.ac.uk/Articles/neilson.htm.

58 Tiziana Terranova, *Network Culture: Politics for the Information Age*, London: Pluto, 2004, pp. 28, 35.

59 Ibid., pp. 36-37.

60 As I write, these are all issues currently being discussed and debated on the collaborative blog Long Sunday <http://www.long-sunday.net/long_sunday/>, with parallel thought on a range of personal blogs, Jon Beasley-Murray's Posthegemony <http://posthegemony.blogspot.com/> among them. See the late July 2006 archives on these blogs.

61 Mario Tronti, *La politica al tramonto*, Torino: Einaudi, 1998. Thanks to Brett Neilson for assistance with translation.

62 Jon Beasley-Murray, 'Politics', Posthegemony: Hegemony, Posthegemony, and Related Matters, 16 July, 2006, http://posthegemony.blogspot.com/2006/07/politics.html.

63 Cf. Beasley-Murray. Virno, *A Grammar of the Multitude*, chapters 1 and 6.

64 Virno, *A Grammar of the Multitude*, p. 40.

65   Benita Parry, 'Internationalism Revisited or In Praise of Internationalism', *Variant* 17 (2003),
     http://www.variant.randomstate.org/17texts/17benitaparry.html. A much harsher critique of *Empire*
     can be read in Timothy Brennan, 'The Empire's New Clothes', *Critical Inquiry* 29.2 (2003): 337-367.

66   See Sassen, *Territory, Authority, Rights*, especially chapter 7.

67   See David Harvey, 'Globalization in Question', *Rethinking Marxism* 8.4 (1995): 1-17.

Chapter 1

1   For a brief genealogy of the term social capital, see Phillip E. Agre, 'Real-Time Politics: The Internet
     and the Political Process', *The Information Society* 18.5 (2002): 311-331. Also available from: http://po-
     laris.gseis.ucla.edu/pagre/real-time.html. For an autonomist deployment of the term, see Mario Tron-
     ti, 'Social Capital', *Telos* 17 (1977): 98-121.
     Over the past decade, however, the term social capital is more often associated with proponents of
     Third Way politics. See Anthony Gidddens, *The Third Way: the Renewal of Social Democracy*, Cam-
     bridge: Polity Press, 1998; Mark Latham, *What did you Learn Today? Creating an Education Revolution*,
     Crows Nest: Allen & Unwin, 2001, pp. 62-100.

2   Gary Genosko, 'Félix Guattari: Towards a Transdisciplinary Metamethodology', *Angelaki* 8.1 (2003):
     33.

3   Chantal Mouffe, *The Democratic Paradox*, London: Verso, 2000, p. 3.

4   Ibid.

5   Ibid., pp. 102-103, 135.

6   Chantal Mouffe, *On the Political*, London and New York: Routledge, 2005.

7   Paolo Virno and Maurizio Lazzarato, 'Multitude/working class [interview]', trans. Arianna Bove, *Mul-
     titudes* 9 (May-June, 2002), http://multitudes.samizdat.net/Multitude-working-class.html.

8   Not even when she is participating with political activists addressing the theme of infopolitics does
     Mouffe rethink her argument on institutions, as on the occasion of the *Dark Market: Infopolitics, Elec-
     tronic Media and Democracy in Times of Crisis* conference held at Public Netbase in Vienna, 2002. For
     full documentation, including Mouffe's paper, 'Which Democracy in a Post-Political Age', 2002, see
     http://darkmarkets.to.or.at.

9   Mouffe, *On the Political*, p. 9. See also Ernesto Laclau, *On Populist Reason*, London and New York: Verso,
     2005, pp. 70-71, 87.

10   See Geert Lovink, *My First Recession: Critical Internet Culture in Transition*, Brussels and Rotterdam:
     V2/NAi Publishers, 2003, pp. 121-126.

11   http://aoir.org.

12   See Scott Lash, *Critique of Information*, London: Sage, 2002.

13   Mouffe, *On the Political*, p. 15. While there are significant differences, the constitutive outside is an op-
     eration similar to what systems theorists and cyberneticists would term 'organizational closure' or
     'noise', which I discuss in chapter 5.

14   Laclau, *On Populist Reason*, p. 241.

15   Those who entertain online systems of voting or 'e-democracy' believe they are transposing the cen-
     tral tenets of representative liberal democracy into 'virtual' settings. Far from it. Such projects high-
     light the evacuation of adversaries engaged in a hegemonic process, and instead embody the very
     failure of representative systems to address the tensions that underscore sociality.

16   Mouffe, *On the Political*, p. 33.

17   See Ernesto Laclau, 'Can Immanence Explain Social Struggles?, in Paul A. Passavant and Jodi Dean
     (eds), *Empire's New Clothes: Reading Hardt and Negri*, New York and London: Routledge, 2004, p. 27; La-
     clau, *On Populist Reason*, pp. 240, 242. Mouffe makes a similar argument to Laclau, claiming the 'the
     constitutive character of antagonism is denied'. *On the Political*, p. 107.

18   See Gilles Deleuze, *Foucault*, trans. Seán Hand, forw. Paul Bové, Minneapolis: University of Minnesota
     Press, 1988.

19   Laclau, 'Can Immanence Explain Social Struggles?', p. 27.

20   Laclau, *On Populist Reason*, p. 245.

21   For a critique of post-political theorists, see Mouffe, *On the Political*, pp. 35-63.

22   Ibid., p. 95.

23 See Ned Rossiter, 'Modalities of Indigenous Sovereignty, Transformations of the Nation-State, and Intellectual Property Regimes', *Borderlands E-Journal: New Spaces in the Humanities* 1.2 (2002), http://www.borderlandsejournal.adelaide.edu.au/issues/vol1no2.html.

24 Wolfgang Kleinwächter, 'Civil Society and Global Diplomacy in the 21st Century: The Case of WSIS or from Input to Impact?', February, Version 1.0, 2005.

25 For a brief outline of some of the tensions peculiar to multi-stakeholderism as the preferred model of governance at WSIS, see Stijn van der Krogt, 'On Multi-stakeholderism', posting to incommunicado mailing list [sent by Geert Lovink], 27 May, 2005, http://incommunicado.info/mailinglist.

26 I recently outlined some of the alternative funding models that have been proposed in the creative industries in the UK and the Netherlands. While I'm critical of these models, which include a financing stream heavily dependent on regulating telcos and ISPs and the expansion of collecting agencies as intermediaries for media productions commissioned under a Creative Commons license, they none the less are indicative of a discussion that organized networks can learn from if they are going to have any possibility of scaling up their operations. For a video recording of my talk on 'Creative Industries, Organized Networks and Open Economies', Kwan Fong Cultural Development and Research Programme, Lingnan University, Hong Kong, 24 May, 2005, see: http://libmedia.ln.edu.hk/media3/www/lib/04-05-3/rossiter050524.htm. Abstract: http://www.ln.edu.hk/ihss/crd/cm200405.htm.

27 See Robin Blackburn, 'The Enron Debacle and the Pension Crisis', *New Left Review* 14 (2002): 26-51.

28 See Ankie Hoogvelt, *Globalization and the Postcolonial World: The New Political Economy of Development*, London: Palgrave, 2001, pp. 181-182.

29 Ibid., p. 184.

30 See Simon Cooper, 'Post Intellectuality?: Universities and the Knowledge Industry', in Simon Cooper, John Hinkson and Geoff Sharp (eds), *Scholars and Entrepreneurs: the University in Crisis*, Fitzroy: Arena Publications, 2002, pp. 207-232; Simon Marginson and Mark Considine, *The Enterprise University: Power, Governance and Reinvention in Australia*, Cambridge: Cambridge University Press, 2000. See also Brian Holmes, 'The Flexible Personality' (Parts 1 & 2), posting to nettime mailing list, 5 January, 2002, http://www.nettime.org.

31 Mary Kaldor, *Global Civil Society: An Answer to War*, Cambridge: Polity, 2003.

32 Rebecca Knuth, 'Sovereignty, Globalism and Information Flow in Complex Emergencies', *The Information Society* 15 (1999): 15.

33 See Alexander Cooley and James Ron, 'The NGO Scramble: Organizational Insecurity and the Political Economy of Transnational Action', *International Security* 27.1 (2002): 5-39.

34 This period is covered in Geert Lovink, *Dark Fiber: Tracking Critical Internet Culture*, Cambridge, Mass.: MIT Press, 2002, pp. 115n41, 296-304. See also the nettime archives, http://www.nettime.org.

35 Geert Lovink, 'Interview with Saskia Sassen on PGOs (for N5M3 TV)', posting to nettime mailing list, 25 February, 1999, http://www.nettime.org.

36 Cf. Cooley and Ron, 'The NGO Scramble: Organizational Insecurity and the Political Economy of Transnational Action'.

37 Ghassan Hage, *Against Paranoid Nationalism: Searching for Hope in a Shrinking Society*, Annandale: Pluto Press, 2003.

38 See Knuth, 'Sovereignty, Globalism and Information Flow in Complex Emergencies', pp. 15-16.

39 Martin Shaw, *Theory of the Global State: Globality as an Unfinished Revolution*, Cambridge: Cambridge University Press, 2000.

40 Manuel Castells, 'Information Technology, Globalization and Social Development', UNRISD Discussion Paper, no. 114, September, 1999. Available at: http://www.unrisd.org/unrisd/website/document.nsf/(httpPublications)/F270E0C066F3DE7780256B67005B728C?OpenDocument.

41 Hoogvelt, *Globalization and the Postcolonial World*, p. 173. See also Heribert Dieter, 'World Economy: Structures and Trends', in P. Kennedy, D. Messner and F. Nuscheler (eds), *Global Trends and Global Governance*, London: Pluto Press and Development and Peace Foundation, 2002, p. 69.

42 Paul Blustein, 'IMF Medicine: the Right Cure?', *International Herald Tribune* 27 September, 2002, p. 9.

43 David and Foray, 'An Introduction to the Economy of the Knowledge Society', *International Social Science Journal* 171 (2002): 9.

44 Ibid, p. 10.

45 See Christopher May, *The Information Society: A Sceptical View*, Cambridge: Polity, 2002, p. 130. Ted Byfield makes this point in quite different ways: '... systems of property are a by-product of the state. extending such a system necessarily involves extending and/or deepening the reach of the state'. Response to the Intellectual Property Regimes and Indigenous Sovereignty thread on nettime, 27
March, 2002, http://www.nettime.org. Byfield sees this as a negative development, though I think
that depends entirely upon one's economic, social-political and geographic situation.

46 Ibid, p. 141.

47 Castells, 'Information Technology, Globalization and Social Development', p. 16.

48 Rossiter, 'Modalities of Indigenous Sovereignty, Transformations of the Nation-State, and Intellectual
Property Regimes'.

49 See Christine Morris and Michael Meadows, 'Indigenising Intellectual Property', *Griffith Law Review*
9.2 (2000): 212-226.

50 Comment made during a panel discussion at the *Dark Market: Infopolitics, Electronic Media and Democracy in Times of Crisis* conference held at Public Netbase in Vienna, 2002, http://darkmarkets.to.or.at.

Chapter 2

1 See Ankie Hoogvelt, *Globalization and the Postcolonial World: The New Political Economy of Development*,
London: Palgrave, 2001, p. 176.

2 Mary Kaldor, *Global Civil Society: An Answer to War*, Cambridge: Polity, 2003, p. 32.

3 Ibid., pp. 31-32.

4 Michael Hardt and Antonio Negri, *Multitude: War and Democracy in the Age of Empire*, New York: Penguin Press, 2004, p. 6.

5 Michael Hardt, 'The Withering of Civil Society', *Social Text* 14.4 (1995): 40.

6 Although the so-called 'decline' of state sovereignty and non-state institutions is peculiar to a modern era of sovereignty. I maintain that state sovereignty has transformed rather than disappeared.
Similarly, the role of non-state institutions can be considered in terms of emergent civil society
movements.

7 In his biographical and biopolitical abecedary undertaken in collaboration with Anne Dufourmantelle, Negri defines 'Empire' even more precisely as: 'The transfer of sovereignty of nation-states to a
higher entity'. Antonio Negri with Anne Dufourmantelle, *Negri on Negri*, trans. M. B. DeBevoise, London and New York: Routledge, 2004, p. 59.

8 Michael Hardt and Antonio Negri, *Empire*, Cambridge, Mass.: Harvard University Press, 2000, pp. 328-
329.

9 See Jürgen Habermas, *The Structural Transformation of the Public Sphere: An Inquiry into a Category of
Bourgeois Society*, trans. Thomas Burger with Frederick Lawrence, Cambridge, Mass.: MIT Press, 1989.

10 See Kaldor, *Global Civil Society*, pp. 15-49.

11 Raymond Williams, 'Dominant, Residual and Emergent', in *Marxism and Literature*, Oxford: Oxford
University Press, 1977, pp. 121-127.

12 Mark Surman and Katherine Reilly, *Appropriating the Internet for Social Change: Towards the Strategic
Use of Networked Technologies by Transnational Civil Society Organizations*, version 1.0, New York: Social
Science Research Council, 2003. Available at http://www.ssrc.org/programs/itic/.

13 Mark Surman and Katherine Reilly, *Executive Summary. Appropriating the Internet for Social Change: Towards the Strategic Use of Networked Technologies by Transnational Civil Society Organizations*, version
1.0, New York: Social Science Research Council, 2003, p. 3. Available at http://www.ssrc.org/pro-
grams/itic/.

14 When I speak of scale throughout this chapter, I am referring to the capacity of actors to operate
across a range of levels of governance and practice. Different scales or spatialities of operation include, for example, supranational, national, transnational, translocal, and intraregional layers of relations.

15 For background information and critical reports on the WSIS, see http://www.itu.int/wsis,
http://www.wsis-online.org, http://www.unicttaskforce.org, http://www.apc.org, http://www.ssrc.org,
http://www.southcentre.org. See also reports and debates on nettime ‹http://www.nettime.org› and
incommunicado ‹http://www.incommunicado.info›. See also Valeria Betancourt, *The World Summit*

on the Information Society (WSIS): Process and Issues Debated, Association for Progressive Communications (APC), 2004, http://www.apc.org.

16 See William J. Drake (ed.), *Reforming Internet Governance: Perspectives from the Working Group on Internet Governance (WGIG)*, New York: United Nations ICT Task Force, 2005. Available at: http://www.wgig.org/docs/book/WGIG_book.pdf. See also Danny Butt (ed.), *Internet Governance: Asia-Pacific Perspectives*, New Dehli: Elsevier and UNDP Asia-Pacific Development Information Programme, 2005. Available at: http://www.apdip.net/publications/ict4d/igovperspectives.pdf.

17 WSIS Plan of Action, Geneva, 12 December, 2003, http://www.itu.int/dms_pub/itu-s/md/03/WSIS/doc/S03-WSIS-DOC-0005!!PDF.pdf.

18 Sasha Costanza-Chock, 'WSIS, the Neoliberal Agenda, and Counter-proposals from 'Civil Society', posting [by Geert Lovink] to nettime mailing list, 12 July, 2003, http://www.nettime.org.

19 Yoshio Utsumi, Secretary-General of the ITU, cited in Constanza-Chock, 2003.

20 Steve Cisler, 'ICANN or UN?', posting to nettime mailing list, 12 December, 2003, http://www.nettime.org.

21 http://www.icann.org/general.

22 See Adam Peake, *Internet Governance and the World Summit on the Information Society (WSIS)*, Association for Progressive Communications, 2004, p. 9, http://rights.apc.org/documents/governance.pdf.

23 See Alexander Galloway, *Protocol: How Control Exists After Decentralization*, Cambridge, Mass.: MIT Press, 2004.

24 Peake, *Internet Governance and the World Summit on the Information Society*.

25 The kind of regionalism constituted by the cloning of root servers raises another interesting issue: namely, the geography of power that attends the complex multilayered dimensions of competing 'regionalisms'. How, for example, does the informational regionalism of the Anycast system reproduce or contest more established regional formations of transnational cultural flows and the diaspora of labour-power, or the regionalisms of multilateral trade agreements and economic blocs, or the subnational, intraregional formations of civil society movements?

26 Peake notes that 'The request of the WSIS Plan of Action to deploy 'regional root servers' was achieved even before the Summit was held' (10). The question remains as to whether this plan is put into effect – something that is still far from certain after the 2005 Summit.

27 Ibid, p. 10.

28 See Carlos M. Correa and Sisule F. Musungu, *The WIPO Patent Agenda: The Risks for Developing Countries*, Trade Related Agenda, Development and Equity (T.R.A.D.E.), Working Papers, no. 12, South Centre, 2002, http://www.southcentre.org/publications/wipopatent/wipopatent.pdf.

29 Carlos M. Correa, *The WIPO Draft Substantive Patent Law Treaty: A Review of Selected Provision*, Working Papers, no. 17, South Centre, 2004, p. 9, http://www.southcentre.org/publications/workingpapers/paper17/wp17.pdf.

30 Civil Society Declaration to the World Summit on the Information Society, *Shaping Information Societies for Human Needs*, WSIS Civil Society Plenary, Geneva, 2003, http://www.itu.int/wsis/docs/geneva/civil-society-declaration.pdf.

31 Peake, cited in Ted Byfield, 'CCTLDS, WSIS, ITU, ICANN, ETC', posting to nettime mailing list, 7 March, 2003, http://www.nettime.org.

32 Byfield, 'CCTLDS, WSIS, ITU, ICANN, ETC'.

33 See WSIS Declaration of Principles, Geneva, 12 December, 2003, http://www.itu.int/dms_pub/itu-s/md/03/wsis/doc/S03-WSIS-DOC-0004!!PDF-E.pdf; WSIS Plan of Action, 2003.

34 Jean-François Lyotard, 'The *Différend*, the Referent, and the Proper Name', trans. Georges Van Den Abbeele, *Diacritics* 14.3 (1984): 4-14; Jean-François Lyotard, *The Différend: Phrases in Dispute*, trans. Georges Van Den Abbeele, Minneapolis: University of Minnesota Press, 1988.

35 John Palfrey, 'The End of the Experiment: How Icann's Foray into Global Internet Democracy Failed', *Harvard Journal of Law & Technology* 17 (2004): 411-412.

36 Daniel Bensaid, 'Sovereignty, Nation, Empire', trans. Isabel Brenner, Kathryn Dykstra, Penny Oliver and Tracey Williams, in William F. Fisher and Thomas Ponniah (eds), *Another World Is Possible: Popular Alternatives to Globalization at the World Social Forum*, London and New York: Zed Books, 2003, p. 317.

37 Palfrey, 'The End of the Experiment: How Icann's Foray into Global Internet Democracy Failed', p. 412.

38 Ibid.

39 Ibid., pp. 412-413.

40 For an argument of how intellectual property regimes hold the potential to advance indigenous sovereignty movements in Australia, see Rossiter, 'Modalities of Indigenous Sovereignty, Transformations of the Nation-State, and Intellectual Property Regimes'.

41 See Thomas Frank, *One Market Under God: Extreme Capitalism, Market Populism, and the End of Economic Democracy*, New York: Anchor Books, 2000; Doug Henwood, *After the New Economy*, New York: The New Press, 2003; Geert Lovink, *My First Recession: Critical Internet Culture in Transition*, Rotterdam: V2/NAi Publishers, 2003, pp. 56-85.

42 Geert Lovink and Jeanette Hofmann, 'Open Ends: Civil Society and Internet Governance [Interview]', posting to nettime mailing list, 12 August, 2004, http://www.nettime.org.

43 http://www.apc.org/english/index.shtml.

44 See Claudia Padovani and Arjunna Tuzzi, *Global Civil Society and the World Summit on the Information Society: Reflections on Global Governance, Participation and the Changing Scope of Political Action*, Social Science Research Council, New York, 2004, http://www.sscr.org/programs/itic/publications/knowedge-report/memos/padovani3-4-30-04.pdf.

45 See Lovink, *My First Recession*, pp. 57-85.

46 Padovani and Tuzzi, *Global Civil Society and the World Summit on the Information Society*.

47 See Betancourt, *The World Summit on the Information Society*.

48 See Hans Klein, *Understanding wsis: An Institutional Analysis of the un World Summit on the Information Society*, Internet & Public Policy Project, School of Public Policy, Georgia Institute of Technology, 2003, p. 3, http://IP3.gatech.edu.

49 My comments in this paragraph and the next are adapted in Geert Lovink and Ned Rossiter, 'Dawn of the Organised Networks', *Fibreculture Journal* 5 (2005), http://journal.fibreculture.org/issue5/lovink_rossiter.html.

Chapter 3

1 Norbert Bolz, 'Rethinking Media Aesthetics', in Geert Lovink, *Uncanny Networks: Dialogues with the Virtual Intelligentsia*, Cambridge, Mass.: MIT Press, 2000, p. 19.

2 Lovink, *Uncanny Networks*, p. 4.

3 McKenzie Wark, 'The Power of Multiplicity and the Multiplicity of Power', in Lovink, *Uncanny Networks*, p. 316.

4 Scott Lash, *Critique of Information*, London: Sage, 2002, p. 220.

5 Or perhaps, more correctly after Baudrillard, a *globalization* of media culture and information flows, since universality, for Baudrillard, is homologous with ethical principles such as human rights, whereas globalization is a term that has emerged with the advent of new icts, post-1989 world events, and the re-scaling of capital. One does not speak of 'global' human rights, for example. Rather human rights are a set of principles that may be idealized, and rarely adhered to. Jean Baudrillard, 'The Violence of the Global', trans. François Debrix, *Ctheory*, a129, May, 2003, http://www.ctheory.net/text_file.asp?pick=385.

6 Lash, *Critique of Information*, p. 8.

7 Ibid., p. 9. See also Andreas Wittel, 'Toward a Network Sociality', *Theory, Culture & Society* 18.6 (2001): 51-76.

8 Ibid., p. 10.

9 Ibid.

10 Theodor W. Adorno, *Negative Dialectics*, trans. E. B. Ashton, London: Routledge, 1990, p. 4.

11 Or as Kafka elegantly deduced: 'Capitalism is a system of relationships, which go from inside to out, from outside to in, from above to below, and from below to above. Everything is relative, everything is in chains. Capitalism is a condition both of the world and of the soul'. Cited in Nicholas Thoburn, *Deleuze, Marx and Politics*, London: Routledge, 2003, p. 69.

12　Danny Butt and Ned Rossiter, 'Blowing Bubbles: Post-Crash Creative Industries and the Withering of Political Critique in Cultural Studies', paper presented at *Ute Culture: The Utility of Culture and the Uses of Cultural Studies*, Cultural Studies Association of Australia Conference, Melbourne, 5-7 December, 2002. Posted to fibreculture mailing list, 10 December, 2002, http://www.fibreculture.org.

13　Here I am appropriating a phrase by Susan Buck-Morss, who is referring to a Derridean sense of the constitutive outside as it operates within secular Islamic discourse in Turkey. Susan Buck-Morss, *Thinking Past Terror: Islamism and Critical Theory on the Left*, London and New York: Verso, 2003, p. 45.

14　At least one of the key proponents of the creative industries in Australia is ready to acknowledge this. See Stuart Cunningham, 'The Evolving Creative Industries: From Original Assumptions to Contemporary Interpretations', seminar paper, QUT, Brisbane, 9 May, 2003, http://eprints.qut.edu.au/archive/00004391/01/4391.pdf.

15　Creative Industry Task Force: Mapping Document, DCMS (Department of Culture, Media and Sport) (1998/2001), London, http://www.culture.gov.uk/global/publications/archive_2001/ci_mapping_doc_2001.htm?properties=archive%5F2001%2C%2Fcreative%5Findustries%2FQuickLinks%2Fpublications%2Fdefault%2C&month=.

16　My claims here are valid for the period in which this chapter was written (2003/2004). Fortunately this situation has changed since then, with a considerable amount of research now being undertaken on the relation between intellectual property and creative industries. See, for example, Terry Flew (ed.), *Media & Arts Law Review*, Special Issue: Creative Commons and the Creative Industries 10.4 (2005), http://www.law.unimelb.edu.au/cmcl/malr/contents104.html. See also Terry Flew, *New Media: An Introduction*, Oxford: Oxford University Press, 2002, pp. 154-159. Though even here there is no attempt to identify the implications IPRS hold for those working in the creative industries sectors. Michael Keane has a body of important work investigating intellectual property issues in China. See Michael Keane, *Created in China: the Great New Leap Forward*, London: RoutledgeCurzon, forthcoming 2007.

17　See Angela McRobbie, 'Clubs to Companies: Notes on the Decline of Political Culture in Speeded up Creative Worlds', *Cultural Studies* 16.4 (2002): 516-531. See also Andrew Ross, *No-Collar: The Humane Workplace and Its Hidden Costs*, New York: Basic Books, 2003.

18　Thomas Frank, *One Market Under God: Extreme Capitalism, Market Populism, and the End of Economic Democracy*, New York: Anchor Books, 2000.

19　See Andrew McNamara, 'How "Creative Industries" Evokes the Legacy of Modernist Visual Art', *Media International Australia* 102 (2002): 66-76.

20　Mathew Arnold, *Culture and Anarchy*, Cambridge: Cambridge University Press, 1960, p. 6.

21　See Graeme Turner, *British Cultural Studies: An Introduction*, Boston: Unwin Hyman, 1990, pp. 41-84; Tony Bennett, *The Birth of the Museum: History, Theory, Politics*, London and New York: Routledge, 1995, pp. 87-101; Patrick Brantlinger, *Crusoe's Footprints: Cultural Studies in Britain and America*, New York and London: Routledge, 1990, pp. 34-67. As one would expect from the 'internationalization' of Cultural Studies, counter-readings of the emergence of cultural studies within Britain, and the significance it holds for local contexts, are inevitable. Interesting work on this topic from a younger generation of scholars writing from an Australian perspective includes McKenzie Wark, 'Speaking Trajectories: Meaghan Morris, Antipodean Theory and Australian Cultural Studies', *Cultural Studies* 6.3 (1992): 433-448; Terry Flew, 'Cultural Materialism and Cultural Policy: Reassessing Raymond Williams', *Social Semiotics* 7.1 (1997): 5-19; Mark Gibson, 'Richard Hoggart's Grandmother's Ironing: Some Questions about "Power" in International Cultural Studies', *International Journal of Cultural Studies* 1.1 (1998): 25-44; Mark Gibson, 'The Temporality of Democracy: The Long Revolution and Diana, Princess of Wales', *New Formations* 36 (1999): 59-76; Mark Gibson, 'The Geography of Theory: Channel Crossings, Continental Invasions and the Anglo-American "Natives"', *symploke* 11.1/2 (2003): 152-166; Tania Lewis, 'Intellectual Exchange and Located Transnationalism: Meaghan Morris and the Formation of Australian Cultural Studies', *Continuum: Journal of Media & Cultural Studies* 17.2 (2003): 187-206; Tania Lewis, 'Stuart Hall and the Formation of British Cultural Studies: A Diasporic Narrative', *Imperium* IV (2004), http://www.imperiumjournal.com/index.html; Melissa Gregg, 'A Neglected

History: Richard Hoggart's Discourse of Empathy', *Rethinking History: The Journal of Theory and Practice* 7.3 (2003): 285-306; Melissa Gregg, *Cultural Studies' Affective Voices*, Basingstoke: Palgrave, 2006.

22 And in this respect, it is possible to draw a parallel between the creative industries project within Queensland and its institutional predecessor, the Australian Key Centre for Cultural and Media Policy, directed by Tony Bennett. For a critique of the tendency by advocates of cultural policy studies – particularly Bennett – to read Foucauldian 'governmentality' as a variation of Althusserian 'ISAS', see Helen Grace, 'Eating the Curate's Egg: Cultural Studies for the Nineties', *West* 3.1 (1991): 46-49. Interestingly enough, McKenzie Wark adopts the position of an 'outsider intellectual' in his critique of Bennett and cultural policy studies. See McKenzie Wark, 'After Literature: Culture, Policy, Theory and Beyond', *Meanjin* 5.4 (1992): 677-690.

23 See Geert Lovink, *Dark Fiber: Tracking Critical Internet Culture*, Cambridge, Mass.: MIT Press, 2002; Geert Lovink, *My First Recession: Critical Internet Culture in Transition*, Rotterdam: V2/NAi, 2003; Graham Meikle, *Future Active: Media Activism and the Internet*, Sydney: Pluto Press, 2002.

24 See Shujen Wang and Jonathan J. H. Zhu, 'Mapping Film Piracy in China', *Theory, Culture & Society* 20.4 (2003): 97-125.

25 Scott McQuire, 'When is Art IT?', in Hugh Brown, Geert Lovink, Helen Merrick, Ned Rossiter, David Teh, Michele Willson (eds), *Politics of a Digital Present: An Inventory of Australian Net Culture, Criticism and Theory*, Melbourne: Fibreculture Publications, 2001, p. 209.
A QUT report commissioned by the Brisbane City Council in 2003 provides some illuminating statistics on the varying concentrations of workers in the Creative Industries across Australia. There aren't too many surprises. Of the seven capital cities in Australia in 2001, Sydney holds the highest proportion of creative industry workers (90,600/40.1%). Melbourne has 63,453 (28.1%), Brisbane (25,324/11.2%), Perth (21,211/9.4%), Adelaide (15,345/6.8%), Canberra (6,916/3.1%), and the Greater Hobart Area (3,055/1.3%). See Stuart Cunningham, Gregory Hearn, Stephen Cox, Abraham Ninan and Michael Keane, *Brisbane's Creative Industries 2003*, Report delivered to Brisbane City Council, Community and Economic Development, Brisbane: CIRAC, 2003, http://eprints.qut.edu.au/archive/00002409/01/2409_2.pdf.

26 See Stuart Cunningham, 'Culture, Services, Knowledge or Is Content King, or are we just Drama Queens?', Communications Research Forum, Canberra, 2-3 October, 2002, http://eprints.qut.edu.au/archive/00000202/01/cunningham_culture.pdf.

27 See McQuire, 'When is Art IT?', p. 10.

28 Creative Industries Faculty, QUT, http://www.creativeindustries.qut.com. A number of research papers and reports can be found at: http://eprints.qut.edu.au/view/subjects/fac_ci.html.

29 Barcan is referring here to the accusation by Australian Prime Minister John Howard regarding 'the idleness of so many in academia'. Barcan is contesting the widespread perception that 'useful' teaching is vocationally oriented and 'useful' research has outcomes with commercial application. See Ruth Barcan, 'The Idleness of Academics: Reflections on the Usefulness of Cultural Studies', *Continuum: Journal of Media & Cultural Studies* 4.4 (2003): 363-378.

30 See Simon Marginson and Mark Considine, *The Enterprise University: Power, Governance and Reinvention in Australia*, Cambridge: Cambridge University Press, 2000.

31 John Hartley and Stuart Cunningham, 'Creative Industries: from Blue Poles to fat pipes', in Malcolm Gillies (ed.), *The National Humanities and Social Sciences Summit: Position Papers*, Canberra: DEST, 2002. Available at: http://www.dest.gov.au/NR/rdonlyres/C785B22C-E7EC-47D0-9781-C5AA68546FCD/1426/summit701.pdf.

32 See Ulrich Beck, *Risk Society: Towards a New Modernity*, trans. M. Ritter, London: Sage, 1992; Zygmunt Bauman, *The Individualized Society*, Cambridge: Polity Press, 2001; McRobbie, 'Clubs to Companies'.

33 Sue Williams, '$A the Villain in Screen Drama', *The Australian Financial Review*, 12 December, 2003, p. 20.

34 Ibid.

35 Chris Chesher, 'FTA and new media?', posting to fibreculture mailing list, 20 January, 2004, http://www.fibreculture.org. For an informative study of free trade agreements between the USA and Australia, and their effect on Australia's cultural economies, see Jock Given, *America's Pie: Trade and Culture After 9/11*, Sydney: University of New South Wales Press, 2003.

36 See Robert Brenner, *The Boom and the Bubble: The US in the World Economy*, London and New York: Verso, 2002; Jean Gadrey, *New Economy, New Myth*, London and New York: Routledge, 2003; Geert Lovink, 'After the Dotcom Crash: Recent Literature on Internet, Business and Society', *Australian Humanities Review* 27 (September-December, 2002), http://www.lib.latrobe.edu.au/AHR/archive/Issue-September-2002/lovink.html; Adam Tickell, 'Unstable Futures: Controlling and Creating Risks in International Money', in Leo Panitch and Colin Leys (eds), *Global Capitalism versus Democracy: Socialist Register, 1999*, Suffolk: Merlin, 1999, pp. 248-277.

37 Lash, *Critique of Information*, p. 24.

38 As Esther Milne has pointed out to me, in many cases practitioners own their own copyright. Furthermore, practitioners are situated differently in relation to intellectual property: a scriptwriter, for instance, holds a relation to IP in a way that a camera person does not. However, the principle of exclusion still holds in such instances: irrespective of whether or not one's labour is ascribed potential value as intellectual property, the point is that labour value is determined by its *relation* to intellectual property rights. In other words, living labour is reduced to labour-power circumscribed within the legal regime of property, and holds no other value other than property or not worthy of property. In which case labour is no more than a service to be traded on the market.

39 Giorgio Agamben, *The Coming Community*, trans. Michael Hardt, Minneapolis: University of Minnesota Press, 1993, p. 68.

40 Gilles Deleuze and Félix Guattari, *What is Philosophy?*, trans. Hugh Tomlinson and Graham Burchill, New York: Columbia University Press, 1994, p. 35.

41 Ibid., pp. 36-39.

42 Chantal Mouffe, *The Democratic Paradox*, London: Verso, 2000, p. 12. Mouffe acknowledges that she is drawing on the work of Derrida for her understanding of a constitutive outside. I am taking quite a different route to an understanding of a constitutive outside by engaging the work of Deleuze, who defines the relationship between inside and outside in terms of the 'fold' and a Foucauldian diagram of power.

43 Buck-Morss, *Thinking Past Terror*, p. 94.

44 Adorno, *Negative Dialectics*, p. 97.

45 Susan Buck-Morss, *The Origin of Negative Dialectics: Theodor W. Adorno, Walter Benjamin, and the Frankfurt Institute*, New York: Free Press, 1977, p. 154.

46 Adorno, *Negative Dialectics*, p. 145.

47 Ibid., p. 182.

48 See Buck-Morss, *The Origin of Negative Dialectics*, p. 249; Peter Osborne, *The Politics of Time: Modernity and Avant-Garde*, London: Verso, 1995, pp. 133-159.

49 Or what Adorno called Benjamin's radical 'negative theology'. See Susan Buck-Morss, *The Dialectics of Seeing: Walter Benjamin and the Arcades Project*, Cambridge, Mass.: MIT Press, 1989, p. 244.

50 Ibid., pp. 218, 246.

51 Buck-Morss, *The Origin of Negative Dialectics*.

52 Deleuze and Guattari, *What is Philosophy?*, p. 16.

53 Karl Marx, 'Excerpt from *A Contribution to the Critique of Political Economy*', in Karl Marx and Friedrich Engels, *Basic Writings on Politics and Philosophy*, ed. Lewis S. Feuer, New York: Doubleday, 1959, p. 44.

54 Here, I am referring to the 2001 federal election in Australia, which was notable for the conspicuous and cynical campaign of fear run by the incumbent government, John Howard's conservative coalition party. Howard played a central role in exploiting a media-generated fear that fed upon the events of September 11 and 'illegal' refugees, many of whom were Afghani asylum seekers arriving in Australian territorial waters, fleeing the ravages of war and political persecution. Many have put Howard's success in gaining a third term in office down to his ability to construct a media-facilitated discourse in which the 'security' of an Australian way of life depended on the capacity of a powerful state to determine which 'outsiders' would be allowed to become 'one of us'. Articulating terrorists with asylum seekers worked as a key strategy in constructing this discourse of fear of the 'outside'.

55 Gilles Deleuze, *Negotiations, 1972-1990*, trans. Martin Joughin, New York: Columbia University Press, 1995, pp. 148-149. See also Gilles Deleuze, *Difference and Repetition*, trans. Paul Patton, New York: Columbia University Press, 1994, p. 37.

56 See Gilles Deleuze, *Empiricism and Subjectivity: An Essay on Hume's Theory of Human Nature*, trans. Constantin V. Boundas, New York: Columbia University Press, 1991; Gilles Deleuze and Claire Parnet, *Dialogues II*, trans. Hugh Tomlinson, Barbara Habberjam and Elliot Ross Albert, London and New York: Continuum, 2002, p. 133. A helpful elaboration of immanent and transcendent traditions in the history of philosophy – with a specific focus on contemporary French philosophy – can be found in Daniel W. Smith, 'Deleuze and Derrida, Immanence and Transcendence: Two Directions in Recent French Thought', in Paul Patton and John Protevi (eds), *Between Deleuze and Derrida*, London and New York: Continuum, 2003, pp. 46-66.

57 Deleuze, *Difference and Repetition*, pp. 40-41; Deleuze, *Negotiations*, p. 146.

58 Deleuze, *Difference and Repetition*, p. 40.

59 Gilles Deleuze, *Pure Immanence: Essays on A Life*, trans. Anna Boyman, intro. John Rajchman, New York: Zone Books, 2001, p. 31.

60 Deleuze and Guattari, *What is Philosophy?*, p. 36.

61 It is ugly, for sure, to adopt parentheses within a word to signal the dual meaning of a term. Here I am following Massumi's technique of translation in *A Thousand Plateaus* for signalling both of the words, 'plan' and 'plane'. In a translator's note to Deleuze's *Spinoza: Practical Philosophy*, Robert Hurley makes the following useful clarification: 'The French word *plan* … covers virtually all the meanings of the English "plan" and "plane". To preserve the major contrast that Deleuze sets up here, between *plan d'immanence ou de consistance* and *plan de transcendance ou d'organisation*, I have used 'plane' for the first term, where the meaning is, roughly, a conceptual-affective continuum, and 'plan' for the second term. The reader should also keep in mind that 'plan' has the meaning of 'map' in English as well'. See Hurley, translator's note in Gilles Deleuze, *Spinoza: Practical Philosophy*, trans. Robert Hurley, San Francisco: City Lights, 1988, p. 123.

In light of this distinction, it might seem more appropriate to adopt Hurley's strategy and use the word 'plane' where referring 'to the plane of immanence', and the word plan, where referring to 'the plan of organization'. However, I will make occasional use of the combinatory form of the two words – plan(e) – rather than deploy them separately, since one does not necessarily preclude the operation of the other; rather, there are complex interleavings, overlaps, and foldings between the plane and the plan. And as Deleuze and Guattari note, there is a 'hidden principle' and 'hidden structure' within the plan(e) that 'exists only in a supplementary dimension to that to which it gives rise ($n + 1$). … It is a plan(e) of transcendence. It is a plan(e) of analogy. … It is always inferred. *Even if it is said to be immanent*, it is so only by the absence, analogically (metaphorically, metonymically, etc.)'. See Gilles Deleuze and Félix Guattari, *A Thousand Plateaus: Capitalism and Schizophrenia*, trans. Brian Massumi, Minneapolis: University of Minnesota Press, 1987, pp. 265-266. Emphasis in original.

It is in this sense in which the plane of immanence subsists, albeit as a supplementary dimension, within that which has emerged as the plan or grid of organization that it remains useful to retain the double sense of the French word *plan*. I will detail this complex relation by way of example below, when I return to the operation of an outside within the discourse of creative industries, as espoused by the CITF and others that adopt their terms of reference.

62 Deleuze and Guattari, *A Thousand Plateaus*, p. 266.

63 Deleuze, *Dialogues II*, p. 130.

64 Deleuze and Guattari, *A Thousand Plateaus*, p. 507.

65 Brian Massumi, *Parables for the Virtual: Movement, Affect, Sensation*, Durham and London: Duke University Press, 2002, p. 69.

66 Deleuze and Guattari, *What is Philosophy?*, p. 50.

67 Agamben, *The Coming Community*, p. 233.

68 Massumi, *Parables for the Virtual*, p. 76.

69 Danny Butt, email correspondence, 23 January, 2004.

70 Gilles Deleuze, *Foucault*, trans. Seán Hand, forw. Paul Bové, Minneapolis: University of Minnesota Press, 1988, p. 43.

71 Ibid., p. 70.

72 Ibid., p. 43.

73 William Rasch, *Niklas Luhmann's Modernity: The Paradoxes of Differentiation*, Stanford, Cal.: Stanford University Press, 2000, p. 106.

74 Michel Foucault, *The Archaeology of Knowledge* and *The Discourse on Language*, trans. A. M. Sheridan Smith, New York: Pantheon Books, 1972.

75 Deleuze, *Foucault*, p. 79.

76 Ibid., p. 119.

77 Ibid. See also Deleuze, *Negotiations*, p. 98.

78 Deleuze, *Negotiations*, p. 98. See also Ian Angus, 'The Materiality of Expression: Harold Innis' Communication Theory and the Discursive Turn in the Human Sciences', *Canadian Journal of Communication* 23.1 (1998): 26-27.

79 Buck-Morss, *Thinking Past Terror*, p. 93.

80 See Rosalind Gill, 'Cool, Creative and Egalitarian? Exploring Gender in Project-based New Media Work in Europe', *Information, Communication & Society* 5.1 (2002): 70-89.

81 Ian Angus, 'The Politics of Common Sense: Articulation Theory and Critical Communication Studies', *Communication Yearbook* 15 (1992): 536.

82 The Innis centenary in 1994 was cause for a revival of interest in the wide-ranging work of Innis, although this was largely a Canadian phenomenon as far as the field of media and communications goes. A special issue of *Continuum* on Innis and dependency theory edited by Ian Angus and Brian Shoesmith is one of the few attempts, to my knowledge, to situate the relevance of Innis's work beyond an exclusively Canadian focus. See Ian Angus and Brian Shoesmith (eds), 'Dependency/Space/Policy: A Dialogue with Harold A. Innis', Special Issue, *Continuum: The Australian Journal of Media & Culture* 7.1 (1993). Also available at: http://wwwmcc.murdoch.edu.au/ReadingRoom/continuum2.html.
    Other notable works include Judith Stamps, *Unthinking Modernity: Innis, McLuhan and the Frankfurt School*, Montreal & Kingston: McGill-Queen's University Press, 1995; Charles R. Acland and William J. Buxton (eds), *Harold Innis in the New Century: Reflections and Refractions*, Montreal & Kingston: McGill-Queen's University Press, 1999; Daniel Drache, 'Introduction: Celebrating Innis: The Man, the Legacy, and Our Future', in Harold A. Innis, *Staples, Markets, and Cultural Change*, ed. Daniel Drache, Montreal & Kingston: McGill-Queen's University Press, 1995, pp. xiii-lix. James W. Carey, 'Space, Time, and Communications: A Tribute to Harold Innis', in *Communication as Culture: Essays on Media and Society*, New York: Routledge, 1992, pp. 142-172; Jody Berland, 'Space at the Margins: Colonial Spatiality and Critical Theory After Innis', *Topia: A Canadian Journal of Cultural Studies* 1 (1997): 55-82. For an interesting example of the migration of Innis into the field of international relations, see Ronald J. Deibert, 'Harold Innis and the Empire of Speed', *Review of International Studies* 25 (1999): 273-289.

83 Ian Angus, 'Orality in the Twilight of Humanism: A Critique of the Communication Theory of Harold Innis', *Continuum: The Australian Journal of Media & Culture* 7.1 (1993): 31.

84 Ibid., pp. 28-29.

85 Harold Innis, *The Bias of Communication*, Toronto: University of Toronto Press, 1951.

86 Harold Innis, *Empire and Communications*, Victoria and Toronto: Press Porcépic, 1986, p. 166.

87 Ian Angus and Brian Shoesmith, 'Dependency/Space/Policy: An Introduction to a Dialogue with Harold Innis', *Continuum: The Australian Journal of Media & Culture* 7.1 (1993): 7.

88 Ibid., p. 13.

89 Angus, 'Orality in the Twilight of Humanism', p. 31.

90 Stamps, *Unthinking Modernity*, p. 85.

91 Jody Berland, 'Nationalism and the Modernist Legacy: Dialogues with Innis', *Culture & Policy* 8.3 (1997): 31.

92 Stamps, *Unthinking Modernity*, p. 80.

93 Innis, *The Bias of Communication*, pp. 33-34.

94 Ibid., p. 33.

95 Ibid., p. 90.

96 See Innis, *Empire and Communications*, pp. 27-31, 36-39; *The Bias of Communication*, pp. 38, 98.

97 Innis, *Empire and Communications*, pp. 34-35, 41.

98 Innis, *The Bias of Communication*, p. 104.

99   Deleuze and Guattari, *A Thousand Plateaus*, p. 268.

100 Innis, *Empire and Communications*, p. 36.

101 Angus, 'The Materiality of Expression', p. 26.

102 Deleuze, *Empiricism and Subjectivity*, p. 107.

103 Adorno, *Negative Dialectics*, p. 182.

104 Deleuze, *Foucault*, p. 89.

105 Angus, 'The Materiality of Expression', p. 19.

Chapter 4

1   *Fibrepower: Currents in Australasian Internet Research and Culture*, Fibreculture Meeting, Brisbane Powerhouse, 11-13 July, 2003, http://www.fibreculture.org/conferences/conference2003/index.html. I posted the questionnaire and preamble to the fibreculture mailing list, 29 June, 2003, http://www.fibreculture.org.

2   See Angela McRobbie, 'Clubs to Companies: Notes on the Decline of Political Culture in Speeded up Creative Worlds', *Cultural Studies* 16.4 (2002): 516-531. See also Rosalind Gill, 'Cool, Creative and Egalitarian? Exploring Gender in Project-based New Media Work in Europe', *Information, Communication & Society* 5.1 (2002): 70-89.

3   See Terry Flew, 'The "New Empirics" in Internet Studies and Comparative Internet Policy', in Hugh Brown, Geert Lovink, Helen Merrick, Ned Rossiter, David Teh, Michele Willson (eds), *Politics of a Digital Present: An Inventory of Australian Net Culture, Criticism and Theory*, Melbourne: Fibreculture Publications, 2001, pp. 105-113.

4   Creative Industry Task Force: Mapping Document, DCMS (Department of Culture, Media and Sport) (1998/2001), London, http://www.culture.gov.uk/global/publications/archive_2001/ci_mapping_doc_2001.htm?properties=archive%5F2001%2C%2Fcreative%5Findustries%2FQuickLinks%2Fpublications%2Fdefault%2C&month=.

5   Richard Florida, *The Rise of the Creative Class: And How It's Transforming Work, Leisure, Community and Everyday Life*, New York: Basic Books, 2002, p. 8.

6   Florida does go on to discuss IP, but not in terms of how its exploitation defines creative industries, as the CITF Mapping Documents of 1998/2001 have it.

7   Pierre Bourdieu, 'Public Opinion Does Not Exist (1973)', trans. Mary C. Axtmann in Armand Mattelart and Seth Siegelaub (eds), *Communication and Class Struggle, Vol. 1: Capitalism, Imperialism*, New York: International General, 1979, pp. 124-130.

8   Scott Lash, 'Reflexivity as Non-Linearity', *Theory, Culture & Society* 20.2 (2003): 51.

9   Ibid., pp. 49-50.

10   My quarrel here is not with Deleuze's concept of a logic of immanence but rather with Lash's shorthand version of it, which conveniently elides the conceptual – and ultimately political and ethical – nuisance of thinking through the operation of the constitutive outside *within* a logic of immanence. See in particular, Scott Lash, *Critique of Information*, London: Sage, 2002.

11   Pierre Bourdieu and Loïc J. D. Wacquant, *An Invitation to Reflexive Sociology*, Chicago: University of Chicago Press, 1992, pp. 68-69.

12   Of course other media do this as well – books, films, TV ads, oral histories, radio interviews – though in ways specific to their material forms, technical features, socio-cultural situations, etcetera.

13   McRobbie, 'Clubs to Companies', p. 519. See also Ulrich Beck, *Risk Society: Towards a New Modernity*, trans. M. Ritter, London: Sage, 1992, pp. 127-150; Zygmunt Bauman, *The Individualized Society*, Cambridge: Polity Press, 2001, pp. 17-30.

14   McRobbie, 'Clubs to Companies', p. 518.

15   See Ankie Hoogvelt, *Globalization and the Postcolonial World: The New Political Economy of Development*, London: Palgrave, 2001.

16   See Michael Hardt, 'Introduction: Laboratory Italy', in Paolo Virno and Michael Hardt (eds), *Radical Thought in Italy: A Potential Politics*, Minneapolis: University of Minnesota Press, 1996, p. 6. See also Paolo Virno, 'Virtuosity and Revolution: The Political Theory of Exodus', trans. Ed Emory, *Radical Thought in Italy*, pp. 196-197.

17 See Ned Rossiter, 'Modalities of Indigenous Sovereignty, Transformations of the Nation-State, and Intellectual Property Regimes', *Borderlands E-Journal: New Spaces in the Humanities* 1.2 (2002), http://www.borderlandsejournal.adelaide.edu.au/issues/vol1no2.html.

18 Manuel Castells and Martin Ince, *Conversations with Manuel Castells*, Cambridge: Polity, 2003, p. 29.

19 Scott Lash and John Urry, *Economies of Signs and Space*, London: Sage, 1994.

20 Ulrich Beck, *What is Globalization?*, trans. Patrick Camiller, Cambridge: Polity Press, 2000, p. 150.

21 Richard Caves, *Creative Industries: Contracts Between Art and Commerce*, Cambridge, Mass.: Harvard University Press, 2000, p. 133.

22 Ibid., p. 132.

23 Thanks to Hugh Brown for bringing the details of this case to my attention. A comprehensive account and documentation of this case can be found at: National Writer's Union (NWU), *New York Times v Tasini*, 2000, http://www.nwu.org/nwu/. See also *New York Times v Tasini*, 533 US 483 (2001).

24 See John Frow, 'Information as Gift and Commodity', *New Left Review* 219 (1996): 89-108.

25 Cited in Steve Wright, *Storming Heaven: Class Composition and Struggle in Italian Autonomist Marxism*, London: Pluto, 2002, p. 84.

26 See Wright, *Storming Heaven*, pp. 84-85. See also Yann Moulier-Boutang and Stanley Grelet, 'The Art of Flight: An Interview', *Interactivist Info Exchange: Independent Media & Analysis*, 7 February, 2003, http://info.interactivist.net/article.pl?sid=03/02/07/1350202.

27 Paolo Virno, 'The Ambivalence of Disenchantment', trans. Michael Turits, *Radical Thought in Italy*, p. 20. See also Mario Tronti, 'The Strategy of Refusal', trans. Red Notes, in Sylvère Lotringer and Christian Marazzi (eds), *Italy: Autonomia, Post-Political Politics*, New York: Semiotext(e), 1980, pp. 28-35. A longer version of this essay is available at: http://www.libcom.org/library/strategy-refusal-mario-tronti.

28 Michael Hardt and Antonio Negri, *Empire*, Cambridge, Mass.: Harvard University Press, 2000.

29 Virno, 'Virtuosity and Revolution', p. 200. See also Paolo Virno, *A Grammar of the Multitude*, trans. James Cascaito Isabella Bertoletti, and Andrea Casson, forward by Sylvère Lotringer, New York: Semiotext(e), 2004, p. 23.

30 Virno, 'Virtuosity and Revolution', p. 201.

31 Antonio Negri, 'Public Sphere, Labour and Multitude', trans. Arianna Bove, *MakeWorld Paper* 3 (2003): 4. My emphasis. Also available at: http://www.makeworlds.org/?q=node/view/11. Initially I read Negri's intervention as belonging to the genre of the manifesto. But as the transcriber and translator, Arianna Bove, informed me: 'Maybe it sounds like a manifesto because it was an oral intervention, the context being one where in my view Negri was questioning the idea of a "public sphere" which Virno seems to hold onto, albeit in a modified form, in some of his writings'. Email correspondence, 29 September, 2003. Negri's intervention took place in a seminar called 'Public Sphere, labour, multitude: Strategies of resistance in Empire', organized by Officine Precarie in Pisa, with Toni Negri and Paolo Virno, coordinated by Marco Bascetta, 5 February, 2003. The version that appeared in *MakeWorld* #3 is slightly edited, and the word-by-word transcript (with part of Virno's response) is translated here: http://www.generation-online.org/t/common.htm.

32 Andreas Wittel, 'Toward a Network Sociality', *Theory, Culture & Society* 18.6 (2001): 51.

33 The notion of cooperation is related to the other autonomist key concepts of the 'general intellect' and 'mass intellectuality'. See Paolo Virno, 'Notes on the "General Intellect"', trans. Cesare Casarino in *Marxism Beyond Marxism*, eds Sareee Makdisi, Cesare Casarino, and Rebecca E. Karl for the Polygraph collective, London and New York: Routledge, 1996, pp. 265-272 and Maurizio Lazzarato, 'General Intellect: Towards an Inquiry into Immaterial Labour', trans. Ed Emery, (n.d.), http://www.geocities.com/CognitiveCapitalism/lazzarato2.html. For a discussion of these terms, see Tiziana Terranova, 'Free Labor: Producing Culture for the Digital Economy', *Social Text* 18.2 (2000): 45-46. For a detailed history of the Italian autonomists, see Wright, *Storming Heaven*.

34 Michael Hardt, *Gilles Deleuze: An Apprenticeship in Philosophy*, London: UCL Press, 1993, p. 110.

35 See Andrew Odlyzko, 'Content is Not King', *First Monday* 6.2 (2001), http://www.firstmonday.org/issues/issue6_2/odlyzko/.

36 See Boris Groys, cited in European Union, *Exploitation and Development of Job Potential in the Cultural Sector in the Age of Digitalisation*, Final Report (Module 1), commissioned by European

Commission/DG Employment and Social Affairs, June, 2001, p. 36. Available at: http://europa.eu.int/comm/employment_social/empl_esf/docs/cult_sector/module1.pdf.

37 Terranova, 'Free Labor', p. 39.

38 Maurizio Lazzarato, 'Immaterial Labor', trans. Paul Colilli and Ed Emory, *Radical Thought in Italy*, p. 133.

39 Ibid. See also Terranova, 'Free Labor', pp. 41-43.

40 Lazzarato, 'Immaterial Labor', p. 138.

41 Hardt and Negri, *Empire*, p. 293.

42 Ibid.

43 This contrasts with Paolo Virno's notion of virtuosic labour in *Grammar of the Multitude*, where there is 'no end product' (pp. 52-53).

44 Henri Lefebvre, cited in Rosemary J. Coombe, *The Cultural Life of Intellectual Properties: Authorship, Appropriation and the Law*, Durham and London: Duke University Press, 1998, p. 133.

45 Scott Lash and John Urry, *The End of Organized Capitalism*, Cambridge: Polity, 1987.

46 See Lash and Urry, *Economies of Signs and Space*, p. 10.

47 Here I am drawing on Timothy Brennan's critique of Hardt and Negri's *Empire*, though Brennan is making a comparison between immaterial labour and the multitude. As I have argued above, the term immaterial labour is one that I see as conceptually flawed, and is better described in terms of disorganized labour. For their part, Hardt and Negri are disappointing in their response to what they fairly address as Brennan's aggressive critique inasmuch as it is heavy on taking a point-by-point refutation of Hardt and Negri's thesis and some examples, yet offers little by way of an alternative. See Timothy Brennan, 'The Empire's New Clothes', *Critical Inquiry* 29.2 (2003): 337-367; Michael Hardt and Antonio Negri, 'The Rod of the Forest Warden: A Response to Timothy Brennan (Critical Response I)', *Critical Inquiry* 29.2 (2003), http://www.uchicago.edu/research/jnl-crit-inq/issues/v29/v29n2.Hardt.html.

48 Brian Holmes, 'The Flexible Personality' (Parts 1 & 2), posting to nettime mailing list, 5 January, 2002, http://www.nettime.org. This text and others by Holmes can be found at Université Tangente, http://ut.yt.to.or.at/site/total.html.

49 Justin Clemens, *The Romanticism of Contemporary Theory: Institution, Aesthetics, Nihilism*, Aldershot: Ashgate, 2003, p. 174. Many of the key proponents of the creative industries, at least in Australia, have had prior intellectual lives and academic careers studying precisely these sorts of cultural phenomena.

50 Lash, *Critique of Information*, p. 167.

51 Hardt and Negri, *Empire*, p. 385.

52 Michel Foucault, *Maurice Blanchot: The Thought from the Outside*, trans. Brian Massumi, New York: Zone Books, 1990, p. 21.

53 Ibid., pp. 21-22.

54 Slavoj Žižek, 'A Plea for Leninist Intolerance', *Critical Inquiry* 28.2 (2002): 558.

55 Régis Debray, *Media Manifestos: On the Technological Transmission of Cultural Forms*, trans. Eric Rauth, London and New York: Verso, 1996.

56 Brown et al., *Politics of a Digital Present*, p. v.

57 Danny Butt, 'Re. Report: Creative Labour and the role of Intellectual Property', posting to fibreculture mailing list, 10 October, 2003, http://www.fibreculture.org.

58 Such a term perhaps best defines the activities of fibreculture, as discussed at the planning meeting in Sydney, 2003. In addition to the annual fibreculture meetings, this was the first face-to-face planning meeting of fibreculture facilitators and other participants (17-18 November, 2003). For a summary of the agenda, see the posting to the fibreculture list by Esther Milne, 13 November, 2003, http://www.fibreculture.org.

Interesting examples of union culture articulating itself in the form of organized networks can be found at the following sites: IT Workers Alliance (AU), http://itworkers-alliance.org and CyberLodge, taking the labour movement open source (USA), http://www.cyberlodge.org/. For a brief discussion of the emergent political consciousness among IT workers – made possible, of course, by the crash in the IT sector which led to a radical change in the material and discursive conditions of programmers, web designers, etcetera – see Verity Burgmann, *Power, Profit and Protest: Australian Social Movements and Globalisation*, Crows Nest: Allen and Unwin, 2003, p. 269.

Chapter 5

1 Michel Serres, *Genesis*, trans. Geneviève James and James Nielson, Ann Arbor: University of Michigan Press, 1995, p. 96.

2 Gilles Deleuze and Félix Guattari, *What is Philosophy?*, trans. Hugh Tomlinson and Graham Burchill, New York: Columbia University Press, 1994, p. 16.

3 Brian Massumi, *Parables for the Virtual: Movement, Affect, Sensation*, Durham and London: Duke University Press, 2002, pp. 38-39.

4 To speak of a field of new media studies is problematic in itself, since 'there is no stable object or ontology around which a conceptual economy can be concentrated'. David Holmes, email correspondence, 23 February, 2003.

5 Gilles Deleuze, *Cinema 1: The Movement Image*, trans. Hugh Tomlinson and Barbara Habberjam, Minneapolis: University of Minnesota Press, 1986, p. 109.

6 Massumi, *Parables for the Virtual*, pp. 1-25.

7 Gregory Bateson, 'Form, Substance, and Difference', in *Steps to an Ecology of Mind*, New York: Ballantine Books, 1972, p. 453. Italics in original.

8 See Jean-François Lyotard, *The Inhuman: Reflections on Time*, trans. Geoffrey Bennington and Rachel Bowlby, Stanford, Cal.: Stanford University Press, 1991; Jean-François Lyotard, *Lessons on the Analytic of the Sublime*, trans. Elizabeth Rottenberg, Stanford, Cal: Stanford University Press, 1994. See also D. N. Rodowick, *Reading the Figural, or, Philosophy after the New Media*, Durham and London: Duke University Press, 2001, p. 20.

9 See Harold D. Lasswell, *Propaganda Technique in the World War*, New York: Knopf, 1927; Elihu Katz, and Paul F. Lazarsfeld, *Personal Influence: The Part Played by People in the Flow of Mass Communication*, Glencoe, Ill.: Free Press, 1970; J. Blumler and Elihu Katz (eds), *The Uses and Gratifications Approach to Mass Communications Research. Annual Review of Communication Research*, Volume 3, Beverly Hills, Cal.: Sage, 1975; J. Fowles, *Why Viewers Watch: A Reappraisal of Television's Effects*, Newbury Park: Sage, 1992. For critical appraisals of these empirical approaches, see Armand Mattelart and Michèle Mattelart, *Theories of Communication: A Short Introduction*, trans. Susan Gruenheck Taponier and James A. Cohen, London: Sage, 1998, pp. 19-42; David Holmes, 'Sociological Theory', in David Holmes, Kate Hughes and Roberta Julian, *Australian Sociology: A Changing Society*, Sydney: Pearson, 2003, pp. 21-87.

10 The first paradigm of Net studies consisted of a techno-utopianism associated with the 'Californian Ideology', the second, unsurprisingly, of techno-dystopianism. Terry Flew provides a useful overview of these paradigms and the emergence of the third paradigm of 'new media empirics'. Terry Flew, 'The 'New Empirics' in Internet Studies and Comparative Internet Policy', in Hugh Brown, Geert Lovink, Helen Merrick, Ned Rossiter, David Teh and Michele Willson (eds), *Politics of a Digital Present: An Inventory of Australian Net Culture, Criticism and Theory*, Melbourne: Fibreculture Publications, 2001, pp. 105-113.

11 Admittedly I'm being very reductive about the diversity within political economy approaches. My point is not so much one about political economy *per se*, as about the lack of reflexivity within new media empirics that adopt political economy approaches. For a useful overview of political economy, see David Hesmondhalgh, *The Cultural Industries*, London: Sage, 2002, pp. 27-48. For a discussion of political economy, the Braudelian *longue durée* and new media, see Terry Flew, *New Media: An Introduction*, Oxford: Oxford University Press, 2002, pp. 52-75. For interesting ethnographic empirical studies, see Elaine Lally, *Materializing Culture: At Home with Computers*, Oxford and New York: Berg, 2002; Daniel Miller and Don Slater, *The Internet: An Ethnographic Approach*, Oxford and New York: Berg, 2000.

12 See McKenzie Wark, *Virtual Geography: Living With Global Media Events*, Indianapolis: Indiana University Press, 1994; Anna Munster, 'Net Affects: Responding to Shock on Internet Time', in Brown et al., *Politics of a Digital Present*, pp. 9-17; Anna Munster, *Materializing New Media: Embodiment in Information Aesthetics*, Hanover and London: University of New England Press, 2006.

13   See Bruno Latour, *We Have Never Been Modern*, trans. Catherine Porter, Cambridge, Mass.: Harvard University Press, 1993.

14   Gilles Deleuze, *Difference and Repetition*, trans. Paul Patton, New York: Columbia University Press, 1994, p. x.

15   Louis Althusser and Étienne Balibar, *Reading Capital*, trans. Ben Brewster, London: Verso, 1979, p. 36.

16   Ibid., pp. 35-36.

17   Ibid., pp. 37-38, 41. See also Martin Jay, *Downcast Eyes: The Denigration of Vision in Twentieth-Century French Thought*, Berkeley: University of California Press, 1993.

18   Karl Marx and Frederick Engels, *The German Ideology*, Moscow: Progress Publishers, 1976, p. 41.

19   Ibid., p. 43.

20   David Holmes, 'The Politics of Negative Theology', *Melbourne Journal of Politics* 20 (1991): 101.

21   Althusser, *Reading Capital*, pp. 37-38.

22   See Raymond Williams, 'The Technology and the Society', in *Television: Technology and Cultural Form*, London: Fontana, 1974, pp. 9-31

23   Scott Lash, *Critique of Information*, London: Sage, 2002, p. 17.

24   Friedrich A. Kittler, *Gramophone, Film, Typewriter*, trans. & intro. Geoffrey Winthrop-Young and Michael Wutz, Stanford, Cal.: Stanford University Press, 1999, p. 206.

25   Ibid., p. 203.

26   Ibid.

27   Ibid., pp. 203, 206.

28   Friedrich Kittler, 'The Mechanized Philosopher', in Laurence A. Rickels (ed.), *Looking after Nietzsche*, Albany: State University of New York Press, 1990, p. 198; Kittler, *Gramophone, Film, Typewriter*, p. 184.

29   Manuel Castells, *The Rise of the Network Society*, Cambridge, Mass.: Blackwell, 1996, pp. 376-428.

30   Lev Manovich, *The Language of New Media*, Cambridge, Mass.: MIT Press, 2001.

31   See Niklas Luhmann, *Art as a Social System*, trans. Eva M. Knodt, Stanford, Cal.: Stanford University Press, 2000, p. 185.

32   Ibid., p. 187.

33   Massumi, *Parables for the Virtual*, p. 6.

34   Ibid., p. 8.

35   Ibid., p. 7.

36   Ibid., pp. 16-17, 208-256. See also Gilles Deleuze, *Empiricism and Subjectivity: An Essay on Hume's Theory of Human Nature*, trans. Constantin V. Boundas, New York: Columbia University Press, 1991.

37   Brian Massumi, *A User's Guide to Capitalism and Schizophrenia: Deviations from Deleuze and Guattari*, Cambridge, Mass.: MIT Press, 1992, pp. 36-37.

38   Deleuze, *Cinema 1*, p. 8.

39   On the role of 'formations', see Brian Massumi, 'Introduction: Like a Thought', in Brian Massumi (ed.), *A Shock to Thought: Expression after Deleuze and Guattari*, London and New York: Routledge, 2002, pp. xvii-xix.

40   Massumi, *Parables for the Virtual*, p. 216.

41   Ibid., p. 152.

42   Ibid., p. 8.

43   In this relation, then, are the seeds to explore the relationship between empiricism, the imaginary and ideology.

44   Louis Althusser, 'Ideology and Ideological State Apparatuses', in *Lenin and Philosophy and Other Essays*, trans. Ben Brewster, New York: Monthly Review Press, 1971, pp. 127-186.

45   See Slavoj Žižek, *The Sublime Object of Ideology*, London and New York: Verso, 1989.

46   John Frow, 'Marxism and Structuralism', in *Marxism and Literary History*, Oxford: Basil Blackwell, 1986, pp. 22-23.

47   Slavoj Žižek, 'Holding the Place', in Judith Butler, Ernesto Laclau and Slavoj Žižek *Contingency, Hegemony, Universality: Contemporary Dialogues on the Left*, London and New York: Verso, 2000, p. 311.

48   See, in particular, Wark, *Virtual Geography*.

49   I am drawing this term from Guattari. For an outline of this concept, see Félix Guattari, 'The Place of the Signifier in the Institution', trans. Gary Genosko, in *The Guattari Reader*, ed. Gary Genosko, Ox-

ford: Blackwell, 1996, pp. 148-157. Gary Genosko's own work is enormously helpful in understanding Guattari. See Gary Genosko, *Félix Guattari: An Aberrant Introduction*, London and New York: Continuum, 2002.

50   Félix Guattari, *Chaosmosis: An Ethico-Aesthetic Paradigm*, trans. Paul Bains and Julian Pefanis, Sydney: Power Publications, 1995, pp. 24, 39, 105, 106.

51   Of course Hall is no slouch, and is the first to acknowledge – in typical reflexive fashion – the limitations of the encoding/decoding model. See Stuart Hall et al., 'Reflections upon the Encoding/Decoding Model: An Interview with Stuart Hall', in Jon Cruz and Justin Lewis (eds), *Viewing, Reading, Listening: Audiences and Cultural Reception*, Boulder: Westview Press, 1994, pp. 255-256.

52   Gary Genosko, email correspondence, 16 December, 2003.

53   Ibid.

54   See Deleuze and Guattari, *What is Philosophy?*, pp. 163-199.

55   Wark's book *Dispositions*, Applecross and Cambridge: Salt Publishing, 2002, is one that I would consider as exemplary of the sort of superempiricism I'm describing. I think Eric Michaels' work also fits the category and maybe even Malinowski's diary. Certainly Serres. Enough names!

56   Genosko, email correspondence.

57   Kittler, *Gramophone, Film, Typewriter*, p. 259.

58   Bateson, *Steps to an Ecology of Mind*, pp. 474-475. Interesting accounts of cybernetics and computer processing can also be read in James R. Beniger, *The Control Revolution: Technological and Economic Origins of the Information Society*, Cambridge, Mass.: Harvard University Press, 1986; Thierry Bardin, *Bootstrapping: Douglas Engelbart, Coevolution, and the Origins of Personal Computing*, Stanford, Cal.: Stanford University Press, 2000; Tiziana Terranova, *Network Culture: Politics for the Information Age*, London: Pluto Press, 2004.

59   Hall stresses that his encoding/decoding paper was motivated by very local concerns: at the level of methodology and theorization, he sought to contest the impasse of traditional uses-and-gratifications content analysis undertaken by the Centre for Mass Communications Research at the University of Leicester in the late 1960s, early '70s. See Hall et al., 'Reflections upon the Encoding/Decoding Model', pp. 253-256.

60   N. Katherine Hayles, *How We Became Posthuman: Virtual Bodies in Cybernetics, Literature, and Infomatics*, Chicago and London: University of Chicago Press, 1999, p. 52.

61   Neil Chenoweth discusses the influence of games theory on Murdoch during his studies at Oxford in the early 1950s. Neil Chenoweth, *Virtual Murdoch: Reality Wars on the Information Highway*, London: Vintage, 2002, pp. 19-21.

62   Bateson, *Steps to an Ecology of Mind*, p. 475.

63   Paul Virilio, *The Art of the Motor*, trans. Julie Rose, Minneapolis: University of Minnesota Press, 1995, p. 125.

64   For a discussion of Maturana and Varela, see Hayles, *How We Became Posthuman*, pp. 131-159. An example of a second-order feedback model applied to the development of open source content and collaboration with African universities can be found in Derek Keats, 'Collaborative Development of Open Content: A Process Model to Unlock the Potential of African Universities', *First Monday* 8.2 (2003), http://www.firstmonday.dk/issues/issue8_2/keats/index.html.

65   Hayles, *How We Became Posthuman*, p. 77.

66   See Niklas Luhmann, *Social Systems*, trans. John Bednarz, Jr. with Dirk Baecker, Stanford, Cal.: Stanford University Press, 1995. See also Massumi, *Parables for the Virtual*, p. 8.

67   Luhmann, *Social Systems*, p. 37.

68   Luhmann, *Social Systems*, p. 42.

69   Keith Ansell Pearson, *Viroid Life: Perspectives on Nietzsche and the Transhuman Condition*, London and New York: Routledge, 1997, p. 141. Genosko also picks up on this point by Pearson in his discussion of how Guattari extends the model of autopoiesis and second-order cybernetics into the realm of social relations and 'machinic autopoiesis'. Genosko, *Félix Guattari*, pp. 195-200.

70   See Massumi, *Parables for the Virtual*, p. 14.

71   Ilya Prigogine and Isabelle Stengers, *Order out of Chaos: Man's New Dialogue with Nature*, London: Flamingo , 1985, pp. 12-14. See also Isabelle Stengers, *The Invention of Modern Science*, trans. Daniel W.

Smith, Minneapolis: University of Minnesota Press, 2000; Albert North Whitehead, *Process and Reality*, New York: Free Press, 1978.

72　Prigogine and Stengers, *Order out of Chaos*, p. 71.

73　Stengers, *The Invention of Modern Science*, p. 72.

74　See Thomas Frank, *One Market Under God: Extreme Capitalism, Market Populism, and the End of Economic Democracy*, New York: Anchor Books, 2000, p. 343.

75　As Chenoweth recounts in *Virtual Murdoch*, 'The Nasdaq composite index of high-tech stocks, which was the surest guide to the state of the tech economy, in the first three weeks of April had dropped 34 per cent down to 3200' (p. 339). By 2001 the fall had increased to 90 per cent. See also Robert Brenner, *The Boom and the Bubble: The US in the World Economy*, London and New York: Verso, 2002.

76　For a rich analysis of the Wall Street stock market crash of October 1987, see Wark, *Virtual Geography*, pp. 167-228. For an idiosyncratic analysis of foreign exchange markets, traders and the role of the computer screen, see Karin Knorr Cetina and Urs Brugger, 'Traders' Engagement with Markets: A Postsocial Relationship', *Theory, Culture & Society* 19.5/6 (2002): 161-185. See also Brian Holmes, 'The Artistic Device: Or the Articulation of Collective Speech', *ephemera: theory & politics in organization* 6.4 (2006), http://www.ephemeraweb.org/.

77　Michael Goldberg, Michael *catchingafallingknife.com*, Artspace, Sydney, 17 October-19 November, 2002, http://www.catchingafallingknife.com. Unfortunately this site has since been taken down and limited documentation can be found at: http://www.michael-goldberg.com. A surprising amount of material is available through the Internet Archive's Wayback Machine, http://www.archive.org. See also Michael Goldberg, 'Catching a Falling Knife: a Study in Greed, Fear and Irrational Exuberance', lecture at the Art Gallery of New South Wales, Sydney, 20 September, 2003, http://www.artgallery.nsw.gov.au/aaanz03/__data/page/2974/Michael_Goldberg.doc.

78　Felix Stalder, 'Space of Flows: Characteristics and Strategies', posting to nettime mailing list, 26 November, 2002, http://www.nettime.org. See also Felix Stalder, *Open Cultures and the Nature of Networks*, Novi Sad: kuda.org and Sarajevo Center for Contemporary Art, 2005. Available at: http://felix.open-flows.org/pdf/Notebook_eng.pdf.

79　Felix Stalder, 'Actor-Network-Theory and Communications Networks: Toward Convergence', 1997, http://felix.openflows.org/html/Network_Theory.html.

80　Geert Lovink, 'Catching a Falling Knife: The Art of Day Trading, Interview with Michael Goldberg', posting to fibreculture mailing list, 16 October, 2002, http://www.fibreculture.org.

81　Lash, *Critique of Information*, p. 112.

82　Wulf R. Halbach, 'Simulated Breakdowns', in Hans Ulrich Gumbrecht and K. Ludwig Pfeiffer (eds), *Materialities of Communication*, trans. William Whobrey, Stanford, Cal.: Stanford University Press, 1994, p. 338.

83　Genosko, email correspondence.

84　Ibid.

85　Doug Henwood, *Wall Street*, London and New York: Verso, 1998, p. 105.

86　Edward A. Shanken, 'Art in the Information Age: Technology and Conceptual Art', *SIGGRAPH 2001 Electronic Art and Animation Catalog*, New York: ACM SIGGRAPH, 2001, pp. 8-15. Also available in *Leonardo* 35.4 (2002): 433-438.

87　Halbach, 'Simulated Breakdowns', p. 341.

88　Michael Goldberg, 'Goldberg Consortium Transcript', 3 November, 2002, http:// http://www.catchingafallingknife.com. Since this link is dead, the report may be recoverable through the Internet Archive, http://www.archive.org.

89　Wark, *Virtual Geography*, p. 189.

90　Ibid., p. 190.

91　Chenoweth, *Virtual Murdoch*, p. 76.

92　Massumi, *Parables for the Virtual*, p. 214.

93　Ibid., p. 8.

94　Kittler, *Gramophone, Film, Typewriter*, p. 115.

95　Serres, *Genesis*, p. 95.

96 For a particularly engaging critique of Lash's book, see Robert Hassan, 'Embrace Your Fate', *Continuum: Journal of Media & Cultural Studies* 17.1 (2003): 105-109.

97 Lash, *Critique of Information*, pp. 72-74.

98 See Lovink's analysis of 'swatch-time' in 'Net.Times, Not Swatch Time: 21st-Century Global Time Wars', in *Dark Fiber: Tracking Critical Internet Culture*, Cambridge, Mass.: MIT Press, 2002, pp. 142-159.

99 Wark, *Virtual Geography*, p. 222.

100 Thanks to David Holmes for reminding me of this idea, among others.

101 See Jay David Bolter and Richard Grusin, *Remediation: Understanding New Media*, Cambridge, Mass.: MIT Press, 1999.

102 Kittler, *Gramophone, Film, Typewriter*, p. 2.

103 David Harvey, *The Condition of Postmodernity: An Inquiry into the Origins of Cultural Change*, Cambridge, Mass.: Blackwell, 1990.

104 Holmes, email correspondence.

105 Paul D. Miller, *Rhythm Science*, Cambridge, Mass.: MIT Press, 2004, p. 88.

106 Antonio Negri with Anne Dufourmantelle, *Negri on Negri*, trans. M. B. DeBevoise, London and New York: Routledge, 2004, p. 49.

107 Ibid.

Chapter 6

1 See Gilles Deleuze, *Empiricism and Subjectivity: An Essay on Hume's Theory of Human Nature*, trans. Constantin V Boundas, New York: Columbia University Press, 1991. See also Gilles Deleuze and Claire Parnet, *Dialogues II*, trans. Hugh Tomlinson, Barbara Habberjam and Elliot Ross Albert, London and New York: Continuum, 2002.

2 See Antonio Negri, 'Public Sphere, Labour and Multitude', trans. Arianna Bove, *MakeWorld Paper* 3 (2003): 4. Also available at, http://www.makeworlds.org/?q=node/view/11.

3 Antonio Negri, 'Towards an Ontological Definition of the Multitudes', trans. Arianna Bove, *Makeworlds Paper* 4 (2004), http://www/makeworlds.org/book/view/104.

4 Briefly, I would suggest two examples that approach how I am conceiving organized networks here: Sarai, a Delhi based media centre ⟨http://www.sarai.net⟩; and Fibreculture, a network of Internet research and culture in Australasia ⟨http://www.fibreculture.org⟩. In their own ways, the conditions of possibility for the emergence of these networks can be understood in terms of the constitutive outside. Both networks address specific problems of sociality, politics, and intellectual transdisciplinarity filtered – at least in the case of fibreculture – through a void created by established institutions within the cultural industries and higher education sector.

5 Gary Genosko, 'Félix Guattari: Towards a Transdisciplinary Metamethodology', *Angelaki* 8.1 (2003): 33.

6 Franco 'Bifo' Berardi, 'What is the Meaning of Autonomy Today?', *republicart*, September, 2003, http://www.republicart.net/disc/realpublicspaces/berardi01_en.htm.

7 Paolo Virno, *A Grammar of the Multitude*, trans. James Cascaito Isabella Bertoletti, and Andrea Casson, forward by Sylvère Lotringer, New York: Semiotext(e), 2004.

8 Chantal Mouffe, *The Democratic Paradox*, London: Verso, 2000.

9 See also Ned Rossiter, 'Modalities of Indigenous Sovereignty, Transformations of the Nation-State, and Intellectual Property Regimes', *Borderlands E-Journal: New Spaces in the Humanities* 1.2 (2002), http://www.borderlandsejournal.adelaide.edu.au/issues/vol1no2.html.

10 See Virno, *A Grammar of the Multitude*, p. 24.

11 See also Andrew Kenyon and Esther Milne, 'Images of Celebrity: Publicity, Privacy, Law', *Media & Arts Law Review*, 10.4 (2005), http://www.law.unimelb.edu.au/cmcl/malr/contents104.html.

12 Virno also recognizes the similarities between these two formations: 'The notion of the multitude seems to share something with liberal thought because it values individuality but, at the same time, it distances itself from it radically because this individuality is the final product of a process of individuation which stems from the universal, the generic, the pre-individual'. *A Grammar of the Multitude*, p. 76. I unpack the distinctions between individuality, its attendant process of individualization, and individuation below.

13 Gilles Deleuze, *Cinema 1: The Movement Image*, trans. Hugh Tomlinson and Barbara Habberjam, Minneapolis: University of Minnesota Press, 1986, p. 8.

14 Michael Hardt and Antonio Negri, *Multitude: War and Democracy in the Age of Empire*, New York: Penguin Press, 2004. See also Negri, 'Towards an Ontological Definition of the Multitudes'. For an argument that identifies class as the primary antagonism and basis for intervention within informational politics, see McKenzie Wark, *A Hacker Manifesto*, Cambridge, Mass.: Harvard University Press, 2004.

15 Virno, *A Grammar of the Multitude*, p. 52.

16 Ibid., p. 68.

17 Mouffe, *The Democratic Paradox*, p. 103.

18 See J. Macgregor Wise, *Exploring Technology and Social Space*, Thousand Oaks, Cal.: Sage, 1997, p. 43; Antonio Negri with Anne Dufourmantelle, *Negri on Negri*, trans. MB DeBevoise, London and New York: Routledge, 2004, p. 124.

19 Negri, 'Towards an Ontological Definition of the Multitudes'.

20 Virno, *A Grammar of the Multitude*, p. 79.

21 See Brian Massumi, *Parables for the Virtual: Movement, Affect, Sensation*, Durham and London: Duke University Press, 2002, pp. 1-25.

22 Franco 'Bifo' Berardi, 'Media, Image, Dispositif', seminar presentation, University of Technology, Sydney, 9 September, 2004, and published as 'The Image Dispositif', trans. Marc Cote, *Cultural Studies Review* 11.2 (2005): 64-68.

23 I am paraphrasing Bifo's conception of the infosphere and psychosphere, based on my notes from the seminar presentation and the abstract of the paper.

24 Michel Serres, *The Birth of Physics*, trans. Jack Hawkes, London: Clinamen Press, 2001.

25 This is a distinction Geert Lovink touches on in dialogue with Trebor Scholz in the newspaper for the Free Cooperation conference that took place in Buffalo, New York in April 2004, http://freecooperation.org. See Geert Lovink and Trebor Scholz, 'A Dialogue between Geert Lovink and Trebor Scholz', *Free Cooperation Newspaper*, 2004, p. 8. Also available at: http://freecooperation.org. Given his own connections with the Social Science Research Council, NYC, Lovink may well be referring to a response paper by Evan Henshaw-Plath, 'Network Technology and Networked Organizations', response paper in Information Technology and International Cooperation research stream, Social Science Research Council, New York City, 2003, http://www.ssrc.org/programs/itic/publications/knowledge_report/memos/evan.pdf.

26 For an original study of the way in which the home computer has shaped domestic living, see Elaine Lally, *Materializing Culture: At Home with Computers*, Oxford and New York: Berg, 2002.

27 This is the category error that so much digital architecture is prone to make. For all the rhetoric among contemporary architectural theorists and designers to escape the modernist iron cage of 'form follows function', it's more often the case that a sad extension of this modernist logic as 'form follows form' occurs under the spectral wonders of digital pixels. The work of New York and Californian architects Greg Lynn and Marcos Novak are standout examples of this tendency.

28 The hugely influential work of people such as John Fiske and Dick Hebdige in the USA, as well as others in the UK and Australia, has spawned countless books, essays, dissertations and postings to listservs that celebrate the 'guerrilla tactics' of subcultural practices. While I can't substantiate the claim, my sense over the years is that the tendency toward a valorisation of so-called everyday tactics as oppositional politics is more pronounced within cultural studies programmes and research in the USA than elsewhere. The concentration of publishers, number of universities, and size of the student and academic population in the USA would be obvious starting points to a study of this phenomenon. Someone else can do the number crunching if they really want to. For a critique of this style of cultural studies, see Thomas Frank, *One Market Under God: Extreme Capitalism, Market Populism, and the End of Economic Democracy*, New York: Anchor Books, 2000.

29 It will be interesting to see the extent to which the Creative Commons licence is adopted by big business – I'm guessing it'll create a suitable amount of havoc, enabling service variation and consolidate an even brighter future for the legal industry. For more information on Creative Commons – an open source style set of standards whereby some rights of authorship and intellectual production are reserved, see http://creativecommons.org.

30 Virno, *A Grammar of the Multitude*, p. 51.

31 Ibid., p. 49-51.

32 Ibid., p. 50.

33 Gregory Bateson, *Steps to an Ecology of Mind*, New York: Ballantine Books, 1972.

34 See http://ocw.mit.edu/index.html.

35 Gilles Deleuze, 'On Gilbert Simondon', in *Desert Islands and Other Texts, 1953–1974*, trans. Michael Taormina, ed. David Lapoujade, New York: Semiotext(e), 2004, pp. 86-89; Adrian Mackenzie, *Transductions: Bodies and Machines at Speed*, New York: Continuum, 2002; Virno, *A Grammar of the Multitude*, p. 76.

36 See Virno, *A Grammar of the Multitude*, p. 80.

37 Mackenzie, *Transductions*, p. 18.

38 See Mackenzie, *Transductions*. See also Andrew Murphie, 'The World as Clock: The Network Society and Experimental Ecologies', *Topia: A Canadian Journal of Cultural Studies* 11 (2004): 117-139.

39 Mackenzie, *Transductions*, pp. 16-19.

40 Murphie, 'The World as Clock', p. 120.

41 Ulrich Beck, *What is Globalization?*, trans. Patrick Camiller, Cambridge: Polity Press, 2000, p. 8.

42 Ibid., p. 8.

43 Ibid., p. 9.

44 Ibid., p. 9-11.

45 Scott Lash, *Critique of Information*, London: Sage, 2002, pp. 39-48.

46 David Harvey, *The Condition of Postmodernity: An Inquiry into the Origins of Cultural Change*, Cambridge, Mass.: Blackwell, 1990.

47 Lash, *Critique of Information*, pp. 39-40.

48 Paul D. Miller, *Rhythm Science*, Cambridge, Mass.: MIT Press, 2004, p. 72.

49 Michael Hardt and Antonio Negri, *Empire*, Harvard University Press, Cambridge, Mass., p. 294.

50 Virno, *A Grammar of the Multitude*, p. 81.

51 Ibid., p. 82.

52 Ibid., p. 49.

53 Deleuze, 'On Gilbert Simondon', p. 86.

54 A comment Bifo makes in the documentary *A World to Invent* (2002), by Florian Schneider. For more information on the *What is to be Done?* series and related media projects, see http://www.kein.org/projects. For a review of this series, see Brett Neilson and Ned Rossiter, 'Report on Creative Labour Workshop', posting to fibreculture mailing list, 30 April, 2004, http://www.fibreculture.org.

55 Virno, *A Grammar of the Multitude*, p. 43.

56 See Raymond Williams, 'Communications Technologies and Social Institutions', in Raymond Williams (ed.), *Contact: Human Communication and its History*, London: Thames & Hudson, 1981, pp. 226-238.

Bibliography

Acland, Charles R. and Buxton, William J. (eds). *Harold Innis in the New Century: Reflections and Refractions*, Montreal & Kingston: McGill-Queen's University Press, 1999.

Admissions Officers and Credential Evaluators' (ACE). Professional Section of the European Association for International Education (EAIE), http://www.aic.lv/ace/default.htm.

Adorno, Theodor W. *Negative Dialectics*, trans. E. B. Ashton, London: Routledge, 1990.

Agamben, Giorgio. *The Coming Community*, trans. Michael Hardt, Minneapolis: University of Minnesota Press, 1993.

Agre, Phil. 'Commodity and Community: Institutional Design for the Networked University', in Kevin Robbins and Frank Webster (eds), *The Virtual University? Knowledge, Markets and Managment*, Oxford: Oxford University Press, 2001, pp. 210-223.

_____. 'Real-Time Politics: The Internet and the Political Process', *The Information Society* 18.5 (2002): 311-331.

Althusser, Louis. 'Ideology and Ideological State Apparatuses', in *Lenin and Philosophy and Other Essays*, trans. Ben Brewster, New York: Monthly Review Press, 1971, pp. 127-186.

Althusser, Louis and Balibar, Étienne. *Reading Capital*, trans. Ben Brewster, London: Verso, 1979.

Angus, Ian. 'The Politics of Common Sense: Articulation Theory and Critical Communication Studies', *Communication Yearbook* 15 (1992): 535-570.

_____. 'Orality in the Twilight of Humanism: A Critique of the Communication Theory of Harold Innis', *Continuum: The Australian Journal of Media & Culture* 7.1 (1993): 16-42.

_____. 'The Materiality of Expression: Harold Innis' Communication Theory and the Discursive Turn in the Human Sciences', *Canadian Journal of Communication* 23.1 (1998): 9-29.

Ian Angus and Brian Shoesmith, 'Dependency/Space/Policy: An Introduction to a Dialogue with Harold Innis', *Continuum: The Australian Journal of Media & Culture* 7.1 (1993): 5-15.

_____ (eds). 'Dependency/Space/Policy: A Dialogue with Harold A. Innis', Special Issue, *Continuum: The Australian Journal of Media & Culture* 7.1 (1993). Also available at: http://wwwmcc.murdoch.edu.au/ReadingRoom/continuum2.html.

Arnold, Mathew. *Culture and Anarchy*, Cambridge: Cambridge University Press, 1960.

Bateson, Gregory. *Steps to an Ecology of Mind*, New York: Ballantine Books, 1972.

Barcan, Ruth. 'The Idleness of Academics: Reflections on the Usefulness of Cultural Studies', *Continuum: Journal of Media & Cultural Studies* 4.4 (2003): 363-378.

Bardin, Thierry. *Bootstrapping: Douglas Engelbart, Coevolution, and the Origins of Personal Computing*, Stanford, Cal.: Stanford University Press, 2000.

Bauman, Zygmunt. *The Individualized Society*, Cambridge: Polity Press, 2001.

Baudrillard, Jean. 'The Violence of the Global', trans. François Debrix, *Ctheory*, a129, May, 2003, http://www.ctheory.net/text_file.asp?pick=385.

Beasley-Murray, Jon. 'Politics', Posthegemony: Hegemony, Posthegemony, and Related Matters, 16 July 2006, http://posthegemony.blogspot.com/2006/07/politics.html.

Beck, Ulrich. *Risk Society: Towards a New Modernity*, trans. M. Ritter, London: Sage, 1992.

_____. *The Brave New World of Work*, trans. Patrick Camiller, Cambridge: Polity, 2000.

_____. *What is Globalization?*, trans. Patrick Camiller, Cambridge: Polity Press, 2000.

Beniger, James R. *The Control Revolution: Technological and Economic Origins of the Information Society*, Cambridge, Mass.: Harvard University Press, 1986.

Bennett, Tony. *The Birth of the Museum: History, Theory, Politics*, London and New York: Routledge, 1995.

Bensaid, Daniel. 'Sovereignty, Nation, Empire', trans. Isabel Brenner, Kathryn Dykstra, Penny Oliver and Tracey Williams, in William F. Fisher and Thomas Ponniah (eds), *Another World Is Possible: Popular Alternatives to Globalization at the World Social Forum*, London and New York: Zed Books, 2003, pp. 317-323.

Franco 'Bifo' Berardi, 'What is the Meaning of Autonomy Today?', *republicart*, September, 2003, http://www.republicart.net/disc/realpublicspaces/berardi01_en.htm.

_____. 'The Image Dispositif', trans. Marc Cote, *Cultural Studies Review* 11.2 (2005): 64-68.

Berland, Jody. 'Space at the Margins: Colonial Spatiality and Critical Theory After Innis', *Topia: A Canadian Journal of Cultural Studies* 1 (1997): 55-82.

_____. 'Nationalism and the Modernist Legacy: Dialogues with Innis', *Culture & Policy* 8.3 (1997): 9-39.

Betancourt, Valeria. *The World Summit on the Information Society (wsis): Process and Issues Debated*, Association for Progressive Communications (APC), 2004, http://www.apc.org.

Blackburn, Robin. 'The Enron Debacle and the Pension Crisis', *New Left Review* 14 (2002): 26-51.

Blumler, J. and Katz, Elihu (eds). *The Uses and Gratifications Approach to Mass Communications Research. Annual Review of Communication Research*, Volume 3, Beverly Hills, Cal.: Sage, 1975.

Blustein, Paul. 'IMF Medicine: the Right Cure?', *International Herald Tribune* 27 September, 2002, pp. 1, 9.

Bojadzijev, Manuela and Saint-Saëns, Isabelle. 'Borders, Citizenship, War, Class: A Discussion with Étienne Balibar and Sandro Mezzadra', *New Formations* 58 (2006): 10-30.

Bologna Secretariat, http://www.dfes.gov.uk/bologna/.

Bolter, Jay David and Grusin, Richard. *Remediation: Understanding New Media*, Cambridge, Mass.: MIT Press, 1999.

Bolz, Norbert. 'Rethinking Media Aesthetics', in Geert Lovink, *Uncanny Networks: Dialogues with the Virtual Intelligentsia*, Cambridge, Mass.: MIT Press, 2000, pp. 18-27.

Bourdieu, Pierre. 'Public Opinion Does Not Exist (1973)', trans. Mary C. Axtmann in Armand Mattelart and Seth Siegelaub (eds), *Communication and Class Struggle, Vol. 1: Capitalism, Imperialism*, New York: International General, 1979, pp. 124-130.

Bourdieu, Pierre and Wacquant, Loïc J. D. *An Invitation to Reflexive Sociology*, Chicago: University of Chicago Press, 1992.

Bousquet, Marc. 'The "Informal Economy" of the Information University', *Workplace: A Journal for Academic Labour* 5.1 (2002), http://www.cust.educ.ubc.ca/workplace/issue5p1/bousquetinformal.html.

Brantlinger, Patrick. *Crusoe's Footprints: Cultural Studies in Britain and America*, New York and London: Routledge, 1990.

Brennan, Timothy. 'The Empire's New Clothes', *Critical Inquiry* 29.2 (2003): 337-367.

Brenner, Robert. *The Boom and the Bubble: The US in the World Economy*, London and New York: Verso, 2002.

Buck-Morss, Susan. *The Origin of Negative Dialectics: Theodor W. Adorno, Walter Benjamin, and the Frankfurt Institute*, New York: Free Press, 1977.

_____. *The Dialectics of Seeing: Walter Benjamin and the Arcades Project*, Cambridge, Mass.: MIT Press, 1989.

_____. *Thinking Past Terror: Islamism and Critical Theory on the Left*, London and New York: Verso, 2003.

Burgmann, Verity. *Power, Profit and Protest: Australian Social Movements and Globalisation*, Crows Nest: Allen and Unwin, 2003.

Butt, Danny (ed.). *Internet Governance: Asia-Pacific Perspectives*, New Dehli: Elsevier and UNDP Asia-Pacific Development Information Programme, 2005. Available at: http://www.apdip.net/publications/ict4d/igovperspectives.pdf.

Butt, Danny and Rossiter, Ned. 'Blowing Bubbles: Post-Crash Creative Industries and the Withering of Political Critique in Cultural Studies', paper presented at Ute Culture: The Utility of Culture and the Uses of Cultural Studies, Cultural Studies Association of Australia Conference, Melbourne, December 5-7, 2002. Posted to fibreculture mailing list, 10 December, 2002, http://www.fibreculture.org.

Byfield, Ted. 'CCTLDS, WSIS, ITU, ICANN, ETC', posting to nettime mailing list, 7 March, 2003, http://www.nettime.org.

Carey, James W. 'Space, Time, and Communications: A Tribute to Harold Innis', in *Communication as Culture: Essays on Media and Society*, New York: Routledge, 1992, pp. 142-172.

Castells, Manuel. 'Information Technology, Globalization and Social Development', UNRISD Discussion Paper, no. 114, September, 1999. Available at:

http://www.unrisd.org/unrisd/website/document.nsf/(httpPublications)/F270E0C066F3DE7780256B67005B728C?OpenDocument.

———. *The Rise of the Network Society*, Cambridge, Mass.: Blackwell, 1996.

Castells, Manuel and Ince, Martin. *Conversations with Manuel Castells*, Cambridge: Polity, 2003.

Caves, Richard. *Creative Industries: Contracts Between Art and Commerce*, Cambridge, Mass.: Harvard University Press, 2000.

Cetina, Karin Knorr and Brugger, Urs. 'Traders' Engagement with Markets: A Postsocial Relationship', *Theory, Culture & Society* 19.5/6 (2002): 161-185.

Chenoweth, Neil. *Virtual Murdoch: Reality Wars on the Information Highway*, London: Vintage, 2002.

Chesher, Chris. 'FTA and new media?', posting to fibreculture mailing list, 20 January, 2004, http://www.fibreculture.org.

Cisler, Steve. 'ICANN or UN?', posting to nettime mailing list, 12 December, 2003, http://www.nettime.org.

Clemens, Justin. *The Romanticism of Contemporary Theory: Institution, Aesthetics, Nihilism*, Aldershot: Ashgate, 2003.

Cooley, Alexander and Ron, James. 'The NGO Scramble: Organizational Insecurity and the Political Economy of Transnational Action', *International Security* 27.1 (2002): 5-39.

Cooper, Simon. 'Post Intellectuality?: Universities and the Knowledge Industry', in Simon Cooper, John Hinkson and Geoff Sharp (eds), *Scholars and Entrepreneurs: the University in Crisis*, Fitzroy: Arena Publications, 2002, pp. 207-232.

Correa, Carlos M. and Musungu, Sisule F. *The WIPO Patent Agenda: The Risks for Developing Countries*, Trade Related Agenda, Development and Equity (T.R.A.D.E.), Working Papers, no. 12, South Centre, 2002, http://www.southcentre.org/publications/wipopatent/wipopatent.pdf.

Correa, Carlos M. *The WIPO Draft Substantive Patent Law Treaty: A Review of Selected Provision*, Working Papers, no. 17, South Centre, 2004, p. 9, http://www.southcentre.org/publications/workingpapers/paper17/wp17.pdf.

Civil Society Declaration to the World Summit on the Information Society, *Shaping Information Societies for Human Needs*, WSIS Civil Society Plenary, Geneva, 2003, http://www.itu.int/wsis/docs/geneva/civil-society-declaration.pdf.

Coombe, Rosemary J. *The Cultural Life of Intellectual Properties: Authorship, Appropriation and the Law*, Durham and London: Duke University Press, 1998.

Costanza-Chock, Sasha. 'WSIS, the Neoliberal Agenda, and Counter-proposals from "Civil Society"', posting [by Geert Lovink] to nettime mailing list, 12 July, 2003, http://www.nettime.org.

Creative Industry Task Force: Mapping Document, DCMS (Department of Culture, Media and Sport) (1998/2001), London, http://www.culture.gov.uk/global/publications/archive_2001/ci_mapping_doc_2001.htm?properties=archive%5F2001%2C%2Fcreative%5Findustries%2FQuickLinks%2Fpublications%2Fdefault%2C&month=.

Cunningham, Stuart. 'Culture, Services, Knowledge or Is Content King, or are we just Drama Queens?', Communications Research Forum, Canberra, 2-3 October, 2002, http://eprints.qut.edu.au/archive/00000202/01/cunningham_culture.pdf.

———. 'The Evolving Creative Industries: From Original Assumptions to Contemporary Interpretations', seminar paper, QUT, Brisbane, 9 May, 2003, http://eprints.qut.edu.au/archive/00004391/01/4391.pdf.

Cunningham, Stuart; Hearn, Gregory; Cox, Stephen; Ninan, Abraham and Keane, Michael. *Brisbane's Creative Industries 2003*, Report delivered to Brisbane City Council, Community and Economic Development, Brisbane: CIRAC, 2003, http://eprints.qut.edu.au/archive/00002409/01/2409_2.pdf.

David, Paul A. and Foray, Dominque. 'An Introduction to the Economy of the Knowledge Society', *International Social Science Journal* 171 (2002): 9-23.

Debray, Régis. *Media Manifestos: On the Technological Transmission of Cultural Forms*, trans. Eric Rauth, London and New York: Verso, 1996.

Deibert, Ronald J. 'Harold Innis and the Empire of Speed', *Review of International Studies* 25 (1999): 273-289.

Dieter, Heribert. 'World Economy: Structures and Trends', in P. Kennedy, D. Messner and F. Nuscheler (eds), *Global Trends and Global Governance*, London: Pluto Press and Development and Peace Foundation, 2002, pp. 65-96.

Di Maggio, Paul (ed.). *The Twenty-First Century Firm: Changing Economic Organization in International Perspective*, Princeton: Princeton University Press, 2001.

Deleuze, Gilles. *Cinema 1: The Movement Image*, trans. Hugh Tomlinson and Barbara Habberjam, Minneapolis: University of Minnesota Press, 1986.

_____. *Foucault*, trans. Seán Hand, forw. Paul Bové, Minneapolis: University of Minnesota Press, 1988.

_____. *Spinoza: Practical Philosophy*, trans. Robert Hurley, San Francisco: City Lights, 1988.

_____. *Empiricism and Subjectivity: An Essay on Hume's Theory of Human Nature*, trans. Constantin V. Boundas, New York: Columbia University Press, 1991.

_____. *Difference and Repetition*, trans. Paul Patton, New York: Columbia University Press, 1994.

_____. *Negotiations, 1972-1990*, trans. Martin Joughin, New York: Columbia University Press, 1995.

_____. *Essays Critical and Clinical*, trans. Daniel W. Smith and Michael A. Greco, London and New York: Verso, 1998.

_____. *Pure Immanence: Essays on A Life*, trans. Anna Boyman, intro. John Rajchman, New York: Zone Books, 2001.

_____. 'On Gilbert Simondon', in *Desert Islands and Other Texts, 1953–1974*, trans. Michael Taormina, ed. David Lapoujade, New York: Semiotext(e), 2004, pp. 86–89.

Deleuze, Gilles and Guattari, Félix. *A Thousand Plateaus: Capitalism and Schizophrenia*, trans. Brian Massumi, Minneapolis: University of Minnesota Press, 1987.

_____. *What is Philosophy?*, trans. Hugh Tomlinson and Graham Burchill, New York: Columbia University Press, 1994.

Deleuze, Gilles and Parnet, Claire. *Dialogues II*, trans. Hugh Tomlinson, Barbara Habberjam and Elliot Ross Albert, London and New York: Continuum, 2002.

Drache, Daniel. 'Introduction: Celebrating Innis: The Man, the Legacy, and Our Future', in Harold A. Innis, *Staples, Markets, and Cultural Change*, ed. Daniel Drache, Montreal & Kingston: McGill-Queen's University Press, 1995, pp. xiii-lix.

Drake, William J. (ed.). *Reforming Internet Governance: Perspectives from the Working Group on Internet Governance (WGIG)*, New York: United Nations ICT Task Force, 2005. Available at: http://www.wgig.org/docs/book/WGIG_book.pdf.

European Union. *Exploitation and Development of Job Potential in the Cultural Sector in the Age of Digitalisation*, Final Report (Module 1), Commissioned by European Commission/DG Employment and Social Affairs, June, 2001, p. 36. Available at: http://europa.eu.int/comm/employment_social/empl_esf/docs/cult_sector/module1.pdf.

Flew, Terry. 'Cultural Materialism and Cultural Policy: Reassessing Raymond Williams', *Social Semiotics* 7.1 (1997): 5-19.

_____. 'The "New Empirics" in Internet Studies and Comparative Internet Policy', in Hugh Brown, Geert Lovink, Helen Merrick, Ned Rossiter, David Teh, Michele Willson (eds), *Politics of a Digital Present: An Inventory of Australian Net Culture, Criticism and Theory*, Melbourne: Fibreculture Publications, 2001, pp. 105-113.

_____. *New Media: An Introduction*, Oxford: Oxford University Press, 2002.

_____ (ed.). *Media & Arts Law Review*, Special Issue: Creative Commons and the Creative Industries 10.4 (2005), http://www.law.unimelb.edu.au/cmcl/malr/contents104.html.

Florida, Richard. *The Rise of the Creative Class: And How It's Transforming Work, Leisure, Community and Everyday Life*, New York: Basic Books, 2002.

Foucault, Michel. *The Archaeology of Knowledge* and *The Discourse on Language*, trans. A. M. Sheridan Smith, New York: Pantheon Books, 1972.

_____. *Maurice Blanchot: The Thought from the Outside*, trans. Brian Massumi, New York: Zone Books, 1990.

Fowles, J. *Why Viewers Watch: A Reappraisal of Television's Effects*, Newbury Park: Sage, 1992.

Frank, Thomas. *One Market Under God: Extreme Capitalism, Market Populism, and the End of Economic Democracy*, New York: Anchor Books, 2000.

Frow, John. 'Marxism and Structuralism', in *Marxism and Literary History*, Oxford: Basil Blackwell, 1986, pp. 18-50.

_____. 'Information as Gift and Commodity', *New Left Review* 219 (1996): 89-108.

Gadrey Jean., *New Economy, New Myth*, London and New York: Routledge, 2003.

Galloway, Alexander. *Protocol: How Control Exists After Decentralization*, Cambridge, Mass.: MIT Press, 2004.

Genosko, Gary. *Félix Guattari: An Aberrant Introduction*, London and New York: Continuum, 2002;

_____. 'Félix Guattari: Towards a Transdisciplinary Metamethodology', *Angelaki* 8.1 (2003): 29-40.

Gibson, Mark. 'Richard Hoggart's Grandmother's Ironing: Some Questions about "Power" in International Cultural Studies', *International Journal of Cultural Studies* 1.1 (1998): 25-44.

_____. 'The Temporality of Democracy: The Long Revolution and Diana, Princess of Wales', *New Formations* 36 (1999): 59-76.

_____. 'The Geography of Theory: Channel Crossings, Continental Invasions and the Anglo-American "Natives"', *symploke* 11.1/2 (2003): 152-166.

Gidddens, Anthony. *The Third Way: the Renewal of Social Democracy*, Cambridge: Polity Press, 1998.

Gill, Rosalind. 'Cool, Creative and Egalitarian? Exploring Gender in Project-based New Media Work in Europe', *Information, Communication & Society* 5.1 (2002): 70-89.

Given, Jock. *America's Pie: Trade and Culture After 9/11*, Sydney: University of New South Wales Press, 2003.

Goldberg, Michael. 'Goldberg Consortium Transcript', 3 November, 2002, http:// http://www.catchingafallingknife.com. Since this link is dead, the report may be recoverable through the Internet Archive, http://www.archive.org.

_____. 'Catching a Falling Knife: a Study in Greed, Fear and Irrational Exuberance', lecture at the Art Gallery of New South Wales, Sydney, 20 September, 2003, http://www.artgallery.nsw.gov.au/aaanz03/_data/page/2974/Michael_Goldberg.doc.

Grace, Helen. 'Eating the Curate's Egg: Cultural Studies for the Nineties', *West* 3.1 (1991): 46-49.

Gregg, Melissa. 'A Neglected History: Richard Hoggart's Discourse of Empathy', *Rethinking History: The Journal of Theory and Practice* 7.3 (2003): 285-306.

_____. *Cultural Studies' Affective Voices*, Basingstoke: Palgrave, 2006.

Guattari, Félix. *Chaosmosis: An Ethico-Aesthetic Paradigm*, trans. Paul Bains and Julian Pefanis, Sydney: Power Publications, 1995.

_____. 'La Borde: A Clinic Unlike Any Other', trans. D. L. Sweet, in *Chaosophy*, ed. Sylvère Lotringer, Semiotext(e): New York, 1995, pp. 187-208.

_____. 'The Place of the Signifier in the Institution', trans. Gary Genosko, in *The Guattari Reader*, ed. Gary Genosko, Oxford: Blackwell, 1996, pp. 148-157.

Habermas, Jürgen. *The Structural Transformation of the Public Sphere: An Inquiry into a Category of Bourgeois Society*, trans. Thomas Burger with Frederick Lawrence, Cambridge, Mass.: MIT Press, 1989.

Hage, Ghassan. *Against Paranoid Nationalism: Searching for Hope in a Shrinking Society*, Annandale: Pluto Press, 2003.

Halbach, Wulf R. 'Simulated Breakdowns', in Hans Ulrich Gumbrecht and K. Ludwig Pfeiffer (eds), *Materialities of Communication*, trans. William Whobrey, Stanford, Cal.: Stanford University Press, 1994, pp. 335-343.

Hall, Stuart et al. 'Reflections upon the Encoding/Decoding Model: An Interview with Stuart Hall', in Jon Cruz and Justin Lewis (eds), *Viewing, Reading, Listening: Audiences and Cultural Reception*, Boulder: Westview Press, 1994, pp. 253-274.

Hardt, Michael. *Gilles Deleuze: An Apprenticeship in Philosophy*, London: UCL Press, 1993.

_____. 'The Withering of Civil Society', *Social Text* 14.4 (1995): 27-44.

_____. 'Introduction: Laboratory Italy', in Paolo Virno and Michael Hardt (eds), *Radical Thought in Italy: A Potential Politics*, Minneapolis: University of Minnesota Press, 1996, pp. 1-10.

Michael Hardt and Antonio Negri, *Empire*, Cambridge, Mass.: Havard University Press, 2000.

_____. 'The Rod of the Forest Warden: A Response to Timothy Brennan (Critical Response I)', *Critical Inquiry* 29.2 (2003), http://www.uchicago.edu/research/jnl-crit-inq/issues/v29/v29n2.Hardt.html.

_____. *Multitude: War and Democracy in the Age of Empire*, New York: Penguin Press, 2004.

Hartley, John and Cunningham, Stuart. 'Creative Industries: from Blue Poles to fat pipes', in Malcolm Gillies (ed.), *The National Humanities and Social Sciences Summit: Position Papers*, Canberra: DEST, 2002. Available at: http://www.dest.gov.au/NR/rdonlyres/C785B22C-E7EC-47D0-9781-C5AA68546FCD/1426/summit701.pdf.

Harvey, David. *The Condition of Postmodernity: An Inquiry into the Origins of Cultural Change*, Cambridge, Mass.: Blackwell, 1990.

______. 'Globalization in Question', *Rethinking Marxism* 8.4 (1995): 1-17.

______. *A Brief History of Neoliberalism*, Oxford: Oxford University Press, 2005;

Hassan, Robert. 'Embrace Your Fate', *Continuum: Journal of Media & Cultural Studies* 17.1 (2003): 105-109.

Hayden, Steve. 'Tastes Great, Less Filling: Ad Space – Will Advertisers Learn the Hard Lesson of Over-Development?', *Wired Magazine* 11, 6 June, 2003, http://www.wired.com/wired/archive/11.06/ad_spc.html.

Hayles, N. Katherine. *How We Became Posthuman: Virtual Bodies in Cybernetics, Literature, and Infomatics*, Chicago and London: University of Chicago Press, 1999.

Henshaw-Plath, Evan. 'Network Technology and Networked Organizations', response paper in Information Technology and International Cooperation research stream, Social Science Research Council, New York City, 2003, http://www.ssrc.org/programs/itic/publications/knowledge_report/memos/evan.pdf.

Henwood, Doug. *Wall Street*, London and New York: Verso, 1998.

______. *After the New Economy*, New York: The New Press, 2003.

Hesmondhalgh, David. *The Cultural Industries*, London: Sage, 2002.

Hesmondhalgh, David and Pratt, Andy C. (eds). *International Journal of Cultural Policy* 11.1 (2005).

Holmes, Brian. 'The Flexible Personality' (Parts 1 & 2), posting to nettime mailing list, 5 January, 2002, http://www.nettime.org.

______. 'The Artistic Device: Or the Articulation of Collective Speech' *ephemera: theory & politics in organization* 6.4 (2006), http://www.ephemeraweb.org/.

Holmes, David. 'The Politics of Negative Theology', *Melbourne Journal of Politics* 20 (1991): 25-121.

______. 'Sociological Theory', in David Holmes, Kate Hughes and Roberta Julian, *Australian Sociology: A Changing Society*, Sydney: Pearson, 2003, pp. 21-87.

Hoogvelt, Ankie. *Globalization and the Postcolonial World: The New Political Economy of Development*, London: Palgrave, 2001.

Horkheimer, Max. 'The Present Situation of Social Philosophy', in *Between Philosophy and Social Science: Selected Early Writings*, trans. G Frederick Hunter, Matthew S. Kramer, and John Torpey, Cambridge, Mass: MIT Press, 1993, pp. 1-14.

Innis, Harold A. *The Bias of Communication*, Toronto: University of Toronto Press, 1951.

______. *Empire and Communications*, Victoria and Toronto: Press Porcépic, 1986

______. *Staples, Markets, and Cultural Change*, ed. Daniel Drache, Montreal & Kingston: McGill-Queen's University Press, 1995.

Jay, Martin. *Downcast Eyes: The Denigration of Vision in Twentieth-Century French Thought*, Berkeley: University of California Press, 1993.

______. *The Dialectical Imagination: A History of the Frankfurt School and the Institute of Social Research, 1923-1950*, Berkeley: University of California Press, 1996.

Joseph, Branden W. and Virno, Paolo. 'Interview with Paolo Virno', trans. Alessia Ricciardi, *Grey Room* 21 (Fall, 2005): 27-37. Available at: http://mitpress.mit.edu/journals/pdf/GR21_026-037_Jospeph.pdf.

Kaldor, Mary. *Global Civil Society: An Answer to War*, Cambridge: Polity, 2003.

Katz, Elihu and Lazarsfeld, Paul F. *Personal Influence: The Part Played by People in the Flow of Mass Communication*, Glencoe, Ill.: Free Press, 1970.

Keane, Michael. *Created in China: the Great New Leap Forward*, London: RoutledgeCurzon, forthcoming 2007.

Keats, Derek. 'Collaborative Development of Open Content: A Process Model to Unlock the Potential of African Universities', *First Monday* 8.2 (2003), http://www.firstmonday.dk/issues/issue8_2/keats/index.html.

Kenyon, Andrew and Milne, Esther. 'Images of Celebrity: Publicity, Privacy, Law', *Media & Arts Law Review*, 10.4 (2005), http://www.law.unimelb.edu.au/cmcl/malr/contents104.html.

Kittler, Friedrich. 'The Mechanized Philosopher', in Laurence A. Rickels (ed.), *Looking after Nietzsche*, Albany: State University of New York Press, 1990, pp. 195-207.

______. *Gramophone, Film, Typewriter*, trans. & intro. Geoffrey Winthrop-Young and Michael Wutz, Stanford, Cal.: Stanford University Press, 1999.

Klein, Hans. *Understanding wsis: An Institutional Analysis of the un World Summit on the Information Society*, Internet & Public Policy Project, School of Public Policy, Georgia Institute of Technology, 2003, http://IP3.gatech.edu.

Kleinwächter, Wolfgang. 'Civil Society and Global Diplomacy in the 21st Century: The Case of wsis or from Input to Impact?', February, Version 1.0, 2005.

Knuth, Rebecca. 'Sovereignty, Globalism and Information Flow in Complex Emergencies', *The Information Society* 15 (1999): 11-19.

Kücklich, Julian. 'Precarious Playbour: Modders and the Digital Games Industry', *Fibreculture Journal* 5 (2005), http://journal.fibreculture.org/issue5/kucklich.html.

Laclau, Ernesto. 'Can Immanence Explain Social Struggles?, in Paul A. Passavant and Jodi Dean (eds), *Empire's New Clothes: Reading Hardt and Negri*, New York and London: Routledge, 2004, pp. 21-30.

______. *On Populist Reason*, London and New York: Verso, 2005.

Lally, Elaine. *Materializing Culture: At Home with Computers*, Oxford and New York: Berg, 2002.

Lash, Scott. *Critique of Information*, London: Sage, 2002.

______. 'Reflexivity as Non-Linearity', *Theory, Culture & Society* 20.2 (2003): 49-57.

Lash, Scott and Urry, John. *The End of Organized Capitalism*, Cambridge: Polity, 1987.

______. *Economies of Signs and Space*, London: Sage, 1994.

Lasswell, Harold D. *Propaganda Technique in the World War*, New York: Knopf, 1927.

Latham, Mark. *What did you Learn Today? Creating an Education Revolution*, Crows Nest: Allen & Unwin, 2001.

Latour, Bruno. *We Have Never Been Modern*, trans. Catherine Porter, Cambridge, Mass.: Harvard University Press, 1993.

Lazzarato, Maurizio. 'General Intellect: Towards an Inquiry into Immaterial Labour', trans. Ed Emery, (n.d.), http://www.geocities.com/CognitiveCapitalism/lazzarato2.html.

______. 'Immaterial Labor', trans. Paul Colilli and Ed Emory, in Paolo Virno and Michael Hardt (eds), *Radical Thought in Italy: A Potential Politics*, Minneapolis: University of Minnesota Press, 1996, pp. 133-147.

Lewis, Tania. 'Intellectual Exchange and Located Transnationalism: Meaghan Morris and the Formation of Australian Cultural Studies', *Continuum: Journal of Media & Cultural Studies* 17.2 (2003): 187-206.

______. 'Stuart Hall and the Formation of British Cultural Studies: A Diasporic Narrative', *Imperium* IV (2004), http://www.imperiumjournal.com/index.html.

Lovink, Geert. 'Interview with Saskia Sassen on PGOs (for N5M3 TV)', posting to nettime mailing list, 25 February, 1999, http://www.nettime.org.

______. 'After the Dotcom Crash: Recent Literature on Internet, Business and Society', *Australian Humanities Review* 27 (September-December, 2002), http://www.lib.latrobe.edu.au/AHR/archive/Issue-September-2002/lovink.html.

______. 'Catching a Falling Knife: The Art of Day Trading, Interview with Michael Goldberg', posting to fibreculture mailing list, 16 October, 2002, http://www.fibreculture.org.

______. *Dark Fiber: Tracking Critical Internet Culture*, Cambridge, Mass.: MIT Press, 2002.

______. *Uncanny Networks: Dialogues with the Virtual Intelligentsia*, Cambridge, Mass.: MIT Press, 2000.

______. *My First Recession: Critical Internet Culture in Transition*, Rotterdam: V2_/NAi Publishers, 2003.

Lovink, Geert and Hofmann, Jeanette. 'Open Ends: Civil Society and Internet Governance [Interview]', posting to nettime mailing list, 12 August, 2004, http://www.nettime.org.

Lovink, Geert and Rossiter, Ned. 'Dawn of the Organised Networks', *Fibreculture Journal* 5 (2005), http://journal.fibreculture.org/issue5/lovink_rossiter.html.

Lovink, Geert and Scholz, Trebor. 'A Dialogue between Geert Lovink and Trebor Scholz', *Free Cooperation Newspaper*, 2004, p. 8. Also available at: http://freecooperation.org.

______ (eds). *The Art of Online Collaboration*, New York: Autonomedia, 2006.

Lovink, Geert and Spehr, Christoph. 'Out-Cooperating Empire: Exchange on Creative Labour and the Hyrbid Work of Collaboration', 2006. Available at: http://www.networkcultures.org/geert/2006/07/08/out-cooperating-the-empire-exchange-with-christoph-spehr/.

Luhmann, Niklas. *Social Systems*, trans. John Bednarz, Jr. with Dirk Baecker, Stanford, Cal.: Stanford University Press, 1995.

———. *Art as a Social System*, trans. Eva M. Knodt, Stanford, Cal.: Stanford University Press, 2000.

Lyotard, Jean-François. 'The *Différend*, the Referent, and the Proper Name', trans. Georges Van Den Abbeele, *Diacritics* 14.3 (1984): 4-14.

———. *The Différend: Phrases in Dispute*, trans. Georges Van Den Abbeele, Minneapolis: University of Minnesota Press, 1988.

———. *The Inhuman: Reflections on Time*, trans. Geoffrey Bennington and Rachel Bowlby, Stanford, Cal.: Stanford University Press, 1991.

———. *Lessons on the Analytic of the Sublime*, trans. Elizabeth Rottenberg, Stanford, Cal: Stanford University Press, 1994.

McNamara, Andrew. 'How "Creative Industries" Evokes the Legacy of Modernist Visual Art', *Media International Australia* 102 (2002): 66-76.

McQuire, Scott. 'When is Art IT?', in Hugh Brown, Geert Lovink, Helen Merrick, Ned Rossiter, David Teh, Michele Willson (eds), *Politics of a Digital Present: An Inventory of Australian Net Culture, Criticism and Theory*, Melbourne: Fibreculture Publications, 2001, pp. 205-213.

McRobbie, Angela. 'Clubs to Companies: Notes on the Decline of Political Culture in Speeded up Creative Worlds', *Cultural Studies* 16.4 (2002): 516-531.

Mackenzie, Adrian. *Transductions: Bodies and Machines at Speed*, New York: Continuum, 2002.

Lev Manovich, *The Language of New Media*, Cambridge, Mass.: MIT Press, 2001.

Marginson, Simon and Considine, Mark. *The Enterprise University: Power, Governance and Reinvention in Australia*, Cambridge: Cambridge University Press, 2000.

Marx, Karl. 'Excerpt from *A Contribution to the Critique of Political Economy*', in Karl Marx and Friedrich Engels *Basic Writings on Politics and Philosophy*, ed. Lewis S. Feuer, New York: Doubleday, 1959, pp. 42-46.

Marx, Karl and Engels, Frederick. *The German Ideology*, Moscow: Progress Publishers, 1976.

Massumi, Brian. *A User's Guide to Capitalism and Schizophrenia: Deviations from Deleuze and Guattari*, Cambridge, Mass.: MIT Press, 1992.

———. *Parables for the Virtual: Movement, Affect, Sensation*, Durham and London: Duke University Press, 2002.

———. 'Introduction: Like a Thought', in Brian Massumi (ed.), *A Shock to Thought: Expression after Deleuze and Guattari*, London and New York: Routledge, 2002, pp. xiii-xxxix.

Mattelart, Armand and Mattelart, Michèle. *Theories of Communication: A Short Introduction*, trans. Susan Gruenheck Taponier and James A. Cohen, London: Sage, 1998.

Miller, Daniel and Slater, Don. *The Internet: An Ethnographic Approach*, Oxford and New York: Berg, 2000.

Miller, Paul D. *Rhythm Science*, Cambridge, Mass.: MIT Press, 2004.

Mitropoulos, Angela and Neilson, Brett. 'Exceptional Times, Non-Governmental Spacings, and Impolitical Movements', *Vacarme* (Janvier, 2006), http://www.vacarme.eu.org/article484.html.

———. 'Cutting Democracy's Knot', *Culture Machine* 8 (2006), http://culturemachine.tees.ac.uk/Articles/neilson.htm.

Morris, Christine and Meadows, Michael. 'Indigenising Intellectual Property', *Griffith Law Review* 9.2 (2000): 212-226.

Mouffe, Chantal. *The Democratic Paradox*, London: Verso, 2000.

———. 'Which Democracy in a Post-Political Age', conference paper, *Dark Markets: Infopolitics, Electronic Media and Democracy in Times of Crisis*, International Conference by Public Netbase/to, Muesumsplatz, Vienna, 3-4 October, 2002, http://darkmarkets.to.or.at/materials/abstract_mouffe.htm.

———. *On the Political*, London and New York: Routledge, 2005.

Mumford, Lewis. *Technics and Civilization*, London: Routledge & Kegan Paul, 1934.

Munster, Anna. 'Net Affects: Responding to Shock on Internet Time', in Hugh Brown, Geert Lovink, Helen Merrick, Ned Rossiter, David Teh, Michele Willson (eds), *Politics of a Digital Present: An Inventory of Australian Net Culture, Criticism and Theory*, Melbourne: Fibreculture Publications, 2001, pp. 9-17.

———. *Materializing New Media: Embodiment in Information Aesthetics*, Hanover and London: University of New England Press, 2006.

Murphie, Andrew. 'The World as Clock: The Network Society and Experimental Ecologies', *Topia: A Canadian Journal of Cultural Studies* 11 (Spring, 2004): 117-139.

Mute Magazine, Special issue on precarity (February, 2005), http://www.metamute.org/?q=en/taxonomy/term/178.

May, Christopher. *The Information Society: A Sceptical View*, Cambridge: Polity, 2002.

Moulier-Boutang, Yann and Grelet, Stanley. 'The Art of Flight: An Interview', *Interactivist Info Exchange: Independent Media & Analysis*, 7 February, 2003, http://info.interactivist.net/article.pl?sid=03/02/07/1350202.

Negri, Antonio. *Insurgencies: Constituent Power and the Modern State*, trans. Maurizia Boscagli, Minneapolis: University of Minnesota Press, 1999.

_____. 'Public Sphere, Labour and Multitude', trans. Arianna Bove, *MakeWorld Paper* 3 (2003): 4. Also available at: http://www.makeworlds.org/?q=node/view/11.

_____. 'Towards an Ontological Definition of the Multitudes', trans. Arianna Bove, *Makeworlds Paper* 4 (2004), http://www/makeworlds.org/book/view/104.

Negri, Antonio with Dufourmantelle, Anne. *Negri on Negri*, trans. M. B. DeBevoise, London and New York: Routledge, 2004.

Neilson, Brett and Rossiter, Ned. 'Report on Creative Labour Workshop', posting to fibreculture mailing list, 30 April, 2004, http://www.fibreculture.org.

_____. 'From Precarity to Precariousness and Back Again: Labour, Life and Unstable Networks', *Fibreculture Journal* 5 (2005), http://journal.fibreculture.org/issue5/neilson_rossiter.html.

Newnham, Mike. 'Foreword', in Paul Miller and Paul Skidmore, *Disorganisation: Why Future Organisations must 'Loosen Up'*, London: Demos, 2004, pp. 9-11. Available at: http://www.demos.co.uk/files/Disorganisation.pdf.

Nietzsche, Friedrich. *Writings from the Late Notebooks*, trans. Kate Sturge, ed. Rüdiger Bittner, Cambridge: Cambridge University Press, 2003.

Noble, David. *Digital Diploma Mills: The Automation of Higher Education*, New York: Monthly Review Press, 2002.

Odlyzko, Andrew. 'Content is Not King', *First Monday* 6.2 (2001), http://www.firstmonday.org/issues/issue6_2/odlyzko/.

OECD. *Governance in the 21st Century*, Paris: OECD, 2001, http://www.oecd.org/dataoecd/41/42/35391582.pdf.

Osborne, Peter. *The Politics of Time: Modernity and Avant-Garde*, London: Verso, 1995.

Padovani, Claudia and Tuzzi, Arjunna. *Global Civil Society and the World Summit on the Information Society: Reflections on Global Governance, Participation and the Changing Scope of Political Action*, Social Science Research Council, New York, 2004, http://www.sscr.org/programs/itic/publications/knowedge-report/memos/padovani3-4-30-04.pdf.

Palfrey, John. 'The End of the Experiment: How Icann's Foray into Global Internet Democracy Failed', *Harvard Journal of Law & Technology* 17 (2004): 410=473.

Parry, Benita. 'Internationalism Revisited or In Praise of Internationalism', *Variant* 17 (2003), http://www.variant.randomstate.org/17texts/17benitaparry.html.

Peake, Adam. *Internet Governance and the World Summit on the Information Society (WSIS)*, Association for Progressive Communications, 2004, http://rights.apc.org/documents/governance.pdf.

Pearson, Keith Ansell. *Viroid Life: Perspectives on Nietzsche and the Transhuman Condition*, London and New York: Routledge, 1997.

Prigogine, Ilya and Stengers, Isabelle. *Order out of Chaos: Man's New Dialogue with Nature*, London: Flamingo, 1985.

Rasch, William. *Niklas Luhmann's Modernity: The Paradoxes of Differentiation*, Stanford, Cal.: Stanford University Press, 2000.

Reagle, Joseph. 'Open Communities and Closed Law', Open Codex weblog, 13 June, 2006, http://reagle.org/joseph/blog/culture/wikipedia/open-discourse-closed-law?showcomments=yes.

Robbins, Kevin and Webster, Frank (eds). *The Virtual University? Knowledge, Markets and Managment*, Oxford: Oxford University Press, 2001.

Rodowick, D. N. *Reading the Figural, or, Philosophy after the New Media*, Durham and London: Duke University Press, 2001.

Ross, Andrew. *No-Collar: The Humane Workplace and Its Hidden Costs*, New York: Basic Books, 2003.

Rossiter, Ned. 'Modalities of Indigenous Sovereignty, Transformations of the Nation-State, and Intellectual Property Regimes', *Borderlands E-Journal: New Spaces in the Humanities* 1.2 (2002), http://www.borderlandsejournal.adelaide.edu.au/issues/vol1no2.html.

Sassen, Saskia. *Territory, Authority, Rights: From Medieval to Global Assemblages*, Princeton: Princeton University Press, 2006.

Serres, Michel. *Genesis*, trans. Geneviève James and James Nielson, Ann Arbor: University of Michigan Press, 1995.

_____. *The Birth of Physics*, trans. Jack Hawkes, London: Clinamen Press, 2001.

Shanken, Edward A. 'Art in the Information Age: Technology and Conceptual Art', *SIGGRAPH 2001 Electronic Art and Animation Catalog*, New York: ACM SIGGRAPH, 2001, pp. 8-15. Also available in *Leonardo* 35.4 (2002): 433-438.

Shaw, Martin. *Theory of the Global State: Globality as an Unfinished Revolution*, Cambridge: Cambridge University Press, 2000.

Smith, Daniel W. 'Deleuze and Derrida, Immanence and Transcendence: Two Directions in Recent French Thought', in Paul Patton and John Protevi (eds), *Between Deleuze and Derrida*, London and New York: Continuum, 2003, pp. 46-66.

Stalder, Felix. 'Actor-Network-Theory and Communications Networks: Toward Convergence', 1997, http://felix.openflows.org/html/Network_Theory.html.

_____. 'Space of Flows: Characteristics and Strategies', posting to nettime mailing list, 26 November, 2002, http://www.nettime.org.

_____. *Open Cultures and the Nature of Networks*, Novi Sad: kuda.org and Sarajevo Center for Contemporary Art, 2005. Available at: http://felix.openflows.org/pdf/Notebook_eng.pdf.

Stamps, Judith. *Unthinking Modernity: Innis, McLuhan and the Frankfurt School*, Montreal & Kingston: McGill-Queen's University Press, 1995.

Stengers, Isabelle. *The Invention of Modern Science*, trans. Daniel W. Smith, Minneapolis: University of Minnesota Press, 2000.

Surman, Mark and Reilly, Katherine. *Appropriating the Internet for Social Change: Towards the Strategic Use of Networked Technologies by Transnational Civil Society Organizations*, version 1.0, New York: Social Science Research Council, 2003. Available at http://www.ssrc.org/programs/itic/.

_____. *Executive Summary. Appropriating the Internet for Social Change: Towards the Strategic Use of Networked Technologies by Transnational Civil Society Organizations*, version 1.0, New York: Social Science Research Council, 2003. Available at http://www.ssrc.org/programs/itic/.

New York Times v Tasini, 533 US 483 (2001).

Terranova, Tiziana. 'Free Labor: Producing Culture for the Digital Economy', *Social Text* 18.2 (2000): 33-58.

_____. *Network Culture: Politics for the Information Age*, London: Pluto, 2004.

Thoburn, Nicholas. *Deleuze, Marx and Politics*, London: Routledge, 2003.

Thrift, Nigel. *Knowing Capitalism*, London: Sage, 2005.

Tickell, Adam. 'Unstable Futures: Controlling and Creating Risks in International Money', in Leo Panitch and Colin Leys (eds), *Global Capitalism versus Democracy: Socialist Register, 1999*, Suffolk: Merlin, 1999, pp. 248-277.

Tronti, Mario. 'Social Capital', *Telos* 17 (1977): 98-121.

_____. 'The Strategy of Refusal', trans. Red Notes, in Sylvère Lotringer and Christian Marazzi (eds), *Italy: Autonomia, Post-Political Politics*, New York: Semiotext(e), 1980, pp. 28-35. I am drawing from a longer version of the essay available at: http://www.libcom.org/library/strategy-refusal-mario-tronti.

_____. *La politica al tramonto*, Torino: Einaudi, 1998.

Turner, Graeme. *British Cultural Studies: An Introduction*, Boston: Unwin Hyman, 1990.

van der Krogt, Stijn. 'On Multi-stakeholderism', posting to incommunicado mailing list [sent by Geert Lovink], 27 May, 2005, http://incommunicado.info/mailinglist.

Virilio, Paul. *The Art of the Motor*, trans. Julie Rose, Minneapolis: University of Minnesota Press, 1995.

Virno, Paolo. 'The Ambivalence of Disenchantment', trans. Michael Turits, in Paolo Virno and Michael Hardt (eds), *Radical Thought in Italy: A Potential Politics*, Minneapolis: University of Minnesota Press, pp. 13-34.

_____. 'Virtuosity and Revolution: The Political Theory of Exodus', trans. Ed Emory, in Paolo Virno and Michael Hardt (eds), *Radical Thought in Italy: A Potential Politics*, Minneapolis: University of Minnesota Press, pp. 189-210.

_____. 'Notes on the "General Intellect"', trans. Cesare Casarino, in *Marxism Beyond Marxism*, ed. Sareee Makdisi, Cesare Casarino, and Rebecca E. Karl for the Polygraph collective, London and New York: Routledge, 1996, pp. 265-272

_____. *A Grammar of the Multitude*, trans. James Cascaito Isabella Bertoletti, and Andrea Casson, foreword by Sylvère Lotringer, New York: Semiotext(e), 2004.

Virno, Paolo and Lazzarato, Maurizio. 'Multitude/working class [interview]', trans. Arianna Bove, *Multitudes* 9 (May-June, 2002), http://multitudes.samizdat.net/Multitude-working-class.html.

Wang, Shujen and Zhu, Jonathan J. H. 'Mapping Film Piracy in China', *Theory, Culture & Society* 20.4 (2003): 97-125.

Wark, McKenzie. 'Speaking Trajectories: Meaghan Morris, Antipodean Theory and Australian Cultural Studies', *Cultural Studies* 6.3 (1992): 433-448.

_____. 'After Literature: Culture, Policy, Theory and Beyond', *Meanjin* 5.4 (1992): 677-690.

_____. *Virtual Geography: Living With Global Media Events*, Indianapolis: Indiana University Press, 1994

_____. *Dispositions*, Applecross and Cambridge: Salt Publishing, 2002

_____. 'The Power of Multiplicity and the Multiplicity of Power', in Geert Lovink, *Uncanny Networks: Dialogues with the Virtual Intelligentsia*, Cambridge, Mass.: MIT Press, 2002, pp. 314-325.

_____. *A Hacker Manifesto*, Cambridge, Mass.: Harvard University Press, 2004.

Whitehead, Albert North. *Process and Reality*, New York: Free Press, 1978.

Wiggershaus, Rolf. *The Frankfurt School: Its History, Theories and Political Significance*, trans. Michael Robertson, Cambridge, Mass.: MIT Press, 1994.

Williams, Raymond. 'The Technology and the Society', in *Television: Technology and Cultural Form*, London: Fontana, 1974, pp. 9-31.

_____. 'Dominant, Residual and Emergent', in *Marxism and Literature*, Oxford: Oxford University Press, 1977, pp. 121-127.

_____. 'Communications Technologies and Social Institutions', in Raymond Williams (ed.), *Contact: Human Communication and its History*, London: Thames & Hudson, 1981, pp. 226-238.

Williams, Sue. '$A the Villain in Screen Drama', *The Australian Financial Review*, 12 December, 2003, p. 20.

Wise, J. Macgregor. *Exploring Technology and Social Space*, Thousand Oaks, Cal.: Sage, 1997.

Wittel, Andreas. 'Toward a Network Sociality', *Theory, Culture & Society* 18.6 (2001): 51-76.

World Commission on the Social Dimension of Globalization. *A Fair Globalization: Creating Opportunities for All*, Geneva: International Labour Organization: 2004, http://www.ilo.org/public/english/fairglobalization/report/index.htm.

Wright, Steve. *Storming Heaven: Class Composition and Struggle in Italian Autonomist Marxism*, London: Pluto, 2002.

WSIS Declaration of Principles. Geneva, 12 December, 2003, http://www.itu.int/dms_pub/itu-s/md/03/wsis/doc/S03-WSIS-DOC-0004!!PDF-E.pdf.

WSIS Plan of Action. Geneva, 12 December, 2003, http://www.itu.int/dms_pub/itu-s/md/03/WSIS/doc/S03-WSIS-DOC-0005!!PDF.pdf.

Žižek, Slavoj. *The Sublime Object of Ideology*, London and New York: Verso, 1989.

_____. *The Ticklish Subject: the Absent Centre of Political Ontology*, London: Verso, 1999.

_____. 'Holding the Place', in Judith Butler, Ernesto Laclau and Slavoj Žižek *Contingency, Hegemony, Universality: Contemporary Dialogues on the Left*, London and New York: Verso, 2000, pp. 308-329.

_____. 'A Plea for Leninist Intolerance', *Critical Inquiry* 28.2 (2002): 542-566.